THE HUMAN CARAVAN
THE DIRECTION AND MEANING OF HISTORY

THE HUMAN CARAVAN

THE DIRECTION AND MEANING OF HISTORY

by

JEAN DU PLESSIS

Translated by

FRANCIS JACKSON

LONDON

SHEED & WARD

MCMXXXIX

NIHIL OBSTAT: EDUARDUS CAN. MAHONEY, S. TH. L.

CENSOR DEPUTATUS

IMPRIMATUR: LEONELLUS CAN. EVANS

VIC. GEN.

WESTMONASTERII, DIE IIᵃ OCTOBRIS 1938

PRINTED IN GREAT BRITAIN BY PURNELL AND SONS, LTD.

PAULTON (SOMERSET) AND LONDON

FIRST PUBLISHED FEBRUARY

BY SHEED AND WARD LTD

31 PATERNOSTER ROW

LONDON, E.C.4.

TABLE OF CONTENTS

FIRST PART

THE SPECTATOR SURVEYS THE SCENE

SECOND PART

THE CARAVAN

CONTENTS

THIRD PART

THE STAGES OF THE JOURNEY

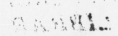

CONTENTS

FOURTH PART

THE LEADERS OF THE CARAVAN

CONTENTS

CONTENTS

B

FIRST PART

THE SPECTATOR SURVEYS THE SCENE

CHAPTER I

THE POINT OF VIEW

I

THE GREATEST EVENTS OF HISTORY ARE LIKEWISE THE MOST
CERTAIN

HUMAN sciences concentrate all their efforts upon an ever-lasting search after the truth, in the course of which they swoop down upon a vast multitude of possibilities and of things merely conjectural, only to reject them on the morrow. In their varied researches they discover a few things which are certainties and can be added to the sum of human knowledge. For thousands of years human sciences have been engaged in their task of erecting, tearing down and tirelessly reconstructing their scaffoldings over the outer face of reality; their theories come ever a little nearer to the truth, but never totally possess it. Man has an inordinate admiration of the sciences of which he is the author and builder, and this is foolish; but if he despised them, he would be guilty of a folly even greater, for they are indeed his support and his glory at the same time as they furnish conclusive and undeniable evidence of all that is lacking to him.

A celebrated inconoclast of the last century stigmatized history as a "poor insignificant, guesswork science". Yet history is no more insignificant and no more the subject of guesswork than any other of the human sciences; on both counts it is much like the others. Its roots, like theirs, thrust downwards into the fertile soil of facts. But it is not from the roots that we shall be able to gather the best fruit. For that purpose we must climb higher. Those doubts which arise in the mind as we concentrate upon the details of any science, have a way of vanishing from our minds as we proceed to take a

broad view of the whole development of it. It is true that on
the ground, beneath the trees, we are never completely in the
dark, nor deprived of all certainty, but higher up certainties
abound and are magnified in our eyes by the light of day. Both
brilliance and purity of vision increase as we rise to greater
heights. History indeed is the final result of many myriads of
tiny human deeds, the vast majority of which, like the work of
coral insects upon a growing reef, are imperceptible in detail,
though they are linked together by a fine network of bonds
which generally escape the human eye; but the assemblages
and total constructions they thus form are, in the course of ages,
vouched for by the unanimous opinion, not merely of the
scientists and savants, but also of the masses of mankind.
There are certain great events whose reality and nature are
beyond denial. Disputes and discussions may indeed arise in
the shadows cast by such events, but they themselves soar upwards into that light where every normal eye may see them as
they are.

Thus there may be debate as to the number of the martyrs
for the faith, the character of the apostolic communities, the
composition of the Gospels, the purpose and explanation in-
volved in the Life and Death of Our Lord Jesus Christ; but of
the existence of the Holy Catholic Church and its civilizing
dominance in the Western world there can be no debate. We
cannot avoid recognizing them, and nothing thought or said
can possibly deprive the Church of the glory of being the
creation of Christ, the Gospels, the Apostles and the Martyrs.
This is a conclusion which we have reached by using the
method of science. If you deny its truth, you bring down about
your ears the whole edifice and construction of science; for you
cannot possibly sustain such a denial without, in effect, under-
mining the very foundation of knowledge, the authority of the
testimony which gives it support—of that testimony indeed
which underlies the complete edifice of human wisdom. The
Science of Mathematics itself has nothing surer, nothing more
solid, nothing that reposes on firmer foundations.

The resemblance of history as a science to physics and

astronomy, is notable also in this that the power of the human will over events in the exterior world is precisely in inverse proportion to their greatness and therefore to their certainty:[1] that is, its power is great only over the less important events.

On the one hand we have before us for consideration a million insignificant facts: many of them must remain doubtful in their causes, their nature and character, their dates, their circumstances and their very existence. This multitude of petty details is the everlasting quarry of those learned men who spend their lives and efforts in research. They are all submerged below the waters of uncertainty. They belong to the category of those phenomena which the unrestrained caprice of contemporary scientists and savants could in fact put forward as part of reality, or withdraw, or modify as research proceeds.

If these innumerable insignificant facts have results which are common to them all, such results will, in the mass, be more certain as well as inevitable. It will be in vain for us to struggle against them. We must acknowledge them and make up our minds to suffer them.

But, on the other hand, if we consider the great movements of history, they will be seen as no less evident to our perception and no less inevitable in their nature than the movements of the great tides of the ocean.

Man is lost in their vastness as in the immensities of space. Even if he dances his own little dance, the countless multitudes of the dead are the leaders of the dance. The profound inscrutable force of accumulated causes carries him away on its waves. If for the moment he should be the leader of the dance, it is only because the force makes a transitory use of him; he is its instrument and if he thrusts himself against the force, it breaks him in pieces and throws him aside.

"If Cleopatra's nose had been shorter, the whole face of the earth would have been changed" said Blaise Pascal, but it is not true. Nothing would have been changed but the fate of

[1] For a summarization of my view on this matter, see the first part of the note at the end of the book (p.353)

Antony and of Octavius Caesar. Even that is not quite a certainty and in any case is of little importance for us. It is the fate of Rome that matters to us. Julius Caesar, Augustus Caesar, or Sulla, what were they, dictators and great men as they were, in comparison with Rome herself and the tides of life and destiny that exalted her? A mighty wave gushed forth from the depths of seven centuries, powerful enough to submerge the world for 500 years, during which time Roman civilization was brought to perfection to dominate a third of the then known world. What could men do to struggle against the power of this imperial wave? True wisdom lies in attempting to sound its depths; true power and grandeur lie in the use of the might and grandeur of that wave. When men comprehend these things they profit from them and are able to achieve their ideas and ambitions. If Julius Caesar, or Augustus, or Sulla had been defeated, other men would have acted differently and if Marius or Cneius Pompeius had failed in their ambitions, others might have perceived and profited; but their will-power changed nothing essential in the destiny of the Eternal City and of the universe—any more than the length of Cleopatra's nose or the treacherous edge of Brutus' dagger.

Great men are masterpieces in the game of life. They possess very great intelligence and they move of their own initiative but they remain on the chequer-board of nights and days, good perhaps for two or three moves in the great game which is being played. We must exaggerate neither their freedom nor yet their servitude to the great forces. The result of the game may indeed depend upon their play: yet their moves are really conditioned by the state in which they find the game at their arrival.

It is true that favourable circumstances are rarely lacking to genius, nor genius to the circumstances which demand its presence and its activities. Genius is gifted with the power to comprehend what is necessary and to fit its actions to the needs of the moment. A human being gifted with genius either accommodates his movements and activities to the circumstances, or controls them to suit his schemes. He must, as a rule, have other men capable of co-operating with him. He draws them to him as a magnet, or he goes out to find them. Sometimes, indeed, they come to him long after his death. Napoleon did not reign in Italy, nor did Peter in Judaea. Only the Middle Ages saw the complete fruition of the works of Aristotle.

Moreover, if a genius is the possessor of great power and of great activity, he possesses them in the present, and only to a limited extent can he exercise his influence over the future. On the other hand the past is beyond the power and activity, even of a genius. It dominates him and fixes for him the path of his career and its limits. The very means of action which he possesses do not originate within himself, but are imposed on him from outside; he neither chooses them nor transforms them to his own whim and fancy. However free and independent of his own nationality and his environment we may think him to be, his knowledge does not go beyond the endowment and traditions of his race, nor that which his surroundings and his epoch bestow upon him. Furthermore we must remember that his followers and supporters are merely the sons of their fathers and the product of their own age and country. At all times and in all places, the deeds and actions which have received the impress of his personality have consequences which reach far on into future ages; but he himself will in that future have no power over them. Just as he was the victim and the servant of numberless consequences without having any power to change them, so others will have to submit to them.

In this world our will never ceases to enjoy its freedom, but in a sphere above this there is another world which penetrates into this and rules over it; it is a world into which our freedom has no entry. In it, as an everlasting law, immutable and without interruption, the Divine Wisdom alone is at work amongst causes and effects, ordering everything, good and evil, to the achievement of the perfect ends and purposes of its activities. It is in that superior world that the Eternal Patience works out the destiny of the human race.

Let us then contemplate this destiny as a whole; for though such contemplation is not the only means of penetrating its divine mystery and of following its path, it is a very sure way. We shall then come face to face with facts which become more certain, the more momentous they are and the wider the vision we have of them; they are forces and unchanging laws, universal, and not to be violated by any passing whim or caprice of humanity. They are indeed constant and universal, because they are born of that human nature which is the same throughout mankind. It is possible that in the course of this contemplation the greatest of events will become clearly defined in our eyes. By following this itinerary of the Human Caravan we should be able to surmise the destination of the world, to have a glimpse of the future and to interpret in a fitting way the experience of the past: above all, to discern the direction and meaning of history.

II

THE SPECTATOR HAS A VIEWPOINT OTHER THAN THAT OF HUMAN SCHOLARSHIP, BUT HE MAKES USE OF IT IN THE FORMATION OF HIS JUDGMENT AND OPINIONS

This is the point of view of all sciences: to arrive at a perfect knowledge we must know the causes, in order that we may foresee the effects. It is a strange fact that scholars and scientists either ignore this principle, or shrink from it in fear. Is it possible that they believe that the real way to know a cathedral is to feel it with their hands, to measure its cubic capacity, to analyse its stonework; to collect statistics with regard to its nature and dimensions and to erect a hasty scaffolding of mathematical calculations with regard to it?

I have not the slightest intention of speaking in a slighting way of their great learning, nor of expelling from historical studies either system or conjecture. All such roads, indeed, lead those men whose intentions and ambitions are sincere to the threshold of truth. Let us not, however, put the cart before the horse and

strive for the means as if it were the end to be achieved however fruitful the means may be.

By all means build hypotheses, but upon the broad, firm base
of facts numerous and certain and universal. Make use of
systems, but they must be supple enough to be in harmony
with the multiplicity of the chances and fluctuations of life.
These creations of our minds are weapons of attack for the
conquest of reality, and lose their value when they lose a
justification of their existence. They lose that justification
when we attach ourselves to them and seek in reality that which
is useful for such systems and methods, rather than make use
of them to achieve and perfect the conquest of truth. For those
whose scholarship is sincere, who have an infinite capacity for
taking pains in the discovery of truth, I am filled with admiration. To descend into the depths of the catacombs and
explore their labyrinths demands a very different and higher
standard of courage from that of the man who in the light of
heaven climbs to the hill-top to the look-out which I have
chosen for my point of view. They till the soil of knowledge
whilst I feed upon the bread they produce.

In historical research, as in all other activities, humble and
patient toil at details is the most arduous, the most ungrateful
and the most necessary of activities. Without it, work which
occupies itself with the whole, the general effect, is only a
painting of mirages; but all that devoted labour is wasted when
the riches which it digs from the sub-soil are labelled and
ticketed in our shop windows and remain there in scattered and
disconnected confusion, like so much bric-à-brac in an old
curiosity shop! It is a necessity to study every scene in the
theatre of life profoundly; therefore such knowledge must be
valued and used; but we frustrate the efforts of dramatist and
publishers if we do not read the play.

The discovery of the truth with regard to an event, a people,
or an epoch does not mean the achievement of our historical
objective; no more than the verification of a formula or an
hypothesis means the solution of all problems in the science of
physics. It is only a means to an end. In order to reach

the objective and to give to the means, and to the labours that provide the means, all their value, we must go beyond the means, rise to the height of the universal and enter the domain of the absolute.

III

THE SPECTATOR'S IMPARTIALITY

There is no need of abnormal strength or courage.

Ever since I could think or read, when I was still at school, I dreamed of what I am now doing. Tacitus, Bossuet and the Bible, the book *par excellence* which unrolls for our eyes to read the destinies of humanity, exercised a great charm upon my awakening faculties. Almost at once I began to gather knowledge, to equip myself, to think upon things with the object of achieving the work on which I am now engaged. It will soon be fifty years since I made my beginning.

At the outset my ambitions were very great. In the simplicity of my youthful mind the plan I had formed was a thousand times vaster than the scheme of this little work and embraced the whole of the universe. I was eager to emulate Victor Hugo and Lamartine and as a historian I hoped to realize the synthesis which the authors of *La Chute d'un ange* and *La Légende des Siècles* had, as poets, merely sketched. The actual experience of my own limitations, of science, and of life reduced my ambitions and I became satisfied with a more modest design; but at any rate, as the consequence of these inordinately vast projects, I gained an exact idea of the difficulties of my task.

For long my eyes and my mind rested upon everything that came within their immediate range. Being extremely sensitive to the abstract beauties of Mathematics, very curious with regard to Nature, very much in love with Religion, the Fine Arts and Literature, I found myself drawn first by the duty of my profession and condition, then by taste, into the study of social economy, of public law, and of the history of law and

political institutions. These numerous studies, however, did
not entirely capture and absorb my mind. My window and
my door remained open. I did not cease to frequent those
places and studies which were my first love. More especially
I did not forget either the tongue or the road which does not
appear in books. I travelled, and as a traveller I made my
observations, I listened to the talk of other men, I worked, I
prayed to God, and I suffered, whilst I was engaged in my
studies. Everything I came across had its uses. As a result of
all this the understanding of the intimate unity of all things
became ever clearer to my vision. Exactly in proportion as my
knowledge grew in extent and in depth, there was constantly
confirmed in my mind the intuition which had given rise to the
conception of the unity of things, as the necessary consequence
and the proof of the existence of the Creator who is infinitely
wise, infinitely powerful, unchangeable and simple in His
essence. In the course of the years which I spent in this
incessant labour I sought for repose only in the diversity of toil
and the joys of activity. I won that repose, it is true, but at the
same time I underwent my test or trial.

Doubts aroused by my labours of research assailed me on all
sides. I could make no statement whatsoever which they did
not fiercely debate. At all times I gave careful consideration
to the reasons they advanced and weighed them scrupulously
and I accorded the same treatment to those of the enemies of
my faith and of my method. I held to the path of truth and I
did not follow my own direction.

Being at all times prepared to abandon my own opinion as
soon as it appeared to my better judgment to be too frivolous
and too light in the scales, I never hesitated to throw off the
bonds of the ideology and the verbiage in fashion in the world
at the moment. Long ago I arrived at the cult of reality which
is the unvarying sign of the Divine Idea.

In this wise this book was not merely carried in my mind;
it is in very truth my life's work and the fruit of my soul. The
reader will therefore feel no surprise when he finds it to be full of
thoughts about God. Let other men divide themselves into

two parts or personalities, being at one time savants, scientists, or scholars to whom the faith is a strange and foreign thing; and at another time, true believers whose faith seems to have scarcely any single point of contact with their scientific knowledge. Let such divided personalities surrender themselves as they think fit to this illogical and cowardly habit of refusing their allegiance to what they believe in their innermost beings to be true, in order that what they say publicly may be looked upon as the truth. With all my being and in all my actions I love and I intend to serve the Lord Jesus Christ. As far as I can see over the path of my life, of my work and of my sufferings, I see myself guided by His attentive providence; instructed, supported, raised up from the depths many times by Him. Towards us He acts with merciful condescension, with penetrating sweetness and limitless patience. Every step I took towards knowledge brought me nearer to the light He radiates around Him; every ascent in the faith helped me to make an advance in my knowledge. Everything I know, everything I can do, everything I am, I owe to Him. If I wrote for other purposes than for His service, I should be guilty of the most despicable ingratitude; if in His service I wrote one word against the truth, I should also be guilty of the grossest folly, since He is very truth.

I have love for the truth and for Him alone. What does anything else matter to me? I have lived too long as the familiar of death not to have taken the true measure of human things. I know our inherent weakness, our universal ignorance, the ridiculous nature of our pretensions to learning, our limited vision, and our wretchedness. The war shed its light upon the lessons which the sordid and oppressive peace of the decadence gave the world before its outbreak. On the 4th of August 1914, the palace of iniquity which we then inhabited began to totter, and the universe still trembles from the long-continuing crash of its ruin. Shall I live to see the end in this world? When will the sacred Fire be lit which shall consume our idols?

Carried away suddenly by the storm far from my past life —perhaps for ever—alone that day I penetrated, as did a host of other men, the shadow of our destiny. I lived from that day through the conflict to the conclusion of peace. I wrote this first chapter, and the whole canvas or scheme of the others, in the desert, and, so to speak, in the depth of the tomb, in any case with the supreme detachment of those whom a brief respite halts on the threshold of eternity. The very plan, and the contents of this little book, gradually achieved precision in my mind in the course of solitary watches, and even during the struggles of trench warfare.

At the far end of the sap, pounded and smashed by bombardment, there remained dominant within the naked soul neither prejudice nor passion, not even against the enemy. It is God who judges between our foes and us whilst we are fighting. Combatants from the first months of the War, thrown hither and thither by the four winds of heaven, harassed, sleepless, foodless in the hurricane of defeat or victory; wanderers in muddy communication trenches, seeking shelter in dark craters, watchers by night, motionless, stricken under the fiery rain of shells; victors upon the stricken field of carnage, at every instant bespattered with the decay of death, we who survived the slaughter were pilgrims through a Dantesque Inferno; how could we not preserve in our souls the complete serenity of pilgrims from the beyond?

Where now are our haughty prejudices; the superstitions born of our faith in science, our pride in our civilization? Alas, the secrets torn from nature only served to amplify the cataclysm and to prolong its sorrows.

As for me who passed through this devastation surrounded by ignorant and unlettered, poor and simple men, I loved them in proportion as my knowledge of them grew, and the difference which separates them from the learned, from philosophers and artists, appeared to me to be ever more infinitesimal. Our common human nature, my interest and theirs, our thirst for progress and light, everything forces me to work unceasingly for *Him who is.*

Beside Him, everything is falsehood, error or darkness. He Himself being Supreme Truth, wants from me the truth, and the truth alone, even if to my mind it seems detrimental to His glory. I am ignorant of His profound designs and I cannot sound the depth. If He allows the triumph of evil, the mixture of evil and of good, even darkness to envelop good, it is because the perfection of His work in this world demands it. It is His work. How should I presume to throw a veil over or close my eyes to the defects which it is His pleasure to allow to be visible in it? "Blessed is he," Christ says, "whosoever shall not be offended in me," "that shall not be scandalized in me."[1] As the trustful servant of that Master Saint who is also the God of Sciences, I must make every effort I can to be led astray by nothing. This book will be offered to Him, only if it sheds rays of pure light. It will shed such rays, only if I think, observe and speak without prejudice and entirely obedient to reality.

IV

THE SPECTATOR'S POINT OF VIEW CAN AND MUST BE PANORAMIC

It has been said, and for a long time I believed, that nothing is more demoralizing than history. In its pages Man cuts no fine figure; but the synthesis which I have attempted, though austere and severe, in spite of everything bears within itself, according to my own experience, an inexhaustible treasure of hope, of power, and of love. It is in the detail that lies the whole horror of the condition of humanity. Let us rise above this detail; if history has direction and meaning, it is God that gives it that direction. He can lead it only to Himself, that is to say, to light and beauty.

It is natural for us to wonder whether the unity of the human race and of its history is a concrete fact, or merely a subjective idea. Does the human mind observe that unity outside itself, or does it add it, for its own satisfaction, to the whole stream of events which in themselves are disparate and fortuitous? Our

[1]Matthew xi. 6

point of view is panoramic; now it often happens that the unity
of a panorama is merely the unity of our own vision and of the
circle which it embraces; but it also happens that this unity,
abstract and personal as it is, rests and forms itself upon another
unity which is real and concrete; as, for example (to use an
analogy), the lake whose surface with its ever changing colours,
framed in its dream-like shores, lies smiling at the foot of the
mountain; the town upon which we look from an aeroplane
flying above it; the distant world which reveals itself to us when
the planet Saturn with its rings and satellites swims into our
ken and is encircled within the field of our glasses.

Is humanity a unity in time as the planet, the town and the
lake are unities in the space within our vision? Or is it indeed
nothing more than an assemblage of various objects, of lines
and of tints which the artist shapes to suit his own taste, as he
places them here and there to form the composition of his
picture? There lies the great question; the answer must come
from what I am to write. If history has both direction and
meaning, of necessity it is a unity; if, on the other hand, it has
no unity, the necessary conclusion is that history has neither
direction nor meaning. Should we accept the latter hypothesis,
then history moves towards no other goal than the collapse and
the perpetual rebuilding of the same card castles. It has then no
meaning and everything which it attempts to teach us can be
taught a hundred times better, for example, by the *Fables* of
La Fontaine.

How can we know for certain, however, whether history has,
or has not direction and meaning, if our knowledge of its
direction, granting it possesses one, does not come to us from
seeing it more? Let us include the whole extent of history,
in a single glance, in order to discern whether or not the great
facts which it presents to us and the great laws which rule them
are really united in a single whole. That indeed is the method,
and the only method.

There is no need to waste time in fruitless controversy. Being
strictly on our guard against everything which might disturb our
view, it is sufficient for us to contemplate the work as it is revealed

c

to us. Though the work is incomplete as long as history has not closed its pages, it must have developed sufficiently during the many centuries of the existence of men and their activities to manifest, in some manner, His plan who conceived it and who follows out that plan before our eyes by marvellous ways. We shall indeed see if there is such a plan, or if everything occurs by chance. Let us turn our eyes upon the history of the human race.

CHAPTER II

THE PANORAMA

I

THE OBSCURITY OF THE DISTANT ORIGINS OF MANKIND

WHAT shall we see from our look-out? Nothing but the face of a shadowy and treacherous water whose tides are in perpetual commotion. There is no solid land on the horizon before our eyes, no gleam of light in the dreary sky; nothing to fix the gaze. Things make a fitful appearance and vanish into obscurity. Everything changes, flees away, sinks into nothingness, only to begin over again its everlasting changes.

"What is it that hath been? The same thing that shall be; what is it that hath been done? The same that shall be done: nothing under the sun is new;"[1] no change in this under a thousand different appearances; neither repose nor rest in the universal becoming. Nothing is fixed or stable, and nothing attains achievement. A few specks of foam flung from vanished waves are all that remain of what once seemed destined to be. Vision is lost and thought falls weary in the midst of the sad lapping of monotonous waters, whose mournful sound fills the whole duration of human history as far as the misty horizons of our sight.

Where shall we see the light? In the sad ray from a mysterious golden age filtering through the sombre, heavy air? The veil of clouds which darken the heavens will not permit us anywhere to see the nature of the light, nor its origin. Where are we to place this golden age? How shall we paint it? Man colours it to suit his own caprice and fancies. Ever since the world was the world, humanity has regretted its disappearance

[1] Ecclesiastes I, 9-10.

and has longed for its return. Even now we are looking for it and are the victims of the illusion that the golden age is close at hand. "Here it is," said Virgil, "the golden age is now returning." But at the very same time his friend Horace deplored the irresistible straying away from the golden rule which separates us from that fabulous golden age: "Our fathers, who were themselves inferior to their ancestors, gave birth to us, still more degenerate than they our sires, and we in our turn shall be the sires of children worse than ourselves."

As far as our vision extends over this panorama, we see nothing but the mediocre and ephemeral; from whatever source the light comes to us which shines upon our obscure destinies— whether from an idle fancy, the hope instinctive in a dream of happiness, a consciousness of our wretched condition, or from the confused memory of an experience and a promise—its path is stained with blood, as its revolving beam shines upon the restless lives of the children of men; at this we need not marvel, for this bloodshed is necessary that man who is born of woman may see the light of day and live. But the golden age is hidden below the horizon; and everything written upon the page of history and everything that history can foretell takes place in the age of blood.

Man remembers Paradise, but seldom thinks upon his Fall. It is so long ago. Can we not explain the effects of that Fall, which are always with us in this world, by causes less catastrophic? Lucretius did not trouble himself about them, nor the Vedas, nor Lao-Tseu, nor Zoroaster, nor Darwin, who indeed unearthed for us another kind of nobility. Man is not descended from heaven; he is climbing up from tertiary forests. An animal who is in the process of becoming a god, he is climbing the tree of knowledge, but he has not left below his instinctive vanity, his cupidity, his lubricity and the cruelty of his four-handed ancestors. There is in these modern doctrines no more Adam, no more original sin, no one couple of human parents at the cradle of humanity, no more divine creation. The traditions of primitive ages and the revelations are nothing but old-fashioned stories, dream-symbols, poetry. The golden age lies before us and will be the result of our own efforts.

This is said and taught in the name of knowledge; but in fact nothing is known about it. The conclusions drawn do not even follow from any premises. The creative evolution of the animal and vegetable world is, as yet, but an hypothesis, rich no doubt in truth, and, like all similar theories, rich no doubt in error. Whatever may be the truth, fix your eyes upon the far distances where all disappears from the vision, even the upheaval of quaternary cataclysms; piercing as your sight may be, you will nowhere see any answering gleam or the slightest dawning of reason in the eyes of chimpanzees, orang-outangs, gorillas, gibbons, or of the anthropoid apes, or the pithecan-thropoids of Java. The men who move in the depths of the prehistoric forests are already men and already numerous. Scattered over almost the whole of the globe, they have no knowledge of metals, but they can make fire and they can build tombs. They manufacture weapons, dress and tools. They think, they draw, they carve and they write.

Whence do they come? It is with difficulty that we catch sight of their original migrations. They are the hunters con-quering the world, and the first shepherds of flocks.

Where was the first furrow driven which fixed them to the soil? When did paternal majesty blossom forth for the first time as priest and king? Is it the truth that "the first man to become a king was a successful warrior"? Was he not rather the chief who imposed himself upon the tribe or the son of the ancestor of the tribe, the priest and sorcerer?

In what time and place, by what hands, shone forth the first flame in the service of humanity, the first metal tool to be made in the flame and, on the clay, when was the first written word traced with bone or pointed stone? On all these mysteries, also, are written great dissertations in the name of knowledge; and nothing is known about them.

The prehistoric man of the type of Canstadt or des Eyzies is our contemporary in Ceylon or in the Australian bush. He was the contemporary of Louis XIV, of Charlemagne, of Pericles and of Sesostris. And the wandering children of the Steppes, how many times, in the lapse of centuries, have they fed their flocks and lived over again the days of Abel on the site of the buried ruins of temples and palaces?

"I do not know": that confession of ignorance is the first and last word in human knowledge. The creators of the arts, the founders of cities, patriarchs, giants, tribes, civilizations, and the slow growth of humanity in its infancy, all fade away into the shadow and are well-nigh invisible in the mists which float far off over the secrets of Asia. But even when we have ransacked the soil whence come the tracks followed by all the races of men in their migrations, shall we ever know more of that history which precedes history, any more than we do of the frozen north of Europe, of the vast desert of the Sahara or of the lands which to-day lie beneath the Indian Ocean, the Atlantic or the Mediterranean Sea? What then existed, He alone sees it as it is, as He sees us in His eternal present. He alone can teach us.

II

THE MOVEMENTS OF THE HUMAN CARAVAN ARE MARKED BY CONFUSION AND INSTABILITY

Within the limits of these horizons, at first we have only legendary or symbolical names to distinguish the scattered heights, visible above the human waves, reduced by distance to one common level; they are the names of the great educators of the human races—men whose greatness was the consequence of their acts, rather than of the extent of their kingdoms or the number of their subjects. They were builders, legislators and civilizers. All the others were merely petty kings and insignificant princelets, embryonic states, nomadic tribes, warlike hordes, scattered clans whom jealousies kept in isolation, adventurous marauders or savages in decadence, lost amidst a hostile nature, the slaves of the exuberance of Nature's power and of the inexhaustible fecundity of her womb.

Very soon the growing kingdoms dissolve into anarchy, then they form again as political units, extend their boundaries and are consolidated, splitting up again only to reform and to extend once more their territories, whilst others elsewhere rise from their foundations, crash down and are restored. On every side there are rising and falling waves and tides of barbarism and of civilization, a confused babel of works, of destruction, of struggles, the echoes of which grow louder in proportion as the generations of men abound and scatter over the face of the globe. Here and there a wave gathers and breaks, a people, a man emerge into prominence for a few moments in history; names which are brought to us on the winds of space; less frequently we see the traces left by them, shining in momentary brilliance or hidden in shadow yet coming into our field of vision, beneath which, however, as elsewhere, all things fall back again at once and disappear in the universal confusion of the perpetual and unceasing movement.

And what remains of it all? Shapeless ruins, broken pottery, weapons, toys, statuettes, paintings which have almost faded away, inscriptions, tombs, useless débris, the scattered bones of cities, of nations, and of civilizations which have disappeared and which others have replaced, only to disappear in their turn. It seems, indeed, that all is delivered over to mere chance and to ignorance. Who, then, ever profited by the experience of his ancestors, or the predictions of the wise? Show to the Assyrian in his hour of triumph the Median tribes and the Persians organizing themselves in their mountain fastnesses: the ploughmen and the merchants of Ionia reposing under their plane trees, near by the fountains of living waters, listening at ease to the heroic songs of the poet Homer: Lycurgus transforming into soldiers the shepherd warriors of Sparta. Your Assyrian would not have understood what you showed him. And he would have had your eyes put out if you had told him that, before the passage of three centuries, Babylon would destroy Nineveh, and would herself suffer crushing defeat a short time afterwards. Great empires indeed have exactly the solidity of great clouds. Death, soon or late,

breathes upon them and they are scattered. What has the
longer life is the spark of thought which charms our desire to
live and to escape, and is multiplied by every breath of the
night air, a gleam of hope and of safety on the face of the com-
plaining waters of life which we are now contemplating.

David and Solomon, if they had not been prophets, would
have reposed like Kheops and Darius with their last breath in
the silence of their glory, but being messengers of divine hope
they live and reign with Moses and all the seers of Israel.

Homer still lives; Herodotus, Sophocles and Demosthenes,
Pythagoras, Euclid and Archimedes, are still our masters. Our
sophists repeat the lessons of Heraclitus, of Parmenides, of
Anaxagoras, of Pyrrho, of Zeno and Epicurus. Aristotle and
Plato are still kings of thought.

All these men, however, amount to little. Consider the names
of the spiritual initiators from whom humanity, has received
religions or the framework of social systems; the Brahmins and
their Vedanta, whose kingdom is in India; Gautama Sakya
Muni, the Buddha, who conquered them and then lost ground,
but is still a guide for the peoples of the Far East; Lao-Tseu
and Confucius, who are rivals and share with Buddha the
Middle Empire; Jesus of Nazareth, the King of the Jews, the
conqueror of the Roman world of Europe and the new world in
the West; Mahomet, whose scarf with its double point includes
Asia and Africa from Siberia and Malaya to the Sudan. They
still survive, and yet, when one thinks of it, how scattered are
the élite who understand them, appreciate them, penetrate to
the depth of their thought, assimilate the substance of it and
really mould their lives on the principles of the doctrines of these
teachers, their precepts and their examples!

I have named only the great names, and half of them the
majority of mankind scarcely knows at all: a name, vague
memories, a few themes with variations embroidered upon
them by the intellectuals, and, for the rest of the masses, a
few far-away influences mingled with many others. That is the
extent of the empire of these chosen spirits.

And as for the other half who were apparently really enshrined in the souls of men, have they indeed made their dwelling with them?

Amongst the Jews, the doctors of the Talmud have supplanted Moses, and his people have been the victims of the dispersion for more than 2,000 years.

The Vedas are works of beauty in the commentaries of Çankarachârya; but the 200,000,000 followers claimed for them are almost all under the tyranny of idolatry, with its train of superstitions and jugglery.

The same must be said of the Buddha and the two Celestials, Confucius and Lao-Tseu, although the main portion of their teachings is more within the grasp of the populace, and has impregnated perhaps, and ruled, more human lives amongst their 500,000,000 votaries. And what can they expect of the future when the exclusively political gospel of Suen Wenn is preached and taught under compulsion in so many Chinese schools? The materialist Chu-Hi, the deadly enemy of their work, must in his tomb feel a thrill of joy.

Jesus and Mahomet also number respectively 600,000,000 and 200,000,000 disciples, but what lack of zeal is in their Faith! The Mahometan prostrates himself five times a day to pray to Allah—the only God; and I could wish that this were not merely a routine practice, a machine-like rite, in which the intelligence and the heart play no rôle, or only a small one. What can Islam do, what has it done, to save the mass of its believers from the vices which are devouring it and making it abominable in the eyes of God? Islam boasts of its stability. Nothing shakes it, in fact nothing breaks into it: there are no more than one or two known schisms in it, and its Faithful scarcely ever break away from it; but it produces nothing from its treasure house for new ages and new things. A thousand years and more have passed by without any addition to its spiritual riches.

And then we observe that after it had driven paganism from the Western world, the Church of Christ saw great numbers of its flock separate themselves and break up into innumerable sects and denominations. The political States which the

Church had brought to birth and educated, one after another drew away from her. The philosophies and superstitions of a renascent paganism stole from her millions of souls.

Amongst those that remain within her fold, there are millions more for whom Christianity is nothing but a collection of formulae and gestures, analogous to the etiquette of everyday civic life and of administrative protocols. "This or that is done"—but one does not draw life from it. Do they even believe in it? Of a surety, this Faith without works is a dead Faith, buried even, and decomposing beneath the mass of contradictions which, little by little, have contaminated it, weakened it, and then choked it: a laicism which confines religion within the temple and so eliminates it from private life; rationalism, the religion of science, agnosticism, occultism, spiritualism, theosophy, esotericism cleverly dosed by secret sects. Once more the gods depart. Man remains in his wretchedness.

III

AT FIRST SIGHT ALL SEEMS VANITY AND HISTORY LACKING IN DIRECTION AND MEANING

With what promises did not the great surge seem swollen which uplifted the human ocean for a thousand years—yet that was but a short phase in the story of humanity—wherein appeared, one after the other, Lao-Tseu, Gautama, Confucius, Plato, Aristotle, Jesus Christ, and Mahomet. Great warriors, statesmen, leaders of the people, founders or reformers of empires, moulding everywhere with powerful hands the clay of Adam's sons, and, that it might receive the breath of life, offering it to the inspiration of the great spiritual leaders. What force is in humanity! What a divine future lies in front of it! And during another millennium that future is prolonged. Along the borders of the Mediterranean, Islam extends her brilliant civilization. Byzantium continues the epoch of the Roman Empire. Rome herself, overwhelmed

by the Barbarians, assimilates them and becomes the embodi-
ment of Christianity. The Mongols conquer Asia.

This time the game seems won. Soon or late, thus lifted high,
the wave will deposit the perfect man on peaceful shores: then
at length will come the golden age. How vain a hope! These
great waves from the depths of the ocean throw only passing
ripples on the culminating points of history. Between the
Middle Ages and us, there is a period of 600 years, a new world
and man's subjugation of the forces of nature. The face of the
universe has changed. The results are wars, revolutions and
famines unparalleled before; it is the reign of gold, and not
the golden age, which is as far off now as ever it was. Asia
has crashed down on herself. The Western world, drunk with
glory, knowledge, power and riches, will in its turn sink into
ruins.

The West, however, has had great builders, but destroyers
have also come to spoil its unity, to undermine its foundations
and to poison and obscure the sources of its force and its light,
although they brought to it, from time to time, a fictitious vigour
and a deceptive illumination. Such men indeed laid claim to
being builders, rather than destroyers. They had faith in their
pretensions. The Great War burnt with fire, shattered to pieces
and ravaged the whole of their proud edifice at the very moment
when the prodigious rise of Japan during the reign of Mutso-Ito
had stirred in the heart of Asia, scornful of her oppressors yet
resigned to her sufferings, the growth of an implacable hatred
and an ardent hope of her future liberation from the tyrannies
of the West. We have seen, on the morrow of the great
cataclysm, to what poor brains Western Democracy entrusted
the destinies of the world. Even if such men had written
nothing, either "at the dawn"[1] or in the evening of what they
called thought, the treaty which they made as the arbiters of a
world would be adequate to give us their measure. Everything disappears, everything dissolves. The cycle is closed until
it begins again. Everything returns with greater fullness and
force and in a different form to its state of yesterday, and to its

---

[1] *At the Dawn of Thought* is the title of the last of Clemenceau's works.

eternal condition. The panorama creates nothing but the impression of an eternal mobility in which everything vanishes in its turn.

Soon when we look more closely we shall discern something different; but the first glance, the first contemplation of the whole inevitably calls to memory the *yinn* and the *yang* of the wise men of China, a succession of things without either beginning or end, without reason or objective, a movement of progress and decadence, of life and death: the universal wheel of the Brahmins which drags with it all living creatures, and rolls on from cycle to cycle, without rest or end. Whether we flatter ourselves that we know little, or much, 7,000 or 700,000 years of human history, what is such an insignificant period of time? And in that time how many billions of people have passed away, in travail, in grief and in their joys more lamentable than their pains—about whom we can know nothing?

Man's complaint and his cry of jubilation are like the laughter and the sobs of a child: they follow one another, are mingled, and the slightest breeze carries them away—and the reason which gives them birth is even more quickly dissipated. Genius emerges and disappears. What remains of it? Our greatness is exactly that of the din of our most terrible battles, which the passing storm obliterates.

We are proud of our power, of our dominion over matter, of our great ships, of our aeroplanes and cannon, of the long range trajectory of our shells: but what are they all, alongside the stream which carries the earth through space, with us upon it in restless commotion and the earth no whit moved by all our agitation?

Measure on this scale the greatest empires and the whole extent of human history, the whole panorama which we have just contemplated: the earth, space, time, force, everything is reduced to an absurd littleness. So long as we remain submerged in it, it seems colossal; that is to say, in comparison with ourselves. But as soon as we escape from the servitude of this environment, to emerge from ourselves and come into contact with sovereign reality, everything takes flight towards nothingness.

Have pity upon us, O Heavenly Father, only true being and only true life! You who pour out eternal compassion upon your creatures, forgive our littleness in having believed in our own power, in our own greatness and its duration. Pardon this illusion in us; dispel this absurd dream. Before death awakens us, take away the veil which hides reality from our eyes; and let our souls, set free in the contemplation of your infinite simplicity, taste at length the nothingness of all that is not You.

SECOND PART

THE CARAVAN

THE TEN LAWS WHICH GOVERN THE DEVELOPMENT OF HUMAN HISTORY

CHAPTER I

THE ORDER OF THE MARCH

I

THE UNITS OF THE CARAVAN ON THE MARCH ARE CORPS OF PEOPLES

THE first impression produced by the panorama of history in a mind sensitive to the facts is of chaos, aimlessness, unceasing disturbance of atoms brought together by blind chance and as blindly dispersed. At first everything appears to be in universal confusion, without end, or objective, or law, devoid of meaning. But this impression is deceptive. The stars in the heavens also seem at first nothing but profusion without order, a chance diversity, a causeless brilliance. Only by 6,000 years of patient investigation, profound thought, and calculations that make dizzy the mind do we begin to catch glimpses of the order of the stellar systems.

Look upon the chaos of humanity, as astronomers look upon the chaos of the heavens: and it ceases to be chaos. It is our ignorance and the weakness of our sight which cause us to miss the order that truly exists. Look beneath the surface; focus your vision with concentrated attention upon that wild medley of peoples and events. You will become aware of an order of light and shade, a perspective, a spectacle seeming to be under the control of certain laws. The limits, it is true, remain insignificant in extent and the personalities of the picture but lilliputian. Their petty agitations, the incoherence and obscenity of their gestures, the conventional hypocrisy with which they conceal their true mind, the complacence of men in their inexpressible baseness, the opinion they entertain of their own importance—the mind may be excused that sees all this as pitiable or ridiculous. Montaigne is amused by the spectacle, Pascal bases a strong argument upon it, Voltaire sneers at the "poor image of the living God". But if all this surface display of animality fills the stage, it must not conceal from us the meaning and the dénouement of the play. Souls are beyond all these petty things; and this drama is a drama of souls. The scene which the narrowness of our vision limits to the measure of ourselves, does in fact open out upon the infinite. What our eyes see before them and what our eyes are not strong enough to see as it passes on into eternity is a grand and tragic matter.

It is no longer an ocean, the blind, vain struggle of the waves. It is a mighty crowd which moves into columns of route, is organized into a caravan and seems to follow a perilous, rough, unexplored but well-defined way, towards some distant goal.

There is an order in the march of the caravan. The men in it are moving side by side, not each for himself on the same road like so many solitary animals driven together by a common instinct of self-preservation when rivers flood. The Caravan, of course, is formed of individuals; but no individual by himself amounts to anything.

This is the first judgment forced upon us by the facts: the individual, as such, does not count, has no place, does not appear in history. The group is everything, whether it remains with its members on the same footing as the crowd, or whether it goes beyond the crowd by raising above it a master who directs its movements: for he can do this only by means of the group.

Let us then turn our attention to the human groups: mobs and unorganized bands, families, clans, tribes, cities, nations, states, administrative bodies, professional bodies, social classes, societies for the preservation of common interests, political parties, intellectual or charitable societies, civil or religious associations: so doing we come to our second observation. Look where you will, from Adam to our own times, you will not find any group of individuals who are truly something apart, to themselves alone. Sociologists and ethnologists, archeologists and anthropologists may discuss at their leisure as to what is to be regarded as primitive—the patriarchal or matriarchal family, the promiscuous or the exogamous tribe, the couple whose union is merely ephemeral, bands of hunters or brigands; behind all this is the solid fact of the insignificance of the part played by such groups in history, so long as they remain isolated.

Their importance only moves beyond the infinitesimal when they enter as elements into groups which are wider and more complex, clans with or without the totem, patriarchal tribes, demes, phratries, villages, communes, the city, nation, state or political federation: the wider unity, absorbing them into its bosom, does but enhance the historical importance of each of them by the value of all the others.

Abraham's family, Romulus' band of adventurers, Mahomet's clan, the tribe of Clovis; the muddy villages of Babylon, Memphis, Benares and Lutetia which became Paris, have played their great rôle in human history.

Others like them whose traces have completely disappeared —obliterated by history in a mood of complete indifference— are numbered by thousands.

Why did the former not suffer the same fate? The reason is in the fact that they did not remain alone and separate. They were united to others that sprang from them, or had their origin outside them and were drawn into or retained within the circle of their influence, or were conquered and held by force. They were at one and the same time the acorn whose seed grows into the oak tree and the spring which increases in volume as it flows along, and in its course receives a thousand tributaries, until it becomes the Ganges, the Nile, the Hwang-Ho, the Euphrates or the Seine. They give birth to numerous peoples, powerful nations, states which lasted long in the world's history, sometimes vast empires and "universal religions". In this way the race of men grew rich on their good fortune and the face of the earth was adorned by their power and beauty.

II

THESE CORPS OF PEOPLES ARE ALWAYS MORE OR LESS POLITICAL

Needs, passions, the power which is in things, the impulse of instincts, the commands of reason, everything unites individuals and human groups in bonds which compel them to collaborate, creating amongst them the organization of common dependence.

Hence a power becomes necessary to direct the action of all towards the common goal, to rule over and maintain the cohesion of the group and so to ensure the unity of its efforts. The greater the independence of this ruling power, the prompter and more direct will be the influence exercised by it and by the organized body of which it is the head, over the march of history. Upon the table where the destinies of the world are diced for, the greatest satrapy of Darius the Mede is merely a bronze penny, whereas tiny Athens, being free, is a gold piece.

All human history is built up in this fashion round these series of groups ruled over by a power free from the control of every other power in its own sphere, a sovereign power in a sphere which is of necessity political. Such large groupings or series are called States.

States, whether great or small, the life of States, their development, their culture, the ideas which they form of themselves and their destinies, their common relationships, their rivalries, their struggles and their alliances constitute the chain and network of universal history. Everything else is but the thread, the preparation, the dye, the design or plan, the gauds or the embroidery of history. In this manner across the apparent disorder of the panorama there becomes visible to the spectator a first law, noted with precision by Aristotle, when he was searching for man's place amongst animate things; he did not classify mankind along with horses and deer which live in herds, nor yet as ants and bees which live in communities associated together by instinct for the performance of the same labours, or for the perpetuation of their species; he placed men apart, as members neither of a compulsory nor a voluntary society, because they are beings irresistibly impelled by their very nature to organize States by the use of the faculty of reason.

"Man is a political animal." It is through politics that history is made. Neither the economic nor the social factor plays a prime rôle in history: the whole of their importance is the result of the fact that they are to be counted amongst the motives, the springs and the conditions of politics and that as such they tend irresistibly to surpass all others. This stands out as a fact. Karl Marx himself supplies the testimony for this indisputable statement and all the dissertations upon the materialist or economic interpretation of history cannot detract from its truth.

The Caravan unrolls its length before our eyes. It moves onward and its component parts fall into ranks and are articulated into companies and columns for the march; their forms take definite shape. Now we can see them distinctly. There are nations organized as distinct bodies, economic and social certainly, yet political in form. Whether they retain the character of a great family, or whether they succeed in minimizing the importance of the family in the organization of the State, these political bodies are States. The more conscious the people become of this organization and the greater the respect and liking they have for it, the more firmly established is the State and the more active and powerful in the Human Caravan.

It happens to the State as to each individual one of us. We are microcosms and the "state of man" is a little kingdom, an abridgment of humanity. Our instincts, our feelings and emotions, our needs and desires, our reason and our intelligence propose, but it is in fact the will-power that disposes. Our other faculties are obedient to the will-power in all its decisions, even if those decisions should be contrary to the advice of reason. Whatever may be their influence it is the free choice of the will and freedom of action which weave the fabric of our lives. And it is the same thing with political nations organized as States, because they alone are the weavers of human life in the community and they alone exercise freedom of choice, judgment and action.

Even religions by themselves can lay no claim to this rôle of directing. They influence action, but it is not they that act. You may very well ask: "What of Islam and Christianity?"— Islam is primarily a political Church formed and developed by force of arms, a theocratic and conquering State. And Christianity differs in its effect from Vedism, Buddhism, Western Paganism and national Churches or religions, precisely in that it is realized in the world through a sovereign Church, universal, independent of the State, superior to it, capable of holding it up when it totters, of replacing it when it slumbers or is dissolved, of restoring it when it falls into ruins, of giving birth to, educating, and directing for ten centuries that family of nations which was once the Western ethnarchy, the State of States, Christendom.

In very truth, religions are forces just as are philosophies, economic needs, social instincts and individual covetousness. They all contribute to form an impulse which is the motive force of States; but it is the great organised groups that move forward and their march constitutes the whole of history.

III

THE CARAVAN AND ITS CORPS OF PEOPLES MOVE IN A CIRCLE

This wonderful organization of the Caravan into great bodies of people advancing across the ages, brings order into the perpetual re-beginnings which at first view seemed to crown the disorder of the human chaos. Henceforth these re-beginnings appear as the successful effort of a second law which presides over the order of the march and is the very law of life on this globe. Generations, peoples, empires, civilizations, each in their turn, take up the thread of life. They are born, they grow great, decrease, break up and are replaced. We cannot speak of constant progress, less still of an indefinite, unlimited progress. The alleged law of progress has no application to history. Cardinal Newman says that there is always a point at which perfection halts: and that the very causes to which things owe their greatness bring them ultimately back to their original littleness. Weakness he sees as merely the result of strength: events form cycles: all things move in a circle.

The curve, however, is not a true circle, for in no part is the curve regular. States are like individual men; as they move along the path of their existence, they pass through incessant alternations of success and failure, illness and health, prosperity and disaster, advance and retreat. The movement is continuous, but this continuity of unequal deviations means that the curve is never moving steadily back to the point of departure.

All humanity is subject to this irresistible law. Not all its changes have meant true progress and, for the race as for the individual members of it, modernity does not necessarily mean excellence. Is it possible for us to entertain the hope that sooner or later the human race may break free from the law of the cycle? Nothing warrants belief in such a possibility; everything warns us of the contrary.

Should the question be asked, we must say that the circle is not yet complete, but that already the arc suggests the full curve. Humanity also revolves in a circle as does each one of the groups organized within it. Thus also the spheres which roll across the heavens or in the immensity of the atoms and the universes they form, are balanced by unceasing oscillations upon their orbits. They are bound together in symmetry without ever passing twice by the same point in space.

Two laws, then, determine the order of the march of the Caravan: *a law of political organization, action and reaction*, by virtue of which the human groupings are united and become subordinate one to the other to form the independent States which make history; *a law of transformation in cycles and oscillating continuity*, by virtue of which history is but an endless series of alternations and fresh beginnings.

At the same time we perceive the dawn of certain other historic laws. How could anything be known of the existence of the first two, if men and groups of men had not increased in great numbers in the course of centuries and their mutual relationships become more complex? This increase and this growing complexity which throw into high relief the laws we have enunciated might quite well, however, have taken place independently of them; just as, if the numbers of the sons of Adam and the simplicity of their social life had remained in fact unchanged for the last 10,000 or 20,000 years, the first two laws would still have remained what they are. It therefore follows that *multiplication of numbers* and *increasing complexity* are also laws.

And yet, even if the elements which form the Caravan grow in numbers and in complexity, the order of the march is in no way changed; it remains the product of those organizations, mutations, re-commencements and vicissitudes which first attracted our attention. The forces and the movements, however, which affect the Caravan on its march grow in number and complexity in the same way. Let us glance at them.

CHAPTER II

FORCES AND MOVEMENTS

I

It is possible that Mr. Wells the romancer had private reasons for affirming in his fanciful *Outline of the History of the World* that there exists not the slightest similitude between the real facts with regard to the origin of man and the world and the account given in the Bible. I know well enough that "concordism" is entirely out of fashion; but I also know that Albert de Lapparent (1839–1908), the great geologist, said not so long ago, "If I had to make a résumé in forty lines of the most authentic advances in geological knowledge, I should copy the text of Genesis, that is to say the history of the creation of the world as Moses traced it."

And if I myself, at the termination of my long period of study, had to summarise in thirty words all the movements of history, the forces which determine them and the first law of such forces, I should copy the text of Genesis which gives God's words addressed to the first human couple: "Be fruitful and multiply, replenish the earth and subdue it, and have dominion over the fish of the sea and over the fowl of the air and over every living thing that moveth upon the earth." The Caravan does not remain encamped. It is neither inert nor sterile. It is moving across the ages. As it moves, it unrolls its length; as it unrolls it grows larger. As time goes on it increases in numbers as well as in length. It covers more and more of the earth and the stubborn soil becomes man's serf and surrenders to him its fruitfulness, its riches and its secrets.

For long ages the sea held out against man; but for centuries the sea has been nothing but his highway. The breezes of the air, caught and tamed in the sails of ships, soon helped humanity to impose its yoke upon the ocean. Three French names— Montgolfier, Renard, Ader—have marked during the course of the last 150 years three stages in the conquest of the air.

The hour will soon be here when the wild beasts of the earth and the creatures of the oceans, the great cetaceans, the rhinoceros, the hippopotamus and the other wild creatures will have to be protected by human laws against human depredations and the annihilation with which they are threatened under human domination, so that they may retain their freedom and live in the Arctic seas, or in a few forest districts, or on the steppes and in the marshes reserved for them.

What shall we call the force that engenders this irresistible movement, this tremendous growth, this multiplication and this empire of man? It is a force inherent and innate in man. It is proper to man and its effects remain in him. Henceforward it will be easy to identify and name it if, as St. Thomas Aquinas writes, "by life we mean the development of oneself by the action of a force which is proper to oneself and is within oneself; and the possession of that development".[1]

The first force, the first movement, the law of laws for humanity is Life; but, let it be clearly understood: *human* Life. Those men will never have any understanding of the Human Caravan who look upon it and study it without admitting any difference between it and a herd of bison, a shoal of sardines, a flock of ducks, a flight of locusts or an invasion of caterpillars. The multiplication of human beings, merely because their life is human, has results which are transcendent in comparison with the multiplication of animals.

Bees swarm as soon as the hive is overpopulated and a second queen has her wings: but that event goes no further in consequences. In the case of mankind, however, the groups which are multiplied by the increase in the population of the earth do not, as a rule, remain in isolation. They co-ordinate

[1] *De Potentia*, q. 10 a, 1. c.

and subordinate their activities. They disperse over the face of the earth to fill it, and yet their tendency is to form regroupings. Human societies in this way grow more complex from age to age; and amongst individuals, groups, and aggregations of groups this complexity very soon produces a partition of historic and social functions which is either automatic or voluntary.

We must not think that things remain there, nor that this division of functions simplifies them. Too many contingencies modify them and render them complex. How could they remain simple when they are controlled by the rule of so many variable and various causes? We have not seen all, nor said all, when we have observed that Rome was made for empire, Greece for dialectic, England for trade, America for production and France to maintain a balance in all such activities. Functions change according to the times; they accumulate or they are scattered and dispersed. One thing alone is constant: the simultaneous growth of human power and of the obstacles it must overcome. Historical movements, like the states which direct them, require ever mightier effort and grow ever wider in extent until they become irresistible.

"When the kingdom of the Assyrians subjugated almost the whole of Asia," says St. Augustine, "it was, it is true, by warfare, but in those days wars could be carried on successfully without excessive harshness, or difficulty, because they were waged against races still inadequately prepared for self-defence and weaker or fewer in numbers than they were later on. On the contrary it was not with such speed or ease that Rome subdued all those nations of the East and the West which we to-day see within her Empire. This was because her tardy growth, in any direction in which she desired to extend, brought her face to face with other nations already powerful and warlike."

To the forces and movements which have a tendency to multiply and disperse the groups and series of groups over the face of the earth, other forces and other movements are added which tend to complicate their organization, their relationship

and their march—but, at the same time they give them a
direction and lead them towards unity. Dominated by the law
of political organization, the laws of *multiplication* and *extension*
which impel the Caravan to develop, engender the laws of
complication and *concentration* which prevent this development
from dying away. Movements and forces balance one another.
In the course of the process they reach a harmony of action.

But this is not effected without breaking another harmony,
another equilibrium. "Man does not live by bread alone."
Being both spirit and matter, he needs a double nourishment;
but it is enough that man should desire the nourishment of the
spirit to find it, inexhaustible and ready for him, at all times;
whilst, on the other hand, it is only with the greatest difficulty
that he drags from a rebellious earth bread for the body. The
more he spreads over the earth the more it becomes necessary
for him, in order to live like a man, to subdue the soil to his rule.
But as he subdues the earth, she in turn seizes upon him,
crushes him down and makes him her slave. He is, so to speak,
absorbed in her mass by the very need he has of her and by
the complexity, the continuity, the fullness and the passion of
their contacts. The materialist or economic interpretation of
history is only a puerile theory; but the materialization of
history is a law directly issuing from the other laws which we
have just observed in action.

In each State as it grows, in humanity, in the passing of time,
the part played by man's preoccupation with economics and the
natural sciences becomes ever more important, because the
weight of matter to be dominated, transformed and set in
motion becomes ever more formidable. The savage has his
limbs and his five senses. They are sufficient for him. The
civilized man, whether a contemporary of Rameses or of
Victoria of England, must, in order to live, have a thousand and
one mechanisms, codes of law, theatres, books, sciences, the
inheritance of centuries, the spoils of the universe. And in this
wise we observe, parallel with the growth of civilization, the
ever-growing importance in history and in politics of the production of wealth in all its forms.

This law of *materialization*, associated as it is with the laws from which it is derived, gives birth in its turn to other laws, by virtue of which there is a constant increase in the speed, uniformity and universality of historic phenomena. Like a body which is falling under the pull of gravity towards an invisible centre, humanity is moving with a constant acceleration of speed towards its invisible goal. The times needed to transfigure it grow shorter and the march of the Caravan is swifter as it progresses along its path. From the age of Kheops to Moses the face of the earth suffered scarcely any change, though from 1,000 to 2,000 years separated them; and another thousand years afterwards its appearance had only just begun its transformation. When the Greeks of Themistocles and Alexander enter upon the stage the play is just beginning.

The rhythm of movement grows more animated in the course of the 2,000 years which follow the age of Alexander. Every 300 years sees decisive events, such as the conquest of the Western world by the Roman power and then by Christ: the coming of Islam and the Holy Roman Empire; of the modern State and Protestant individualism. There was certainly no delay for rehearsals. The Greeks raised the curtain and turned up both the headlights and the footlights. At once the actors walked the boards and the plot of the drama was developed in three acts and six scenes.

Scarcely three and a half centuries ago this epoch reached its end. Already, near its conclusion, there had come into the world the invention and use of cannon in warfare, the art of printing, and the discovery of America, all three in rapid succession. These were followed by the newspaper, machinery, and the wonder of modern finance, which have brought about as many changes in the world as took place within the whole cycle of the twenty centuries of the preceding age.

That is not all: for if two centuries intervened between the disruption which terminated the preceding epoch and the Declaration of American Independence, the French Revolution and the accession of England to the hegemony of the world, one century has sufficed since then to mature that other cluster of events of supreme grandeur:—the commercial and colonial expansion of European Nations, the progress of the United States and Japan who have thrust forward and taken their place amongst the leaders of the Caravan; the first World War; the Russian Revolution; the awakening of Asia and the enfranchisement of Islam.

The tragedy is in truth becoming ever more violent in its nature, more complex, profound and painful. The action moves swiftly. If we were present in a theatre I should say that the dénouement was close at hand. The *acceleration* of events must be apparent to all observers. The process of *universalization* is equally manifest.

Whereas long before the age of Kheops men were already scattered over the whole area of the ancient continent of Asia, the empire of the Pharaohs merely covered the Nile valley and a small portion of western Asia. It went no further than the partition of Syria with the Hittites and the extension of its influence from Ethiopia to Jerusalem, Crete and Mycenae. The Egyptian power, therefore, was of interest to a small portion of the globe only; its contemporaries also in Mesopotamia, Asia Minor, India and China operated in comparatively restricted spheres.

Alexander was the first monarch and statesman to have anything like a real vision of the earth and to covet domination over the whole world. In the vigour of youth he rushed into action. He furrowed the earth with his conquests and scattered the seed with swift hands. He fell a victim to death before he had overrun one quarter of the then known globe.

The Romans obtained dominion over one-third of the ancient world. They retained it and organized it. They were its constructors, erecting it as a vast Forum with a multitude of basilicas where in the future *comitia*, or assemblies of the human race, might come together; but we must bear in mind that during that epoch only those peoples profited from its organization and development who dwelt round the shores of the Mediterranean Sea.

It was in this manner that the *Two Ways* of Buddha, the

Gospel of Jesus Christ and the *Koran* of Mahomet—which appealed to all men and were in the course of time to have more influence than Greek wisdom and Roman discipline on the march of history—during long centuries were messages of the Spirit only for the East or the West, or those lands which lie between them on the confines of the great deserts.

Everywhere in the same way events that are purely local and of limited consequences are succeeded by other events which are of much longer and at the same time of much wider range. They are indeed local sowings of harvests which are slower to achieve maturity, but destined to be universal.

These events which follow—the invention of artillery, the discovery of America, the beginning of the press, the coming of Protestantism and of democracy, of the machine and of English imperialism—though still local in themselves, become immediately universal through their direct consequences. The most recent—the expansion of European power, the accession of the United States of America and of Japan to the rank of the Great Powers, the War of 1914-1918, the Russian Revolution, the Asiatic awakening, the liberation of Islam—are events of world-wide influence. The relations between men and between peoples grow in number, in frequency, in importance and in extent, as men multiply and the number of nationalities increases. Their common interests tend to unite them ever more closely, but the field of the rivalries which divide them becomes constantly vaster.

At the same time and for the same reasons the differences that separate them grow less important and of less effect. Dress, usages, amusements, knowledge of the arts of war and peace, industrial and commercial operations, even laws and social and political institutions, from one end of the world to the other, all move more frequently and more quickly towards a perfect uniformity.

All the races of eastern Asia ended by following a life more or less in the Chinese manner; as all those of southern Asia, the Hindu mode of existence. Conquered Greece conquered the

Romans and put her mark with theirs upon half the ancient world.

More deeply still Islam stamped its own image upon the conquests it made. And then we see the European type, unified from the Middle Ages, extended to America in modern times, then to Africa in the nineteenth century, in our own time extend its dominion into Asia which for thousands of years had resisted invasion.

Let us, however, be sure that we understand: variety in human things has neither wholly nor everywhere disappeared. We may quibble on the more or less that still exists: it is a matter of appreciation; but the growth of uniformity is a fact, startling in its certainty. To prove it or to verify it, neither lengthy observations nor minute statistics are necessary. It is self-evident and the Law of *Unification* which its consequences display is indisputable.

In addition, when one works beneath the surface, it is seen that this law is not merely derived from the others. Like the other laws and along with them, as much and more than on the surface, it plays a part in the depth of things. All have their origin in the same surge of vigour. After all, it is the unchanging and permanent identity of human nature in men which brings them to unity in proportion as their empire grows over the material universe; just as matter, when it exercised its power over men, bent them by its brute force to its changing diversity, by making of their very multiplication a cause for their dispersion.

II

THE SPIRITUAL, INTELLECTUAL AND FREE FORCES OF LIFE ARE PREPONDERANT IN THE CARAVAN

The movements of human history are not then produced, like those of the animal world, by the sovereign play of exterior forces. On the contrary they have as beginning and end the subjugation of such exterior forces by the interior force of the soul. For 10,000 or 300,000 years, in spite of all the corporeal resemblances which make of us, if we persist in the idea, just simple primates, the unanimous voice of facts is evidence of our transcendence and of our spirituality.

Does that transcendence mean that nothing of the beast pushes itself to the front of our Caravan? To answer this question it is sufficient for us to look inside ourselves to find certainty. The moving force within us is *need*, which generates passion: now, passions and needs equal in power to those of the animals are not indeed lacking in our natures. We have them even more than they have, but we feel passions and needs which are more numerous and more powerful, having nothing in common with the animal, which are of another order, foreign to those of the animal world, superior to them, inaccessible to their nature, beyond all development that such a nature could possibly achieve in the future.

Besides, whether they are transcendent or not in relation to animality, our needs have this in common, that their influence over our history is much less the result of the individual or collective passions which they engender, than of the manner in which they are used, ruled, directed, exploited by a small number of men—thinkers, artists, men of action, statesmen—who are guided by those very passions, and also by the idea which they entertain in their own minds of their tasks and our destinies, of God and the Universe.

What then do we find under the ten laws which control the order of the march and the movements of the Caravan? The fatality of matter? Animal determinism? By no means. Everything moves in liberty of mind, ruled and directed by the power of the intelligence and by love. Therefore it is by no means surprising that the very action of these ten laws causes such profound forces to surge upwards and to extend, in proportion as the human race grows more and more intricate in its nature, more concentrated on itself, more universal, shaped in its course towards unity. The beliefs and the aspirations, the knowledge and the prejudices of a certain number of men, a minority, continue to acquire strength, as in the end do those of

E

the masses of the people, the great majority, and in this way achieve an importance which is ever greater, more powerful and of higher value. In a word, the process of the growth of public opinion extends to more and graver things. Opinion which in a way has always been the ruler of the world continues in the development of its power and the spread of its influence.

This is inevitable in the order of things, although in that order democracy does not exist as of divine right, nor is it even postulated at any moment whatsoever by this new condition of the world. But, whether this be so or not, at any rate it is a fact that the "emotion of the ideal", as Benjamin Kidd calls it, has an ever growing tendency to take prime place amongst the forces of history and, as a consequence, "the science of power"—or better, the art of controlling the march of the Caravan—consists, to an ever-increasing extent, in knowing how to make use of the home, the school, books, newspapers, the spoken word and the theatre to create and manipulate public opinion.

The "emotion of the ideal" is, most certainly, not a modern discovery. It played its part in the Punic wars as in the Crusades, in the expedition of the Argonauts as in the deeds of Joan of Arc, in the expansion of Buddhism and of Islam, as in the growth of Christianity. We must, however, wait for the period of the Renascence to see it operating on a grand scale upon a whole civilization, and upon all orders of men at the same time: upon art, science, philosophy, religion and politics.

In the eighteenth century all the power of the "philosophic church" was the work of this "emotion of the ideal", as well as the power exercised by the secret societies and the clubs. The French Revolution which was their work marks this triumph. We know what its influence has been since then, in the universal advent of political régimes where public opinion and the world-wide dominion of the press are the paramount phenomena. We understand how much "propaganda" costs and how much it brings by way of profit to States intent upon winning or holding an empire.

And so it happens that the intelligence and love which in

their freedom give movement to the whole Human Caravan become identical, though in varying degrees, with the intelligence and love of a multitude whose tendency is to become one with the whole of humanity. If only it were always an intelligence that seized upon truth and was guided by it; and a love having good things for its object!

III

LIFE AND ITS FORCES ARE NOT IN THEIR NORMAL CONDITION IN THE CARAVAN

It is exactly at this point that a strange disorder becomes evident. Outside the human race there is no organism of any rank or degree whatsoever which at any moment is divided against itself. If it changes, develops, declines, or dies, it is always according to the essential principle of its being and nature. It is never false to itself.

If it is material, it will be transformed or disintegrated in matter; but the forces which determine its existence will never cause it to vanish into nothingness.

If the organism is vegetable, the forces which co-ordinate its creation and cause its sap to circulate, can indeed cease to act, but, so long as they operate, it will be to prevent the organism from disintegrating into its mineral elements. If it is an animal organism, from the very moment of the fertilization of the germ it moves towards death; but the forces which support its life and which sometimes bring about in it most remarkable metamorphoses will never have the least tendency to transform it into a vegetable.

There are scientists who demonstrate that the mammals, including man, are great-nephews of the reptiles and the molluscs; but no one has ever regarded for a moment the possibility that we may have snails and lizards as great-nephews. Nature has her caprices and her monsters: but even amongst them there is to be found no example of such retrogressions.

Man, if he is a spirit and transcends the animal, as history assures us he does, has then only to let himself go and follow his bent. The whole universe advises him: "Follow nature, and you will then develop, in the order in which she has placed you. She has created you both an angel and a beast in order to harmonize in you the spiritual with the material: confidently and perseveringly, you will, as is right, train the beast in the service of the angel and you will subdue what is material in you to the empire of the mind." But there is for man no promise more false and no advice more pernicious.

If he follows nature, he goes astray. If he allows himself to follow his bent, he is lost. None of the forces which control him and his actions will advance him surely and constantly in the direction of his transcendence over the animal world and of his spirituality. All his developments tend, more or less, to drag him out of his own order. He must in fact react vigorously and tenaciously, in order that the conquests of his spirit shall not profit the materialism of his nature; and such reactions within man are not always immediate, spontaneous and decisive. The angel has wings, but he likes to cohabit with the beast and to crawl along the ground with it, more often than he chooses to carry the beast upwards with him in his flight.

In its skilful analyses psychology reveals to us the whole of this tendency in man; but with what relief, in what clear light, with what fullness and what perseverance does history disclose the vision to our eyes!

If it is in the nature of man to multiply, to unite in groups, to subjugate the earth to his empire as well as the sea and the empyrean above; to be constrained to unity by the needs of his common humanity and disciplined for progress by the emotion of the ideal; how then does it happen that the groups into which men organize themselves are never developed without reducing men themselves, sooner or later, to the status of domestic animals, the slaves of a master, of the soil, or of the State! What is the cause of the fact that their empire over matter in proportion as it grows wider increases men's need of matter and debases their nature to the pre-occupations of the beast?

How does it come about that men's tendency to achieve a unity scarcely ever creates any organization which is not a coalition of selfishness, individual or collective, united and moved by bestial passions, such as cupidity, envy, hatred of other nations, class-hatred, a mad lust for domination and the joy of destruction or fear?

How does it happen that the emotion of the ideal is so much more powerful and easy to arouse, to stir up in the multitude and to prolong, in proportion as the ideal is false or inhuman?

To all these questions generally speaking only one superficial reply is given. We are satisfied to say: "Man is free, but limited, hence he is fallible; his will power is subject to its inherent faults, just as his mind is to error." In answering thus we do no more than skim over the surface, we almost side-step the problem.

In point of fact our natural limitations keep us from the knowledge and understanding of many things; but the matter we are now discussing is our own errors in matters which we know and understand quite well. Our liberty consists in being able to make a choice of that action which we regard as the best amongst all those which are presented to our judgment; and at this point the faults of which we are guilty in choosing those actions which we well know to be evil in their nature and consequences come into question.

This then is the reason why to all questions with which history confronts us, as we see on the stage of the world this division of man against himself—these disorders born of movements, forces and laws, whose normal play should bring nothing but order into things universally—I do not make the same reply as the philosophers who say: "The reason is that man is an animal." or: "The reason is that man is a free entity." On the contrary my reply to such questions is that which is found in the Bible and the Gospel: "The reason is that man has sinned."

When? Where? How? These questions have no importance in the matter, given that the consequences, otherwise inexplicable, lie before our eyes. The three passions with which we were endowed so that we may continue to live—the passion for a knowledge of the truth, the passion to enjoy that which is good, and the passion to achieve excellence by surpassing ourselves—have become three fatal appetites which fill the whole course of the ages with crime and all baseness. The angel in our nature does wrong to the beast that is also there. The angel is no longer what he should be, that man might be perfect in his kind like other created things. Clearly then it follows that the angel within man is a fallen angel.

Hence the development of man throughout the ages is not merely motion in a circle with deviations to this side and that as with all other created beings, but disordered and misdirected.

The forces and impulses which have been designed to assure man's progress fetter and trammel him. They turn him away from his road or arrest his movements. The Caravan has lost its way. In the darkness and shadows it is vainly searching for the road. Those who compose the Caravan are incapable of any harmonious disciplined efforts towards making any advance along the road of progress; but, on the contrary, its movements are stimulated by the bitter struggle and the fierce and violent contentions of the groups and series of groups amongst themselves. The Caravan is thrown into confusion and a state of anarchy is the result.

Each element in the Caravan strives its utmost to develop at the expense of the others and to elevate its will and desires into supreme laws. Hence in every state there exists a triple tendency: in the first place it puts forward all its efforts to dominate other states; secondly there is the tendency to disintegrate within itself; and finally it endeavours to destroy its rivals by first dividing them and then absorbing all autonomous elements. Imperialism, Individualism and Statism, such is the threefold historical fruit of the Law of Internal Contradiction to which the original degradation of man gives birth by dividing human nature against itself in the scale of mankind.

IV

THIS DISORDER AND THE MOTION IN A CIRCLE INSTEAD OF
ALONG A STRAIGHT PATH RAISE THE QUESTION OF THE
DIRECTION AND MEANING OF HISTORY AND MAKE THE MEANING
OF PROGRESS THE KEY OF THE PROBLEM

Disorders, discords and internecine struggles are then added
to the vicissitudes of nature and its perpetual new beginnings.
Order and disorder are confounded and born one from the
other; such is the prodigious spectacle which the Caravan offers
to our eyes in contrast with the harmony, the regularity and the
clearness of universal order.

Hence a question is propounded and a principle emerges.

If, in spite of all that has been said against it, history has a
definite path; if in its entirety, as a whole process, it escapes
from the law of death and the law of sin which impose their
inexorable decrees upon every detail in history; if there
emerges from the chaos of facts, not merely a certain order
which is particular and relative, such as we have in these pages
just perceived, but also general and absolute order, within
the unity of which contrasts and contradictions, obscurities and
anomalies, as well as death and sin, are resolved and disappear;
then this transcendent order of things and events implies a
transcendent End, or goal, towards which, ever since the
creation of the world of men, all humanity has been making its
way.

In its turn this End, this "far off, divine event", reveals an
Intelligence which has conceived, and a Will which in the
course of the ages performs upon earth and amidst humanity,
a work which, like the End, is itself transcendent. There is,
indeed, a divine wisdom which "rejoices and takes its delight
in dwelling amidst the children of men".

If the direction of history and its meaning remain constant,
in spite of all the contradictions and retrogressions mentioned
already, and in spite of the new beginnings of history, it can

only happen by the intervention of God who by the super-abundance of His perfection corrects and neutralizes the excess of human imperfections and actually makes use of that excess for the purpose of correction. Along with such men as St. Augustine, Bossuet and de Maistre, or, if you should consider these as having an inadequate knowledge of our modern discoveries, then with G. K. Chesterton and Berdyaev, one must recognize in the unity of history alongside and above human facts, other facts, divine facts which dominate them, penetrate them and saturate them with divinity.

In a few words, amongst so many combined and collective movements which compose the warp and woof of history, if there are discovered any threads which develop with constancy in a straight line and which avoid the laws of contradiction and death, inherent in the law of life in this world, let us have no doubt—it is the Master of Life and of Death who liberates them from those common laws which otherwise obtain.

Progress is the sign or mark of God.

CHAPTER III

THE OBJECTIVE OF THE JOURNEY

I

THERE IS NO ABSOLUTE PROGRESS FOR THE CARAVAN EXCEPT THE
PROGRESS TOWARDS PERFECT JOY

PROGRESS, the sign of God, is a word flattering to our ears, an idea confusing to our minds. It is important to fix the sense of the word, to define it, in order to avoid bestowing our adoration upon idols. All development is not progress, all change still less so. What is progress? Of what does it consist—collective or individual progress? To progress, to advance, are they two words for the same idea? Whatever moves advances. But is all movement progress?

Let us be on our guard against the cheat of words. Is it true that whatever is moving is advancing? If it is moving in a circle it advances only along the circle and returns to the point of departure. What sort of an advance is that? Its progress is purely and simply an appearance; it is in your mind that you create the idea by imagining on the circumference of the circle a fixed point which the being that moves has either passed, or is about to reach. This being, in truth, does not advance. Yet it is not falling back. It is simply moving.

What does it need in order that it may advance? Precisely that fixed point, that term, that end, which your imagination deludes you into seeing where it does not exist. The horse that is made to go round and round the track of the riding school is not advancing; it is moving. The horse that gallops at random in order to exercise its limbs, or to frisk upon the prairie, is moving; it is not advancing. All progress postulates an end: the horse which walks round and round in the process of drawing up two tons of water by means of a bucket-chain advances towards his last turn round the track he follows; the horse that gallops over the meadow to escape by an open gate or a fallen hurdle advances towards that exit from the field. Food, rest from work, escape from restriction and restraint, such is the objective towards which progress is made by every movement in its direction. See now where these four horses are taking us.

The first two horses who move vigorously without going anywhere in particular, are the very living symbol of humanity as seen by the materialists. For them there is no object whatsoever in life because there is no finality in the universe. Finality, they say, is purely and simply an illusion of the human imagination. When they speak to us of progress we shall return the compliment, since progress and finality are one and the same idea. Progress as conceived by them is therefore an illusion of the human imagination.

The two other horses which move, one round and round in a circular track, the other galloping along in a straight line, but both of them towards an objective, illustrate the two kinds of progress and the means of judging them. They signify what the Human Caravan is ever on the look out for and towards what distant goal it directs its march.

The two horses are making progress, one towards the open gate or barrier, the other towards the precise point where his hooves will rest, when the last quart of water in his allotted task has been drawn up and the merry-go-round has been stopped; but in neither case is it the final end. Out beyond the open gate, or the hurdle that is down, and after the completion of the task of drawing up water, there will be liberty and rest, or the peck of oats as a reward; these are the secondary ends, more important objectives in comparison with which the first are merely the conditions, or means.

The provender, repose and liberty towards which our horses move are in themselves but intermediary ends or objectives. The horses move towards them as the means of satisfying a third end, viz: the need they experience of eating, sleeping, or of wandering at liberty; and the satisfaction of this need is in itself but the means to a fourth, or ultimate end: life, healthy, normal life; the happy life of horses whose needs are satisfied. Thus they realize the double progress of every living creature: absolute progress in the accomplishment of its destiny; a relative progress in the possession or use of the means that can accomplish it. Outside these means and ends we can indeed speak of changes and movements, of complications and differences, but neither of achieving perfection, nor of progress. In reality after we have considered all the evidence it seems that relative progress is not progress, unless it contributes something towards the achievement of absolute progress. What an absurd business it would be to have everything, and yet to fall short of that absolute progress. As a matter of necessity, therefore, before we declare that a certain movement or change means progress, it is necessary for us to know two things: the type of creature that changes or moves, and its destined end. How is that end to be attained?

We know the reason for the existence of comparatively few creatures. What is the end or purpose of the vegetable world? Why does the animal world exist? What reason lies behind the innumerable universes which people the vastnesses of space? We have no scientific knowledge of such ends or purposes and we shall in this life remain ignorant of them. We may be quite aware of what their existence means to us; but the existence of innumerable multitudes of things and beings which never have served and never will serve in any way whatsoever the needs of sublunar humanity makes it difficult to assert that the purpose of the celestial bodies, or of vegetables, or animals is to be defined by their utility or non-utility for mankind. What are we to say of the multitude of other things of which we know exactly this: that we know nothing about them?

Where there is no known end, there can be no recognizable progress. I marvel that a believer in the doctrine of evolution dare affirm that man, in comparison with the oyster, constitutes an advance. What does he know of the matter? Why does he speak of inequality when the system or theory to which he pins his faith allows him to see mere differences? It is only in an arbitrary way that he takes as sufficient evidence of progress in organic life the multiplicity of organs, their complexity, the duration of life, its intensity, its expansion and action on other lives and organisms and its extension into time or space.

Though St. Augustine was not a disciple of Lamarck, nor of Darwin, nor yet of Herbert Spencer, he already knew that "God created the angels in heaven and the worms on the earth, without being himself smaller in the latter, or larger in the former". In itself the oyster is as perfect an organism as man, even more perfect, perhaps, since its organs and its rudimentary life are better adapted to the purpose of its existence than are the incomparable body and the prodigious life of man to human ends and purposes. "What a piece of work is man! How noble in reason, how infinite in faculty, in form and movement how like an angel!" But what savant or scientist can tell us the purpose of the oyster?

Let us now classify the mollusc in nature upon its bed of iridescent pearl, and by its side man with all his implements. What scientist will be able to tell us the end or purpose of this fine piece of work, "the beauty of the world, the paragon of animals", so that Science out of its own mouth may instruct us in what respect man, rather than the oyster, brings the universe nearer to its final end or purpose? On this matter Science is mute.

All that Science can in fact say is that the whole fabric of nature appears to move round and round along a circular track, developing in cycles, passing and repassing, indefinitely perhaps through a state of infinite subdivision of the cosmic matter, returning to that state in order to recede, and receding in order to return without anyone being able to perceive any real progress either in the recession or in the return.

Science is cognizant only of varieties, differences, movements and changes infinite in variety. And it is for this reason that the materialists have come to place in change the ultimate end and purpose of all things. If one is to believe them, the living are not made for life, nor man for joy; every creature has as its destiny to evolve as we see it evolving, and nothing more. This

---

comes back to declaring that every change is progress, every difference a superiority and every development an improvement subject to the sole condition that it is more recent, more modern in date. This is indeed nonsense, since it implies confounding and confusing things as manifestly distinct and often opposed in nature as quantity and quality, the end and the means, the essential and the accidental.

Of final or absolute ends Science is ignorant. To contemplate such ends and to be able to speak intelligently of progress, we must turn from Science to Metaphysics.

Without weakening our own position we concede that the Human Caravan is on the march; and on their own principles the materialists must—I do not say define, for that is entirely a question of Metaphysics—but recognize the end or purpose of the journey.

Will they deny that every man is on the look out for joy? Those very men pursue it who most proudly declare that they are not interested in it. The most confirmed pessimists, even if they deny speculatively that we are born to be happy, cannot in practice prevent themselves from striving their utmost to attain happiness, provided that melancholy has not completely turned their minds. Joy, perfect Joy: even if no one knew where it really is to be found, and no one ever attained it; even if no two individuals could agree as to its nature; yet the end of the world will come before we can discover a single person who does not ardently desire it. It is the centre towards which everything conscious in the universe irresistibly gravitates. There is no exception to this rule. This indeed is the very fact which compels us to identify happiness with the proper goal of man; and as there is nothing else in the communities or collectivities of the Caravan than the men of whom they are composed, these communities can have no other final end or purpose than fullness of joy for the men who constitute them.

It is indeed the law of human nature for men to live in groups that their individual lives may be happy. Their groups and series of groups have no other basic reason for existence. From this it follows that such groups and series are merely the means to an end and that as a result their progress as a whole is relative.

Families, tribes, cities, nations, societies, States, ethnarchies, civilization and humanity, the whole indeed, for many thousands of years has kept on developing. But is this constant development in itself, everywhere and at all times, the same thing as progress? That men find in it the means to achieve in an ever increasing degree the life of the community, or to win happiness with greater ease, is too easy a solution of the question. It would still be necessary that these means should not be applied at the wrong time, should not move or turn against the current, should not take the place of the objectives to be achieved, and should not obscure the goal to be attained.

We have a desert to cross, why therefore should you bring me pearls for the journey? Rather fill the leather bottle with water, and when we are on the road do not hinder me from drinking it under the pretext that the soil of the desert would become fertile and blossom like the rose if we watered it from our bottles.

Whatever may be the definition of happiness, what we dream of and pursue under this magic name is in very fact complete and perfect joy, fullness of satisfaction without end, without satiety, of all our needs and desires. This is what the Human Caravan is searching for.

CHAPTER IV

THE ITINERARY

I

ALL RELATIVE PROGRESS IS HARMFUL, IF IT IS NOT INCORPORATED AS PART OF ABSOLUTE PROGRESS

THE Caravan marches onwards towards Joy. On the Chart of Progress, which is no less artificial and ridiculous than the famous Chart of Love, many places bear the name of Joy. Which one amongst them all is worthy of that name? Many roads lead towards them. The Human Caravan follows them all. It is an army whose many columns advance to the assault in a series of movements, carried out in the grand style, simultaneously, towards all those points which the staffs and the leaders have marked out for immediate attack and capture.

Routes, marches, combats; victories gained at every moment yet still remaining to be won; the highway to felicity. It is all one! And the word for it is Civilization. The words which are successful are never selected by chance. Civilization is derived from *civilis*, which in turn is derived from *civis*. The *civis* is man looked at as a member of a *civitas*, of a State, of a political society. Civilization, the action which civilizes, or the effect of that action, operates in the first place by the development of political society.

This development is progress when it contributes to men's happiness. It does not always contribute to this happiness. It is sometimes in opposition to it. It cannot be denied that it is in the normal order of human things; but is it necessary?

Mgr. Le Roy met in the African forest a negro dwarf who on this very subject made certain remarks which are full of a judicious philosophy. "Your inventions are marvellous," said

61

in effect this almost naked chief of a tribe of pygmy hunters; "but does your civilization, of which you are so proud, make you happier? You possess a hundredfold more than we do; yet you have need of a hundred other things. As far as we are concerned we have our bows and the forest around us; we have our families and the tribe and with that we lack nothing. What is the good of your knowledge, your anxieties, your weapons which art has brought to perfection? Life is short. We have the better lot!"

And this is the oracle of good sense. No! civilization does not make men happier at all points. It is precisely for that reason that it is developing. We are on the look out for happiness: if civilization does not find it for us, we shall go on inventing new means, new combinations of means to conquer happiness.

We should have no history; nor would civilization, without these new inventions; for all this swarm of marvellous inventions, you may be sure, is civilization herself. With them she began; by them she is defined. How then does it come about that, being better and better equipped for this hunt, she pursues it without ever reaching her quarry?

Satisfaction complete and perpetual of needs and desires, in other words, perfect joy, is only the constancy of an equilibrium; but the problem is to establish such an equilibrium.

Shall we attain to it by annihilating, as far as possible, our needs and our desires, as the Yogis do? Or, are we to multiply the means of satisfaction, like Croesus and Solomon? Everything has been tried out. Both ways have been found painful and delusive—two labyrinths ending in an impasse. Disillusioned Ecclesiastes sits down at the end and declares: "Vanity of vanity. All is but vanity and vexation of spirit." We have certain needs and desires which are inherent and essential in our very being; he who reduces them, or atrophies them, at the same time destroys or diminishes himself.

This is a remedy, of a sort: to kill the sick man does infallibly end the sickness; but if to gain happiness I maim myself in the very faculty or quality which makes me a man or makes me myself, what happiness have I won? My own? No, not at all. It is the happiness of another creature, I know not what—dog, pig, ant, jelly-fish—which naturally lacks what I have artificially removed. In this metempsychosis I miss the end or purpose of my being.

With what kind of animals, you will say, must we then classify the prophets of Israel, the hermits of the desert, the Stylites, the Cenobites, the little poor man of Assisi, men like Nicholas of Flue, women like St. Catherine of Siena, men like Peter of Alcantara who lived for years without food and without sleep; in every instance without according to nature the satisfactions for which she is greedy, delivered over to super-human contemplation and to indescribable sufferings?

These were indeed angels. But let us not forget the lesson of Felicity, the well-named, who cried out in the pangs of child-birth, on the eve of her martyrdom, and said to the jailers who were mocking at her: "To-day it is I who suffer; but to-morrow there will be another in me who will suffer for me, because I, I shall suffer for him."

Let us not forget the lesson that Paphnutius was taught in the Thebaid when he wondered how much of a saint fifteen years of solitude and self-mortification had made of him. The Lord showed him that the virtue on which he prided himself was no greater than that of a mountebank who gained his living by juggling and tumbling. The men who heroically deprive themselves of the necessities of life in penance and self-discipline, would be mere acrobats unless they were more than themselves. We shall see later on whether there is any way by which we may escape from ourselves and pass through Him. For the moment we shall stay in our own natures!

What experience does that civilization bring us which for centuries has multiplied for our use the means of satisfying our needs and desires? It has multiplied our desires and our needs in the same proportion. He who has drunk, will drink. The fact is that nothing satisfies us; that one satisfaction produces two lusts; that we create for ourselves unceasingly fresh neces-saries out of "the superfluous which is so necessary". The

F

fictitious needs which are multiplied by these misuses in the end distort our nature. They bury our humanity under a mass of habits which become our second nature, superhuman, if we listen to the misusers, but in fact often inhuman or bestial.

The end so achieved is no longer *our* goal, nor is such a happiness, if indeed it be happiness, *our* happiness. Where then is the distinctive sign which will enable us to form a sound judgment of civilization, to know its quality, to discern the nature of progress, to discern the real decadence under the appearance of progress?

We possess an intelligence whose unconquerable tendency is to know, a heart whose unconquerable tendency is to love, a will-power whose unconquerable tendency is to act. Must we reach the conclusion that all that develops these faculties, all that increases for each man or group of men the extent of his knowledge, the greatness of his love and the width and scope of his actions, merits the name of progress? The temptation is to say, yes; but let us be on our guard; intelligence, heart, will, knowledge, love and action, all are but means to an end. The misuse which falsifies them or atrophies them in us, and even the use which satisfies our thirst, augment that thirst, or turn it into a worse thing. Our goal is to know, to love and to do something: but what? Shall we look to our tendencies for the solution? We have already observed that they contradict one another, drag us hither and thither, ourselves, our families, our groups and our series of groups. We must either choose some among our tendencies to the exclusion of others, or be torn asunder; we must chain up some tendencies and so destroy them; liberate and develop others; tame, discipline, check and guide still more.

It is admitted that mankind is created to live, and to live happily. But universal experience attests that for us the happy life does not consist in gratifying the impulse of the moment, nor the passing need, nor yet in allowing instinct to have its own way as with the animals. "That which is nature in animals, in man is vice", says St. Augustine. Our own human nature rests upon the free choice amongst the impulses, needs, instincts, whims and thoughts which appeal to us. But this freedom of choice is denied in the name of "science". What is the basis upon which rests this negative answer? Merely an hypothesis and assertions which are without proof. We, on the contrary, have before us facts which cannot be disputed.

The free decisions we make are, it is true, not always good, nor are the judgments of our reason always sound. Both induce us, only too often, to enter upon roads which lead inevitably to degradation and unhappiness. Even when our decisions and choice are at their best and achieve excellence, taking no account of those mistakes which render their imperfections manifest to us, they find nothing to free us from desires.

Hence it is clear that there is nothing in the universe, not even the universe itself, the knowledge of which, the love of which, and the free choice of which can possibly be sufficient for us. The people who are contented in it and live happily, so that their joy is full and constant and unending, are few.

The goal of the generality of men and consequently of mankind is not then within the universe. That is something which we have added to our knowledge; and this as well: in the march of the Human Caravan towards this mysterious goal where true happiness is, if the Caravan is turned aside ever so little from the path of absolute progress, then all relative progress accelerates decadence, aggravates it, or becomes its occasion or cause. If it is not to be harmful, relative progress must follow the same track as absolute progress, must be part of it. If then the progress is such as never to cause harm and never to have the power of causing harm; if amongst those movements which men realize and which enter as elements into civilization, we find one whose universal nature excludes all idea of misuse or excess, then in it lies the key to absolute progress; it is the condition and the testimony of that true progress. It will bring us to the knowledge of our end, our true happiness, and will reveal at once the road to our goal and the points at which the Human Caravan has strayed from the road.

II

THE PROGRESS OF CIVILIZATION IS ONLY RELATIVE

The roads which the Caravan follows are tortuous.

In our days it is sufficiently apparent in the Western world that grandiose civilizations, political societies which are extremely complex in their constitutions, cultured in their habits, very refined, humane, organized on a rational basis, scientifically equipped, capable of realizing prodigies in the extension of their powers alike over natural forces and over men, may yet behind this splendid façade conceal unbelievable barbarisms.

I am not thinking only of the Great War. Yet the flood of heroism which that war let loose over the world has not cleansed the Western world of moral and social stains; nor does it wash from our hands all the blood unjustly spilt in colonial expansion, in the revolutions and persecutions which we have tolerated, encouraged by our inertia, provoked by our doctrines, excited or subsidized in Europe, in China and in Mexico. From these blemishes, which one of us can say that he is completely exempt? I know that all these matters are extraordinarily complex; that there are just wars, legitimate and beneficent conquests, as well as misery and ruin which it is impossible to prevent. But too often civilization is directed towards barbarism, used for barbarism, becomes barbarism.

In short, the true way for the Caravan to follow, if it is not to be found along the roads that lead to animalism, is not necessarily to be discovered along those ways that take us away from it. Let man be distinguished more and more from the animal, let him become more man, that without any doubt is progress; but what kind of progress? Absolute or relative? We must see what the progress consists of.

In what then does man differ from the animal? If there is nothing in either save matter, then there is no essential difference between them. The abyss which we think we see between them, is entirely unreal. Their bodies are diverse from ours and yet like ours; their faculties, being completely corporeal, must also be like ours. But the moment we see those faculties at work, the similitude disappears; the abyss, the real abyss, between man and the animal yawns wide.

The animal is capable of discernment; but he neither reasons nor judges. He knows, but without ever seeing beyond the senses. He loves, but by inclination and not by choice. He chooses, he desires, he acts; but always by instinct, ever amenable to the strongest impulse. His soul is not a mind. In these phenomena lies the distinction between us and the animals. Mind, liberty, reason, create between us and the animal a greater distance than the faculties of movement, of knowledge and of love between the animal and the vegetable.

Our progress, that which fosters the growth and the blossoming of all true civilization, is marked by a growth in the spiritual life, the life of the intellect, our empire over passion and instinct, the clear-sightedness and the sureness of our reasoning faculty, the liberty of our wills and the wisdom of our soul and its dominance over matter. Only thus is man's progress fully and exclusively human.

We see it working under our eyes. "The whole series of men during the course of so many centuries," says Pascal, "must be considered as one and the same man, who always exists and is continually learning"—and, alas, continually forgetting. Every comparison is halting; but it is none the less true that tradition and the novelty which is born of it are the elements of our progress. The marks and signs which reveal our own proper faculties and show the development of them can blossom forth neither on the branches which the new springtime has not touched, nor on those wherein the sap generated in the roots of tradition no longer flows. These are signs not numerous, but remarkable. Who is there who does not know these transcendent facts? For reason, fire and the tool; for the intelligence, science and art; for liberty, laws; for spirituality, the worship of God.

Of all this the animal is ignorant, just as he is ignorant alike of tradition and of novelty. He never lights a fire and he

makes no use of tools. His stupidity is often greater than the
wonder of his instinct and he remains enclosed within this
wonder and within the narrow limits of his stupidity. He
invents nothing and he perfects nothing. He is imitative. He
finds things by chance. He fills the earth, but he does not
subdue it to his needs. He knows nothing whatsoever of heaven.
Older than we are, he has yet never reached the Stone Age,
the age of the chipped, flint stones. We on the other hand have
outstripped the machine. The miracles of electricity have put
under our control invisible waves of power. We have searched
into space, numbered and weighed the stars and penetrated the
secrets of their structure, movements and history.

The animal neither ploughs nor sows. If he sings he is
recognized by his song; a few notes of which the mode and style
scarcely ever vary. If he speaks, his language is limited to
translating, by inarticulate sounds which do not vary, elementary impressions; either of joy or desire, fear or grief, or a call to
a mate. He neither writes not draws, neither carves nor paints.
Whether he leads a solitary life or not—a couple, a pack, a
troop, a shoal, a colony, a swarm, an ant-heap—he makes no
rules or laws. His existence, whether it is lived alone or in
common, develops in its order, without his being under any
necessity to regulate it. The laws which exist for him he obeys;
neither he nor any of his kind make them. Everything comes
to him from outside himself.

Everything comes to us from within ourselves, for even that
which comes to us from outside receives its value and its human
form from within. We order our own lives. We regulate our
acts. Our laws which have been established under the empire
of nature are none the less our own work and the work of our
kind. Man is a law-maker. Man is a priest. In order to live
and die he must have a conception of life and death, create for
himself an idea of himself and beyond the limits of his own self
catch sight of what lies beyond such limits. He prays. He
offers sacrifices. Where are the altars and the temples and the
tombs of the animal? Worship, legislation, philosophy and the
order that they introduce into life; the soul and societies of

men; letters and arts, sciences, trades, industries, commerce:
so it is with just reason that their development in quality—even
in quantity if the quality does not suffer as a result—is looked
upon as the progress of civilization. It is a relative progress,
however: here is nothing which necessarily leads to our goal,
producing only joy. This is only too evident to us. It is matter
for derision when philosophers assign as the end or purpose of
our life, at one time vague hypotheses based upon arbitrary
postulates such as the non-existence of God and the automatic
evolution of nature; at another time simple means such as
society, the State, the fatherland—or even thought, knowledge,
love and action—considered apart from their ultimate object.

The whole of history furnishes evidence against such follies.
Yet we do not read the evidence. We admit the degradations,
abortions, catastrophes, horrors of the past, but we think to
make up for our losses by setting our happiness in some prob-
lematic future. Humanity will then be happy, happy to be
the master of itself in the splendour which our works and our
sufferings shall have made, but in which we ourselves shall
have no more part than humanity of the future has in our
pains. I know scarcely any idolatry which is more sinister,
more derisive and more monstrous than this.

III

ABSOLUTE PROGRESS AND MORAL PROGRESS ARE ONE AND THE SAME

So much for relative progress. It is a fact, constant and
undeniable, that the need of the absolute is no less spontaneous,
no less universal, no less irrepressible in mankind than the need
of food. There is a being within us who cries out towards God.
If we put a gag into the mouth of this importunate guest, if we
use him despitefully, or deny his very existence—he is there all
the same. It is alleged by some that he is a stranger to certain
races of men; and to a few individuals. Even if this were true,

it would prove only that they are unconscious of his existence within them; but it is by no means certain. What is sure and decisive is the vast multitude of ancient religions and their importance in human history. There are tombs which date perhaps from 200 centuries ago. The men who dug the graves and made the tombs seem to have been so barbarous and so oppressed by the yoke of nature that some have even questioned, in spite of the testimony of the monuments and other remains, whether they were indeed men. Yet all these things were born with humanity and will only disappear with man. Sepulchres, menhirs, dolmens, sacrificial stones, subterranean graves, sphynxes and pyramids, symbolic idols, altars, temples, pagodas, marabouts, mosques, convents, cities of the dead, churches and calvaries, such are the things left behind by the Human Caravan. Its course can be followed by them, by these innumerable traces which give eloquent testimony of what the Caravan is seeking and what is its great business and object.

Even those who deny for the Human Caravan this need of the absolute, bear witness to it in this—that their conception of civilization and progress includes, as ours does, a transcendent idea, that of a moral kingdom in which there shall be nothing but peace, kindness, justice, compassion, fidelity, loyalty, mastery of self and temperance. They deck these splendours with strange names, such as solidarity or altruism, reduce morality to the science of customs and law to the art of legislation in spite of themselves, they make confession of the need we have of the absolute.

The song they sing, the song of fear and self-interest, is useful to beat time for our steps, but cannot always and everywhere take the place of the voice of conscience. Man is rather so constituted and made in every age and in all climes that he insensibly transposes the sound, as it becomes familiar to him, into the major key of duty. "It is necessary," or "I am obliged," may at first mean, "I am compelled," or "I am afraid," "I want to be like everyone else," or "I go that way to get what I want." Sooner, or later, if the remark is repeated and prolonged, it inevitably takes the sense of: "It is my duty."

Consider the evidence: civilization and progress imply the moral law; the moral law implies duty; duty implies the existence of an authority which has the right to command, because it has a duty to command. And so we are in an endless circle until we discover, above all legislators, an authority which is the cause of its own duty, the source of its own right. All moral progress, always and everywhere, whether we like it or not, and whether we know it or not, is making its way towards God, the perfect One. Such progress then is the only one which does not and cannot do harm. Adequate for the destiny of humanity, as for human nature, it alone leads to the end or purpose of existence. When the Christian catechism says that every man is created to know, love and serve God which is life eternal, the catechism does not enunciate a theory; it states a fact, the most magnificent in history—and it defines true happiness.

IV

MORAL PROGRESS, TRANSCENDENCE (I.E. BEING IN ANY MANNER ABOVE AND BEYOND EARTHLY THINGS) AND RELIGION ARE BOUND UP TOGETHER IN THE HUMAN CARAVAN

What is it then throughout all countries which directs the intelligence, the will, and the action of men towards this divine end, or purpose, which develops them in uprightness and in purity by faith, love and service? What name are we to give to the guardian and the artisan of moral progress? Philosophy, science, sociology, metaphysics, or morality? No, although sometimes we allow ourselves to disguise it with one of these pseudonyms. It is called religion. Through it passes the true road, the only way of progress. It traces not only the itinerary of the soul towards God, but also the itinerary of the human race towards joy.

By what then are we to recognize it in the complexity of history and life if so many false names hide it, and if its true name too often covers nothing but our morals, our philosophies, our metaphysics, even our lusts and our imaginings? We desire to follow the Caravan across the ages: how shall we form a judgment of its march, if one must judge of it according to moral progress, and if true religion, which is the arbiter of this progress, remains hidden from our eyes?

True religion must manifest itself, or it cannot exist. If it exists, we ought to be able to distinguish it with ease from that which surrounds it or is like it. "The artisan is known by his work", unless there is neither artisan nor work and we are condemned to be always ignorant of what it concerns us most to know. We have before us certain men and certain groups of men, who represent human kind and who lay claim to transcendence: certain societies, which represent humanity, which proclaim themselves to be cities of God.

If none of these claims is justified by history, then history has neither direction nor meaning; the idea of direction is a delusion, existing only in the mind; the armies of peoples and humanity are of no account; each one of us follows his way alone to his destiny, an atom thrown among a chaos of atoms, we know neither why nor how, in this inexplicable universe.

If, on the contrary, the facts show that several amongst these claims are well founded, then men can draw the divine from more than one spring and make their way by more than one way to their final end or goal—but these ways must converge, for it is possible that there are many ways and also many Caravans, but the end is one—history has a direction.

All the more certain is it that history has a direction if it carries within itself the proof that there is only one beginning and only one way to follow, and that since the dawn of human life all reason for existence, all hope and all destiny, are bound up in one same city.

Let us test these three possibilities to see what truth is in them.

THIRD PART

THE STAGES OF THE JOURNEY

CHAPTER I

THE STEEPLE CHASE

I

THE STAGES OF THE CARAVAN ARE MARKED BY ITS PROGRESS
TOWARDS UNITY AND DOMINATION

THE Journey is a far one and by a winding road. Nor does the
road lie completely under our vision. We catch a distant
glimpse then lose it for long stretches. But always the Caravan
moves on.

There is no halting stage, no rest for humanity. The
Caravan must go on to the end of the journey, to the City of
Life lit by joy where there is day without time and without
nightfall.

The Caravan has never stopped. It will never stop. The
changes which go on in it, the different phases of its movement,
the detours of its itinerary, may well help our classifications,
our weak memory, or our need of analyzing the facts accumulated in its passage across time. But that passage is marked by
no halting places; there is no time for slumber. The drama
will be played through, from the prologue to the dénouement,
without the curtain being lowered for the shortest interval.
Stand where you choose; all points of view are permissible as are
all the pictures you see from the position you select as the action
of the drama unfolds without intermission. These stages of the
march, which in reality are not stages, are perfectly real. It is
not merely in dreams nor yet only on the shores of the Mediterranean that "you see", with Bossuet, "the Assyrians of the old
world or of modern times, the Medes, the Persians, the Greeks,
the Romans", and their like, "present themselves before your
eyes one after another". The same picture is offered to you,

75

under other names, in China, India, Japan, northern and
western Europe, in Russia, in Asia, in the Americas and in
Australasia. All the divisions into periods and all classifications
of fact are useful, convenient, suggestive and moulded upon
reality.

They are often put aside with scorn as empirical and
arbitrary, but what shall we say with regard to those divisions
and classifications of history which the moderns claim to put in
their place? Spengler's laughter is very much to the point at
"professional historians who see universal history under the
image of a tapeworm which lengthens out ceaselessly in epochs
placed end to end". "As for myself," he adds, "I see in it the
image perpetually changing of a perpetual creation, of a
wonderful flow of organic forces in a perpetual state of becoming."

And thus he arranges his pictures. There are, for instance,
the seasons of the spirit—*springtime, summer, autumn, winter*
—which preside over the evolution of the sciences, philosophies,
and religions, and ebb and flow over the surface of the earth;
which come by periodical returns and make people who are
separated by thousands of years in point of time actually contemporaries in point of culture. There are the four ages—the
primitive *infancy* of mankind, the culture of the cities and
provinces of its *youthful age*, the *maturity* of the great capitals
marked by an activity of building and construction and a
teeming cosmopolitan civilization and, in the final stage, the
giant cities of complacent *old age*.

All this is ingenious, poetic, pleasing, but not so new as
Spengler thinks and not solidly based. Withal, it is not less
empirical and less arbitrary than other views. I admit that
it is complete; and that history is greatly respected; henceforth
history will keep its place above every other discipline of the mind.
But if the development of humanity has no more end, idea, nor
plan than that of the butterflies or the orchids: if "flourishing
and fading away, cultures, peoples, languages, truths and
gods grow, in a superiority directed to no end, like the flowers
in the fields", what matter ages and seasons? History, human

history, has no less and no more importance than the history of butterflies and orchids. It is then only a vain and empty word without sense or direction: it does not exist.

That alone has a history which is at one and the same time manifold and yet one, temporal and without recurrence, changing yet directed towards the unchangeable, from a beginning to an end, according to a plan and a thought. To see and to study only certain acts of the great drama; to classify empirically, arbitrarily to separate the rôles, the scenes and the changes of fortune, is not assuredly to write universal history; yet it renders service to the art of universal history and it is more "real", more historical, than disjointing the whole of the play from one end to the other; and then reassembling the bits according to their analogies, as if each one of them had not its proper place in the plot of the action; and then to tell us: "Here's your universal history. What you take for drama is only the inevitable chain and the everlasting return of the same seasons."

If we would omit nothing and distort nothing in our picture of life and of living men, we must adopt a different proceeding. Let us look at the panorama, the march of the Caravan, the forces, laws and movements which are there manifested; and leaving aside what is now in question—transcendence and progress—let us see what everything comes back to, what are the general, constant and universal tendencies of humanity in history. According as they appear to us thwarted or favoured in their actions by the wide and varied events which we must contemplate, we can mark the points at which progress wins, loses, goes off the track, finds its way again, accelerates or slackens speed.

These tendencies are only two. The man of small learning can discern them as easily as the savant. Their power has already been manifested to us in the ten laws which control the whole of history. God has put them into the human race by creating our first father in His own image. *Unus et Dominus.* They direct all the sons of Adam *towards unity* and *towards domination.*

Of all the men who are scattered like seeds by thousands of millions as far as we can see along the ways of past centuries, not one is identical with another; yet they are all the same. They differ among themselves infinitely less than the coleoptera or the papillonidae, whilst they are infinitely further from the other primates than the polyps or the sea-anemones are from sea-weeds. Under the most different skies, over the widest stretches of time, under the most varied conditions of life, they solve the same problems in the same manner, are pleased by the same fables, retell the same proverbs and hide the same realities under the same symbols.

Little Red Riding Hood had probably been round the world before the building of the Pyramids, and the men of Mycenae hunted the lion in the manner of the Zulus who were contemporaries of Livingstone. Does there exist a race of men who have no heroes, take no interest in personal decoration, are without the spirit of intrigue, men who do not covet riches, or desire praise, or rare and glittering things, or empire over their fellow-men? They do not all use the same gestures, their eyes are not all of the same shape, nor their cheek-bones, nor all human lips as prominent as those of the negro, nor their skins of the same colour, but human brotherhood is a fact, not merely an idea. We are one in Adam's race; and every man, in himself, is one. Our pains, our misfortunes arise from the things that divide us. From the beginning to the end and at every moment of life, the passion for unity shines in the eyes of humankind, at first split up into a multitude of families, of scattered tribes, then grouped into kingdoms, empires, federations of States, to-day impelled by irresistible forces towards still vaster associations, fewer in number.

The passion for unity has become manifest in each one of the political groups with which everything is connected or subordinated in the course of the ages. Every group owes its origin, its growth, its achievements and its splendour to the fusion within it of foreign elements which at first lived parallel with it, subsequently joined with it and other groups, and finally united with them in a single whole.

In this lies the basic element of our nature. Separation, disruption and hatred are merely decay. That factor in human nature which tends towards disintegration and hatred, whether in nations, states or humanity, tends towards destruction. It would be absurd and irrational to seek in this tendency towards annihilation and death for the key to the various phases of our development.

It is then, in the first place, on the track along which the Caravan is making its way towards *Unity* that the real stages of its progress must be found; and, in the second place, since it is only necessary to have two lines to determine the position of a point, along that track which it is following towards *Domination*.

Unity, in effect, in our souls and in our lives, in each group and series of groups, as in the whole of mankind, is realized only by domination, by sovereign authority. He who is not master of himself falls, injures his whole being, and so ceases to be himself. If he did not exercise power over nature, man would be the most miserable of animals. Society without any sovereign power to rule it would be dissolved in anarchy. The nation, in the measure in which it loses its independence and surrenders all effort to regain it, or to preserve its traditions, will very soon lose its nationality. The state remains a state only in the measure that it preserves its sovereignty. The struggle for life which amongst the animals is individual, amongst men is also social and political. It is a struggle for sovereignty and domination.

"*Increase and multiply, and fill the earth, and subdue it.*" We must always come back to that. Whether God said these words; whether Moses or someone else put these words into His mouth; whether the story in Genesis is human allegory, or divine symbol or the evidence of revelation, yet the words throw a clear light upon the depths of our nature, its most potent forces and the essential destiny of humanity. They are the perfect résumé of history. Since the beginning the sons of Adam have multiplied to replenish the earth, they grow in numbers in order to subdue it; and the great crises through which they pass show that there is nothing worse than that men should multiply

G

and not have unity or should dominate and not increase in numbers.

To be one, in order to rule; to rule, in order to be one; such is the circle in which they turn. To that point all the movements of their Caravan return, all the forces of which these movements are the effects and the ten laws which rule or determine the play of such movements and forces. The real stages in their multiplication, their extension and their growth can only be stages towards unity and towards domination.

CHAPTER II

EDEN AND BABEL

I

ADAM, THE FALL OF MAN AND THE DELUGE

MYTH or symbol, according to the taste of "advanced exegetes," the Biblical Adam is certainly not a fable. The picture that Genesis gives us of him is true from the feet to the head and from one end to the other of the story. Why should he not be an historical reality? Is there so much difference between him and the men of Chelles, the Neanderthal or the Cro-Magnon men?

Shame was no stranger to him; though in that respect his ingenuity did not go much further than the fig-leaf: he dressed himself and his wife with an apron of fig-leaves. God must have intervened to clothe them or teach them to clothe themselves in the skins of beasts. They reduced the loving kindness of God to the image, the manners and the language of a man, in order to express what they felt about Him. He heard them when they were walking in the garden. He called to them. He put questions to them and uttered His judgment when He heard their replies. They, on their part, hid themselves, as if He did not already see them, or would be at some trouble to find them. They excused themselves with the naïve awkwardness of children caught red-handed. They were more ashamed of their nakedness than of their guilt. Their eldest son believed in the virtue of the offering to God, but he had no conception of the offering of virtue. God had to intervene to teach him that it was purity of heart, of life and intention which gave value to sacrifice. Shortly afterwards he murdered his brother. He was an insolent sullen brute. Only in the third generation of men did they begin to invoke God under the name of "Him who is".

It is not credible that the first human family was depicted with such features simply to give pleasure to the contemporaries of Esdras, of Moses or of Abraham. This tradition squares with all that we know of them. It is altogether out of accord with the inveterate leaning of human beings to glorify their origins. It is evident that those who transmitted it to us, themselves received it and did not invent or correct it. It comes from a much more remote antiquity.

On the other hand, it is in agreement with what we see to-day amongst the uncivilized descendants of the first occupants of the Southern world—the Negrillos and San of Africa, the Negritos of Malaya, the Australian savages—all of them from the North, that is to say from the confines of the Persian Gulf and the Mediterranean. And can we find in the description in Genesis anything inconsistent with the man of Grimaldi, of La Chapelle-aux-Saints, or of Heidelberg?

It is indeed said that primitive man had no other tools than flints roughly chipped and fashioned; but nothing is known for certain. All we know of him is from the remains of these primitive tools and they do not by implication mean that he had no other. It is said that he could neither read, nor write, nor think abstractly; but we have no certain knowledge on this subject. In this respect we could find many of his contemporaries in our own days, living in the very bosom of the most advanced civilizations.

What was he? A "supermonkey" or the descendant of some poor human stray lost in this recess of the northern forests and brutalized by misery? Those who attempt to solve this question have no real knowledge of him; but the author of Genesis knew and tells us that the Adamites, up to the seventh generation, were as ignorant as their father of the art of working copper and iron. Cain tilled the soil and with what did he plough the stubborn ground, if not with some rough plough-share of wood hewn out with a stone axe? With what weapons did these first human beings defend themselves against ferocious beasts, if not, as their great nephew of Piltdown, with stones, with stakes sharpened with flint knives and hardened

in the fire, or with brands that glowed and flamed in the darkness of the night?

Abel the shepherd seems to have been the owner of his sheep
as Cain of his harvests. We do not read that he ever guarded
his father's flocks. It was he and Cain who offered sacrifices.
The land and the pasture were the property of the first occupant
as long as he occupied them. What could there be more
primitive? The patriarchal family grouped in obedience and
respect around the ancestor, the only priest and chief, the only
master of his people and possessions, had clearly not come into
existence. As for the nomadic tribe, Genesis tells us in precise
terms that it appeared for the first time much later, five generations after Cain. It is true that the latter built the first town,
but how many inhabitants could have been in it?

"The first man," said St. Thomas Aquinas, "was established
in the perfection of his body, so that he might immediately
produce offspring, and in perfection of soul in order immediately to be able to govern and instruct other men. He knew
all that it was natural for a man to learn"—that is, of course,
according to the state in which he and his first descendants
were then living. The author of the *Summa Theologica* expressly
allows this restriction with regard to the *supernatural* knowledge
allotted to the first man. The story of Genesis and logic itself
oblige us to make the same restriction, although St. Thomas
seems to set it aside, with regard to natural knowledge. See
now the nature of their coarse, brutish, material state immediately after the fall of man; the nature of the earth over which
and of the heavens under which the advance-guard of the
Human Caravan must travel; the way men dispersed, either to
retain their independence or for the chase, for conquest or for
discovery!

Forests, steppes and mountains, all are virgin. For hundreds
of centuries everything has been given up to the exuberance of
life. Where then is man's place amongst this luxuriant growth
of the vegetable world and amongst the beasts of the wild? He
has hands, feet and a mind, and that is all, to make a place for
his naked self in this fierce struggle for existence, without

help or support except his wife, as miserable and naked as himself.

Two creatures against all the world. And under their feet the earth trembles. Many convulsions have agitated it since it began to grow solid slowly beneath the boiling liquid of the primitive waters. The mighty forces that have hardened its frame have only now begun to abate their activity. They have not yet completed the modelling of its face. Both seas and oceans are still seeking their definite beds. Great islands, broad isthmuses and continents surge up from the depths and disappear again into them. Rivers roll their muddy waves in impassable floods, or sink away into impenetrable marshes across plains formless and limitless. All this immense activity seems to have been scaled down. Our present floods, glaciers, tidal waves, cyclones, volcanoes and earthquakes are tame and shrunken when compared with those which the prodigious saurians and giant mammals had to confront in order to survive. Indeed our first ancestors, much later in the history of the world, faced a universe hardly less violent. At that remote time everything changed more quickly and over greater areas than the geological quietists are pleased to admit. The rhythm of human movement accelerated and was accentuated in a geometrical progression as the ages passed on, and we have seen why this happened; but it is an inverse progression which the rhythm of the universe has followed in the same order of time.

Man exiled from Eden was most pitiably placed. His kingdom awaited its conquest, but what a kingdom! More than once the glaciers of the Arctic regions descended almost midway from the Pole to the Equator. The glaciers from the mountains invaded the plains. Without respite, from year to year they advanced and then fell back, piled up their icy wastes and then dissolved. The whole of the hemisphere not covered by the oceans passed thus in turn from heat to cold and from icy cold to tropical heat in alternations, the rigours of which we can imagine only with great difficulty because of the relative mildness and certainty of our climates during the last 10,000

years. In point of fact, there were men living between the Alps
and the Atlantic during the last ice age. There were men there
before that age. Quite recently there have been found men
who were their contemporaries, if not their predecessors,
towards the other side of the Asiatic continent on the shores of
the Yellow River. Others have been discovered in South
Africa, in western Asia, in Java and in Australia. One must
then go back to the last ice age but one, and further perhaps,
in order to find our first parents—men who waged a terrible
and unequal struggle for existence.

Two beings pitted against a whole world, says religion. And
science does not contradict. The antiquity of our species, its
boldness and its ingenuity, its indifference to climate, its power
of endurance of all kinds of toil and wretchedness, set against
the fact that so many countries do not yet to-day carry the half,
the quarter, the tenth part, sometimes even the hundredth
part of the population which might live in them; the rarity of
human fossil remains, in spite of their being scattered in all the
corners of the old world; the convergence of civilizations, of
languages and races towards a common origin—type, instincts,
time and region—in spite of profound differences and the
dispersion already manifested in the oldest vestiges of men; all
these contradictions and the riddles they propound become
completely insoluble, if one holds that the human stream gushed
forth from innumerable sources.

Their solution remains difficult enough with the Biblical
account; but on any other it is hopeless: a single couple as
the first creation and, much later on, the new beginning
of everything by "Noah, the eighth to be saved from
the flood", when "all that which was on the face of the
earth was destroyed, from man to beast and disappeared from
the earth".

It is curious that the scientists, who as a matter of course
assign to the rhinoceros, the horse and the tapir a single origin
at the end of the tertiary period, yet see insurmountable
difficulties in the idea that men, white, black, yellow, long-
headed, square-headed, round-faced, oval-faced or lozenge-

faced, broad-nosed or thin-nosed, should have originated from one and the same couple of human beings.

They are ready to declare that our direct ancestors had as other descendants, opossums and shrubs: the influence of environment, the changing conditions of existence and the multiplication of individuals, the repetition of efforts, the constancy and diversity of habits, the hereditary accumulation of imperceptible differences, the creation of the organ by function, the struggle for existence, the survival of the fittest have worked this miracle: no other explanation is required. But that the same causes, joined with the dispersion of the first men over the whole extent of the continents and with the isolation of vast regions during the last of the ice ages, either before or since that age, can account for diverse races in the human species, they will not grant.

Those who believe are freer and less credulous. Did the Word by whom all things were created call each species, or each kingdom, or life, directly out of nothing into its proper being—or did he only create matter, fertilizing it in such a way that by the development of this germ it brings forth all that is less than spirit? Of this we are completely ignorant; but the author of Genesis knew and said and repeats to us that the plants, animals and man were drawn by God, all of them, from the "dust of the earth". These ancient texts can be interpreted in twenty different ways. There is one, the simplest and the most literal, which gives them a sense and a meaning to turn the fiercest evolutionists green with envy. For what they can present only as an unproved and indeed unprovable hypothesis, takes upon itself in Genesis the figure of traditional truth, inherited from the first man; come down, not without a certain admixture, through the many centuries to the country of Sennaar and the cities of Chaldaea; collected by Abraham and re-established by him in its original purity, when, rejecting all but one of the gods worshipped by his ancestors, he left his father's house at the call of *Him Who is*.

The Book which bears in our days this venerable message to all peoples of the globe—1,700,000,000 of the sons of Adam—

if they have the will to hear it, is not of course a treatise on geology, anthropology, or pre-history. It is a brief and popular chronicle, written with a religious and national purpose in view. It bears the impress of the Jews and for its first readers was written in their own language.

One must be doubly blind not to recognize in it, here and there, superhuman depths from which shine pure and ageless the splendours of reality. The only God, the good God, the infinite Being, the Creator of all things; man, the king of nature through his humanity, one father and one mother for the whole human family, their innocence and their fall, and, in the disorder that followed, an assurance of salvation; justice, pity and divine providence always at work amongst us. This clear light compels our attention; and there may be others in it which the normal weakness of our vision alone prevents us from seeing. "God made man in His own image," says Voltaire, "and man has well repaid Him." To clothe God in the garments of humanity is, in effect, the natural impulse both of our own wretchedness and of God's infinite pity for us. But to attribute to God the complex and continuous multitude of our wishes and our acts is merely the result of our own wretchedness.

Thus it seems to us altogether divine and not without reason that each individual, each really distinct being, should come from nothing by a separate creation. But surely it is a still mightier proof of divine power to create the oak tree from the acorn, humanity from one man, and all the life that is in matter from lifeless matter. Now this is but a far-fetched analogy, a childish image of what God does, who is pure, unique and simple Actuality, who is *thought* which alone can understand itself, who realises Himself by thinking Himself in the plenitude of being and expressed Himself eternally by giving reality to the universe, while yet not identifying Himself with the universe, nor confounding His being with its, nor limiting Himself by assigning to the created universe its frontiers.

And after such a creation what does it matter how man comes

from the dust? He is "the son of Adam who was the son of God". His first parents squandered his heritage. They sinned and he in them. They lost the divine gift that no one amongst their descendants could reconquer. That we should regain it, it was necessary that God "should dwell amongst us", Son of Man, a new Adam born of a new Eve, in order that we who have become His brothers, might, if we so desired, have a share in the heritage which by nature belongs to Him, although the first Adam had received the first-fruits and the promise of it only by a supernatural gift.

That is the reason that we are born and live in wretchedness. What remains to us is less than nothing, without taking into account what we lack. In us and by us, our inmost inconsistencies disturb the whole of creation in its balance. This is a fact we cannot doubt. Our common ancestor reduced all his descendants to extreme misery. Whether man risks the poor remnant of his fortune upon an apple, a card, a horse, or a speculation on the stock exchange, the result of the gamble cannot be less painful for him than what has come to be his natural condition.

The forbidden fruit and the serpent disturb you? Your mind is resolved upon seeing in them nothing but myths? But remember: every myth expresses realities, and these stories, even if they were no more than myths, are full of meaning. We have but to keep our eyes and ears open to know to what depth man has fallen, even if we did not find adequate proofs of his fall in history and the recollections of humanity. Look back at the Caravan at any moment. In nearly every tent, when fears whirl about in the shadows, under the swarms of lusts which clamour for satisfaction, amidst the cries and groans which are the accompaniment of childbirth and death, at all times since men wandered and struggled, the burden of the song which delights them in their weariness, their sufferings and their toil is the myth of the golden age.

The primordial happiness of the human race; the earth a vale of tears, though once a paradise; evil, the origin of which is explained by sin; regrets, full of desires, sheltering vague hopes;

there has been no age and scarcely a single race of men in which all these phenomena did not occur under some form or other though there are some who have preserved no recollection of the original fall. All this, you may say, is because humanity is old; and the old man always glorifies his past life. But mankind used to say the same thing when it was young—I do not mean young in age, for what it said in that far-off day we know not, but young in character, feeling and customs.

Tradition passes from century to century and none among the centuries lends to the golden age its own beauty, its own riches, ambitions and pleasures. All are of accord in depicting the golden age the perfection of equilibrium in order and simplicity; Adam and Eve under "trees goodly to look upon and full of fruit good to eat"; primitive people happy without needs, in the peace of their innocence, of their physical, moral and intellectual harmony in the company of the creatures of the earth and of the Creator. The theorists have slipped in, as a foundation for this conception of the golden age, the idea of an original civilization of which all other civilizations are merely the decadent descendants. The soil which the Caravan has trodden tells a different story, a story of innumerable comings to maturity and decline following after everywhere. As the earth continues to give up to us the ancient vestiges of humanity, we observe that for weapons and tools, iron has succeeded bronze; bronze copper, often copper succeeded polished stone, more than once polished stone has taken the place of stone roughly chipped and cut. But man is revealed to us as identical in all men: the same obstinacy, the same boldness, the same instinct to conquer, to surpass and to survive; but his life was always too brief for art which remained unaccomplished. It took millenaries to make him grow and multiply according to his nature. But this is the universal progress of things, and the way God would have it. The Caravan and all civilizations originated in the country couple who cultivated, around their home on the border of a river, the Garden of Eden.

The Fall and the Flood were only episodes, notable enough, one must agree, to be engraved upon the memory and indefinitely to furnish matter for popular stories, mythical songs, theological speculations and sacerdotal controversies. It goes without saying that tongues have often embroidered on the primitive canvas arabesques of fiction and conjectures; but the canvas itself is made up of realities. Without the Fall neither our present condition, nor our history are conceivable; and floods are innumerable in the history of the world. It is improbable that any of these inundations ever submerged he whole earth since the time that it revolved "without form and void" upon its orbit "in the darkness of the abyss". Yet is it so improbable that one or other of the inundations which have flooded the earth did in fact cover all the inhabited plains and submerge what the plain dwellers called the "tops of the mountains"? In the same rise of the waters?—Why not?— One after the other?—Perhaps. Earthquakes, tidal waves, earth subsidences, encroachments of the sea upon the land; geologists are acquainted with more cataclysms than are necessary to make this credible. It is easy to dispense with these catastrophic explanations. It is enough that it happened towards the Ice Age: it is scarcely possible to date it from any other time.

The monstrous rainfalls which these ages must have seen and of which the Nile valley, Mesopotamia, Siberia, China, the Indian peninsula, the greater portion of Europe and of North America offer traces; the torrential general inundations produced by the melting of the snows and the ice accumulated in this way as far as 40 degrees from the pole or 100 kilometres from real mountains—these would release more water than was actually necessary to account for the three or even twelve months of Noah's voyage upon the face of the waters as easily as for the seven days of the Babylonian Xisuthros, and to drown the peoples everywhere scattered on the borders of lakes and rivers, or at least never far from water. In any case the occurrence of the Flood is certain; and its indelible tradition is scarcely less perennial or less universal, both in the Old World and the New, than the tradition of the golden age within the mind of man.

II

THE DISPERSION OF THE TRIBES

Contemplate all this. Reflect upon the duration of the early ages of the globe, their remoteness in the past, the obscurity in which they are lost, the astonishing brilliance spread over all things by the few luminous points we can see, the strange harmony breathed forth to fill this night of ages, by the concordances and discordances of tradition, the myths, legends, histories, relics of the past exhumed in every direction; evidences raised up out of the depths of the soil. In ourselves we are aware of a confusion of ignorance, hypotheses, probabilities and certitudes; but there appears too, though blurred in outline, the image of the Human Caravan at the beginning of its march.

The first of its stages, happy but of short duration, ended in disaster: the leaders of the rank and file, led astray by deceitful voices, disobeyed the order which they had received, abandoned the right road and took all who followed them along the wrong road which leads to disunion and to slavery. Henceforth it is in suffering and blood that unity is born; by blood and toil that domination is achieved.

This is clearly seen from the beginning of the second stage of the journey—which is long and terrible. The Caravan marches under the banners of murder, lust and violence. In this stage everything goes from bad to worse. Life becomes harder and yet harder. The Caravan seems to turn its back on the goal of its journey and to multiply its ranks merely for the purpose of quarrel and rioting. In this respect the story of the Bible is confirmed by mythology, geology and palaeontology.

At the outset there was "a warm climate, a rich vegetation and a magnificent fauna of mammals; in other words the surroundings were most favourable to humanity"[1]—throughout

---

[1] Boule, *Les Hommes Fossiles*, pp. 51, 159.

the whole of the inhabitable and inhabited lands. Eden was
very near. Later on, ice and rain divided the globe between
them. The animal life from the higher altitudes and the polar
regions descended to the shores of the Mediterranean, invaded
North America and in Siberia took the place of the tropical
fauna. The fossil men of that period, of the Quaternary and
the Palaeolithic ages, to judge by their skeletons, the attachment of their muscles to the bones of their legs and their arms,
their craniums and their faces, evoke in our minds the image of
scarcely anything but brute force, violent instincts and weariness upon an earth which was under a curse.[1]

Is there anything else we shall find in the stories related by the
traditions of the Gentiles and the Hebrews, referring to almost
all the heroes, giants and titans of the antediluvian world?
Their valour and might overwhelm us—but it is an individual
might, belonging rather to the order of matter. They are
overgrown children, leaders of daring bands, hoisted on to
mythical pinnacles by the muscular vigour of their legs
and the power of their fists, their names inscribed (perhaps
by their own hands like the kings that came after them) upon
the list at once of idols to be worshipped and of founders
of dynasties.

Of unity there was none, though unities swarmed. There
were innumerable unwieldy kingdoms, principalities and
powers. The swarm aimed at leaving the hive; the hive rejoiced to see the swarm fly away. The departing colony
wandered about, or established itself at will, according to its
needs and its temper. If the place was already occupied
it wandered off still further; space is vast and the soil a
desert.

There were certainly regions which were habitable and there
were regions which were inaccessible, fewer perhaps than is
generally believed. Neither mountain, forest nor desert remained everywhere and for ever insurmountable barriers to
the primitive man whose fire, bow and arrow, skill and patience
preserved his life and carved his way. It needs neither much

[1] Genesis v. 29.

room nor a long time for a handful of human ants to make a passage when their leader has courage, or necessity gives wings to their heels.

In fact man made his way everywhere, before as well as after the Flood; and, up to that final irruption of the great waters and after they had receded, the whole of western Asia from Persia to the Mediterranean, Siberia, China, the peninsula of India, Malaya, Australia; the two Americas, from the great lakes to Tierra del Fuego; Europe to its southern boundaries from the northern seas, and to the west from the shores of the Black Sea, presented to him, alongside swamps and impenetrable jungles, an abundance of plains, valleys and table-lands both habitable and accessible.

To a greater or less extent and rather early in the story of humanity the major portion of these lands was inhabited, together with the deserts—Australian, Kalahari, Sahara, Syria and Gobi—which were then fertile, and of the lands since swallowed up by the waters—Atlantis, the Aegean, the submarine plateaux which surround Sicily and Corsica, Provence, the Channel and the North Sea—where river-beds, the bones which are brought to the surface by dredges, prehistoric traditions, legends and history itself furnish evidence that the elephant, the rhinoceros, the mammoth, the reindeer, and man once wandered in the light of day.

As far as possible I omit mere possibilities and stick to certainties. Yet on this or that point in the above list further discoveries may prove me wrong; but the main fact, the only one that is of any importance to the direction which history takes, will remain indisputable: the first state of man from the time that he began to multiply is like that of the universe, a state or condition of great dispersion.

Babel is indeed the symbol of that state, whichever may be the signification of that name: the "Gate of God" opening upon virgin space, which one passes through in order to fill the earth, according to the Creator's command, by spreading over it; or "Confusion", diffusion without unity, concord or method, without rule or dominion, nor any chief whose power is of any real extent, to the day when, according to the traditions of the Chaldaeans, "royalty came down from heaven" and, according to Genesis, became incarnate in Nimrod, the builder of mighty cities.

In their anxiety to achieve distinction, to maintain their independence, to preserve, to increase and, especially, to surrender no share of their common tribal property, the tribes of men dispersed over the earth. This force of expansion was all-powerful and was the main factor in the creation of races. It separated the shoots from a single tree, transplanted them in different soils, scattered them in different climates of completely opposite characteristics and isolated them, each in its different type of life, its particular mentality, its customs—in a more lasting and efficacious manner than all other barriers imaginable.

Invented by certain learned ethnologists as the imaginary basis of their theories and hypotheses, such barriers were never really closed at any point or insurmountable; but the force of heredity, nevertheless, did its work in a multitude of compartments closed up by instincts, habits and distances. It worked for long ages as an additional force to defeat the achievement of unity and of domination, affirming and strengthening independence amongst tribes and races, multiplying and ceaselessly accentuating varieties of taste, aptitude, character, forms, features and colour.

All this is still going on under our eyes. And how indeed can we entertain any doubt of the primitive anarchy of mankind when we find it everywhere as soon as we begin digging into traditions and excavating the soil and so drawing nearer to human origins in Chaldaea, Elam, Egypt and Judaea—in Persia, India, Greece, Italy, in Celtic countries and in Germany —amongst the Negroes and Negrillos, the Chinese, the Redskins, the Aztecs, the Mayas and the Incas? Berosus, the Chaldaean priest, assigns to this period, by an artifice whose secret is perhaps not impenetrable, a duration of 223,000 years: we might do with a shorter period—but we cannot reduce the period to zero.

In several places we still to-day possess images of that world as it then existed, here almost effaced, there still fresh and vivid, as also the drawings painted by the cave-dwellers on the walls of the caverns of the Reindeer Age, drawings still fresh and vivid in spite of the lapse of many thousand years. And even to-day in China, in Japan, in the Indies, in the United States and in Europe itself we can find true "primitives" living amongst people long civilized.

Little by little the tide of civilization gains on them, absorbs them or destroys them; but in the meantime their presence warns us not to form too hasty a conclusion, from the condition of certain men, as to that of the whole of humanity in the same period. For the most widely contrasting ways of life can be found co-existing almost side by side. A few miles up in the hills men as primitive as the man of ages long ago are the neighbours of our engineers and our modern mandarins. We supply them with the rubbish of our civilization until they disappear, exterminated too often by our schools, our vices and our poisons, against which they have no defence. Go to Brazil, Venezuela, Colombia, to Argentina, Malaya, the Sudan, the Congo, South Africa; the situation is reversed. It is now the tide of the primitives which surrounds the centres of civilization—an ebbing tide, assuredly, tending to vanish away and leave only a continuity of civilizations.

Shade the picture slightly; accentuate or simplify certain traits; touch up the colouring; and you have the world in its early times, the Human Caravan on its march on the stage of Babel. Like a spring of water spread out fan-shape in a thousand little streams over the meadow it seems to be lost for ever over the face of the earth. There were as yet no deserts to cross, but everywhere steppes, pampas, savannahs, or forests. In the midst of these vast extents of country, somewhere along the borders of great rivers where animals come down to slake their thirst, civilizations began to be outlined, planned and built. The soil was fruitful: man could eat the produce of the

H

fields and multiply the best plants by eliminating thorns and
thistles with the sweat of his brow.

But the soil has always been more tractable to man than his
own soul! As the house he was building for himself began
to rise above the level of the earth, envy, discord, hatred and a
thousand unrepressed growths upset the foundations, invaded
the works and drove away the builders. It was Babel. And
so they separated. The world is wide: some of them set off
to discover fresh places, others stopped where they were.
Why? We are not certain of the reason, but we can perhaps
catch a glimpse of it.

There are instincts which drive men to movement and others
which prompt them to settle in a fixed place of abode;
Bohemians, Gypsies, Tziganes have been wandering for
centuries, untamable nomads in spite of their fewness in our
sedentary Europe, without either the wish or the power to
settle down.

There are also forces in nature more powerful than the forces
of desire. The Eddas and the Avesta are in agreement in
relating to us that at the beginning of the earth the ancestors
of the Scandinavians and the Persians were driven from the
lands already occupied by them by the rigour of the winters
and the invasion of ice. The great book of nature which the
geologists study attests that many other men have suffered
the same compulsion.

Lastly, there are political, economic, social and moral
necessities which compel migrations: such as those which later
drove the Israelites towards the Promised Land, the Goths
towards the western Mediterranean coasts, the Arabs towards
the regions of Turania and Magreb, the Mongols towards
China and India, the Conquistadores of Spain, the Puritans
of England, the Catholics and the poor of Germany towards
the riches and the freedom of the Americas.

Bold spirits, the conquered, the proscribed, fugitives and all
those who are carried away by the great winds of fear or of hope,
face a hostile nature. They depart, uprooted, until they find
if they are searching for it, a fixed and stable dwelling-place.

They multiply and in their turn they throw off swarms. The antediluvian strata of Croatia, the Rhineland, Belgium and Sussex; Picardy, la Brie, la Correze, the Dordogne and Charente; the Riviera and Gibraltar, the upper Ienissei, the mouth of the Yellow River and Java; probably also those of Australia and the Transvaal; perhaps those of eastern Africa and America; reveal the remains and traces of these migrations. Other finds will be made elsewhere, or in the same countries, and it seems certain that many a group has disappeared, leaving no traces or remains behind it. And there are stones and human skeletons which will never be dated with any certainty. But of the significance of all these things there can be no doubt: they are tiny islets, like those of the Pacific, lost in an ocean of solitude. Scattered, or in archipelagos, they are evidence of the existence of greater human islands, still unknown—the communities from which they must have come.

Diverse and changing, it is quite impossible that, amidst so many changing and diverse circumstances, all such communities progressed in the course of the centuries, or all lost ground, or all retained in perpetuity the inheritance they had received from their ancestors and from the lands that they or their fathers had quitted, by their own choice or through compulsion, for those lands where we find them. Some, perhaps, remained unchangeable, in spite of the difference of climate and of their environment. It is certain that the majority experienced rise and decadence, either one or the other, or perhaps both in their turn.

Were those hunters degenerates whose traces we light upon at times at all the ends of the habitable world? It is possible; nothing is known of them. Did they mark a progress of our species? It is so stated, but we are not sure. It is not even known whether they were as stupid and as bestial as men say who have studied their hand-chipped flint instruments or their small brains and prognathous jaws.

To-day the first imbecile who comes along in a motor-car can knock down and kill anyone on the high roads. But the

men of the Chellean period, the naked, badly armed hunters
of elephants and lions, or the Neanderthal men, victors with
no great equipment over the rhinoceros and the mammoth,
were doing something considerably more difficult. In any case
more reflexion and perseverance were necessary to light the
first fire, to hack out the first stone-axe, to invent the boomerang,
the javelin and the bow and arrow than to imagine the wheel-
barrow after the wheel, cannon after gunpowder, the aeroplane
and the motor-car after the kite, firearms and the steam-engine.

To this we should add that under our own eyes, many
alleged "primitives", far from presenting the traits of a fresh
healthy infancy, remind us rather of the twisted abortions,
vicious or sub-normal and undeveloped creatures, which the
most normal of civilized couples with the least tainted of
lineages sometimes produce as offspring. Visibly some factor,
either within themselves or exterior to them, has spoiled,
arrested or distorted their growth.

Many others, on the contrary, more backward still—
Yagans of Tierra del Fuego, Pygmies, Australian aborigines—
exhibit, in the extreme simplicity of their existence, a penetrating intelligence, pure and lofty ideas about God, the soul
and the universe, and a morality which, taking all into consideration, is less corrupt than the morals of civilized man.
It is evident that such ideas date from antiquity and are those
which are to be found everywhere behind the depravement,
the superstitions, the brutishness and the complications of the
real "savages" of the world, when one goes far enough back
into their past.

This new simplicity, rich in possibility of development,
undoubtedly shone forth in the dawn of prehistory, if not
amongst the scattered people whom we exhume, at any rate
amongst their ancestors, in the regions where families developed
into clans and for a long time remained neighbours. Amongst
them civilization in its rudimentary forms grew and put forth
its leaves little by little.

Traditions, preserved more or less faithfully to a limited
extent everywhere, in Chaldaea, Egypt, Judaea, Persia, India,

China and America, whose origin is lost in the most remote ages, affirm that this second stage in the journey of the Caravan saw the beginning of the art of making use of herds, of cultivating the soil, of working copper, gold, silver, bronze and iron, of spinning and weaving and finally the tribal discipline which from the earliest times ruled over the people settled in the "towns" and, later, the shepherds leading their flocks to pasture in the mountains or wandering over the earth in their journeys.

The Chaldaeans, the Egyptians, the Chinese, speak to us of kings, emperors, even of "divine dynasties"; but we must not forget that, following the judicious formula of Paul Viollet, " the first kings were almost patriarchs, and the first patriarchs almost kings ". The lofty deeds and misdeeds of these legendary sovereigns seem to apply rather to brilliant family leaders raised to the rank of heroes and gods after their demise, by the gratitude, the pride, the respect and the superstition—or the politics—of their descendants. They are canonized and deified for having taught the arts which I have just mentioned; procured for their tribes what was necessary to slake their thirst, satisfy their hunger and clothe themselves; they established peace, put an end to disorder, destroyed some formidable monster and won for their progeny the benevolence of some superhuman power. Undoubtedly they waged war, and they celebrated their victories ; but was the *gens Fabia* a kingdom, when, giving battle by itself, it put into line 306 warriors well-armed and practised in the use of weapons? Shall we trick out Abraham with a crown he never claimed, because as the ally of authentic kings, with 300 warriors of his own household, he routed the troops of Chedorlaomer?

Very soon the primitive family grew into a tribe and following that a State; but in fact and in the thoughts of men these developments remained for long incoherent and confused. The father's authority was dominant; sometimes it was the mother who exercised power, or the council of those who were of the lineage, the elders, when tribes had formed a confederation. The true royalty indeed does not seem to have "descended from heaven" until after the Flood and only, at first, in a few places. Up till then traditions did not designate as royalty any other form of government than the widest type of domestic authority which was on its way to give rise to royalty.

Once this point has been recognized, these traditions undoubtedly take within their field the whole content of the more credible sources of history, especially when they touch upon other beginnings of civilization. The extreme antiquity of such traditions, their verisimilitude and their points of agreement one with another, rendered more persuasive by their very discordancies, grow clearer as one disentangles them from the later additions and decorations which distort them. After having considered them in their most recent expression we must look for them in their original form. Everything connected with them invites us to take such traditions seriously and to classify them amongst the documents we can reasonably believe, especially when verifications from another order of evidence confirm their truth.

The position then comes to this: it is indisputable that everywhere the remains hidden underground, when excavated, reveal great differences between men as they existed before the Flood and those that followed it. It is to be observed that almost everywhere, between the disappearance of the former and the coming of the latter, for a long time dwellings awaited uninhabited the guests that were to come. And when they came these were the guests: men who knew how to draw, to model, to carve, to paint, to spin the thread and weave it, to plough, to tame animals, to hew hard stones with extreme fineness and polish, to smelt and hammer copper, and, in the East at any rate, to harden it with arsenic. They made use of conventional signs, of symbolical figures, of combinations analogous to those of our rebus, real inscriptions before the advent of letters, and the first germ of ideographic or phonetic characters, cuneiform or linear. They practised a host of superstitions—sexual, phallic, totemic, zoolatric, magic and orgiastic—the origin of which amongst all the most recent of peoples where they are met with is to be found in the decadent complications and the perverse degeneration of what had been simple, pure and natural customs.

The Caravan has once more made a start. It is at the end of the second stage of its journey. There is no need to follow it very long to observe the appearance, in the course of the dispersion of men and the general anarchy, of many centres of unity and dominion. Babel has now been left behind.

CHAPTER III

MEMPHIS AND BABYLON

I

APPEARANCE OF THE CITY

ONLY by doing violence of one sort or another to the facts can we fit them into a *Table of History*, such as Oswald Spengler drew up in his *Decline of the West*—in parallel series, spaced out with intervals of from eight to ten centuries and endlessly repeating themselves, varied somewhat but analogous, like scales or gamuts in music strummed out on the table of harmonies, in all keys, modes and harmonics. I do not mean that all is false in such a conception; on the contrary, the analogies and the repetitions are indisputable; but so also are their contrasts and the way facts have to be shaped to them. To undertake the systematization of these inconsistencies is a delusive enterprise, like carving the sea with a sword, or writing on the sands, or painting on the clouds!

It would be a mistake, less learned indeed or perhaps less pedantic, but equally erroneous, to believe that every part of the Human Caravan completes every one of its stages regularly and simultaneously. The majority of its advance-guard have left Babel far in the rear; but the main body still lags behind; and numbers of those who wandered astray, the lame, the laggards and the late-comers, are still on the road, drifting along on a thousand different by-paths. There are some who will never escape from these culs-de-sac. Others, on the contrary, who for some time trudged along but slowly, will now go at top speed for one, two, or three stages, urged on when the day is come by that impulse which gradually, division by division and column by column, seizes all humanity on the march.

Thus as the centuries pass those groups which have still remained in the age or *Cycle of Dispersion*—the cycle of the family, of the clan, of the tribe, of the fellowship, of the horde (what we have called the Cycle of Babel)—become fewer and rarer. The area offered to adventurers as their prey, to the weak as a refuge, becomes ever more restricted. Progressively the conquered cease to be hunted down, to be offered as a sacrifice, or to be reduced to slavery. They are no longer outlawed, nor absorbed into the household as serfs, nor into a patrimony as human property. They are incorporated as subjects and then as citizens into a political society.

This society develops from contractual groups, either neighbouring or domestic. It smelts from the ore the cast-metal of which nations are made; it makes alloys, forges, tempers the new metal. Here and there in this political society, unities, hitherto scattered and separated, are assembled; and its chiefs, hereditary or elective, ruling for life or only for a term, gather the ancient dominions into groups to form their own realms.

Under divers names they are kings and the society they govern is the State. Concentration begins. Men do not, of course, cease to multiply and to replenish the earth; but conquest and dominion now become a prime political motive. The Caravan now enters the *Cycle of Organization*— the age of the city, the nation, and the race, the cycle of Memphis.

If I take this name as a symbol, it is not because the town of the Pyramids can be regarded as the first capital of the first kingdom of the world of men. More ancient cities than Memphis are known to us. It was, however, the head of the first great body of people with many limbs differently formed and harmoniously articulated, developing as one whole, on the banks of a great river and extending for 300 leagues of country. The others at that time, some 3,000 years before Christ, had not yet so successfully reduced the various peoples and lands under their rule to unity.

II

WHENCE CAME THE NATIONS OF ANTIQUITY?

It is elsewhere, however, that one must look for the source of those civilizations which, some time after the Flood, invaded the universe. Everybody is agreed upon the fact of this coming of civilizations; but there are a multitude of theorists with regard to the source. But when all has been weighed and considered—their arguments, sound and unsound, their methods, learned or fantastic, the facts that they advance, neglect, or invent and the interpretations simple or forced that they bring forward—this is what seems most probable. Go back a little along the roads followed by the Caravan: we shall not follow them for long without perceiving that they seem to come from a single point. They certainly have their detours, now towards South Africa or northern Europe, now towards Siberia or the Americas, again towards some land which has since been swallowed up by the sea in the East or the West, Atlantis or Gondwana. The roads run into dead-ends or vanish altogether. Suddenly—in the open country or near glacial moraines, sometimes on the shores of seas or the edge of deserts which appear untried and untouched—the traces we are following back cease, leaving no hint of where the men came from who left those traces, men who were branches of a trunk already old. We shall never know the answer unless we find it in another direction and recognize the original trunk.

But on these blind lost roads, as on the others, the traces seem to point all one way—towards the mountains where the figurative ark came to rest bearing the destiny of the human race. To this point we are brought back from everywhere by the bits of flint and obsidian which are scattered

like Tom Thumb's pebbles. The most ancient of artisan's
and cultivator's tools, in Elam, Chaldaea, Syria, Egypt, Crete,
in the centre and in the west of Europe as in Iran and Turania
whence they made their way to China and the Indies, seem
indeed to have come from that source. At times their names,
often certain peculiarities of their structure which cannot be
explained save as imitations, assign to them this origin in the
mountains of Ararat. It is certainly from that place and from
the neighbouring province of Anatolia that the blacksmiths
came, those who subdued fire and metal to their uses, to teach
men who cut out things in hard stone how to smelt and to
work gold, silver, copper, bronze and iron.

Where was "archaic Greek art born with its taste for the
animals of the East and its circular friezes"? Where the
universal art of heraldry with its geometry, its stylization and
its symbolism? Where "the art of the Far East with its special
combinations of vases without handles and of added supports
and its predilection for fantastic imagery"? Had they not their
origin amongst the Sumerians of Chaldaea, "that reservoir
whence the best known forms of art have poured out over
the world"?[1]

And whence indeed did the Sumerians and Elamites come,
bringing their gifts as artists, their talents as goldsmiths, as
workers in ceramics and as sculptors? They came from the
north, they came out of the mountains, they followed the
retreat of the waters. That is the reason why the animals we
see upon the first pottery made by them on the plains—"asses,
oxen, wild goats with glossy horns, argalis with knotted horns
and sheep with long hair"—had their origin in the high lands.
Did not Europe recruit its first domestic animals amongst the
species of the Near East? And there from the remotest antiquity
the three types of human language were spoken side by side:
the monosyllabic tongue which the Chinese declare they
brought from the West; the agglutinative languages of Elam
and of the plateaux which dominate the Black Sea; inflected
languages from each direction, Semitic in the south and Aryan

[1] E. Pottier, ap. *Revue de l'Art ancien et modern*, 1910.

in the north. The ancient idioms of the Sudan derive their origin from northern Africa; but their previous genealogy like that of the Egyptian language goes back to the interior of Asia.

It is indeed possible that the lineage of the Aryan tongues takes us to Lithuania rather than to Turania in central Asia or the Caucasus; yet how is it possible to believe that this country which was still covered with floods and ice, when humanity and civilization had already spread through the world, was a point of departure or even an initial stage? If the earliest roots of these languages are there, I have no doubt that they were brought there from elsewhere and, perhaps, from regions where more recent languages have supplanted them.

It is probable that the art of writing was born at different times in several different countries and we may doubt whether the hieroglyphics of Yucatan are in any way related to those of Egypt or of Chaldaea; but it seems certain that the alphabets which alone have, for a long period, been in use in the remainder of the world come from common ancestors, born between the Mediterranean, the Red Sea, the Gulf of Oman, the Sea of Aral, the Caspian and the Euxine.

The oldest of the sciences—the science of the stars and the science of numbers—bring to us the same evidence. The Egyptians made use of a calendar founded on the conjunction of the rise of Sirius with the sunrise every 1,400 years. Perhaps they had it from the Chaldaeans who, before them, were great astrologers; but the constellations of the Zodiac show that this knowledge, in Chaldaea as well as in Egypt, was brought from the north, from a well-defined region, and that Armenia answers to the definition.

The great migration of the barbarians with square heads, brachycephalics, who spread over Europe some time after the end of the Diluvian period, along with their dolmens, their menhirs and their cromlechs, set out from the East. Those stones tell us that in the East they did not inhabit the steppes where rocks are very few and far between; such customs could never have come into existence amongst them there. It is very unlikely that they came from Persia, from the Pamirs, from the Hindu-Kush or the Tian-Shan, which like the Siberian chain were then scarcely freed from their age-old glaciers along the marshes which formed their border. They could hardly have descended by any other route than the valleys of the Araxis and the Koura, the Phase and the Acampsis. They too must have come from the confines of Ararat.

Skirting the shores of the Black Sea, then the banks of the Danube and its tributaries, they mingled with the scattered descendants of the cave-dwellers with long heads who lived in Europe before them. These men lived in families, or perhaps in tribes, hunting the mammoth, the seal, the reindeer, the bear, the chamois, the bison and the aurochs. Many of them migrated towards the north, or towards the south, giving way before the new arrivals. Many, on the other hand, remained and produced stocks by mixture with the invaders, autochthonous people with hybrid features; whilst a completely new kind of life—a sky which became ever more gloomy and covered with clouds, long winters, the monotonous flat immensity of the steppes or the forest—transformed into northern people their eastern brothers who ascended the course of the Dnieper, the Don and the Volga towards the Baltic and the White Sea.

Later on, the multitude of their offspring—Celts, Mycenaeans, Hellenes, Aryas of India (who are simply one branch of all this people and not, as used to be thought, its ancestral root), Medes and Persians; Scythians, Germans, Hiung-Nu and Tou-Kiue (Huns and Turks)—were to people the two Gauls and the two Britains, the Balkans and Greece, Persia, half of India, Turania and northern China. The multitude flowed back towards the south and west. Of a truth it was to these people that "God gave space," intelligence and knowledge, reason, beauty, empire, the whole heritage of Memphis, of Babylon, of Jerusalem as far as Korea and Japan.

The Sumerians, the Accadians, and the Hittites who increased and multiplied perhaps at that time on the southern slopes of the Armenian mountains gradually descended towards Anatolia and Syria by the Euphrates and the Lycus.

Others before had followed the same routes: Aegeans, Etruscans, Ligurians, Iberians, Northern Africans, Egyptians, Elamites pushing in front of them on one side the Dravidians towards India, on the other side, the sons of Ham towards the Sudan.

Further away still, driven back everywhere, the Primitives—Negritos, Tasmanians, Tierra del Fuegans, Bushmen, Negrillos—the survivors from ages long ago and the first occupants of the soil, as their traditions attest in agreement with the tradition of the new-comers—took refuge in the extremities of the southern world; they sought a refuge in the forests of Equatorial Africa, in Ceylon and Malaya; whilst some went back again in the direction of southern China.

There, slowly, by the development of its ancient seed, with the co-operation of the climate, the soil and mode of life, emerged the yellow race of to-day. They were the result of repeated interbreedings and crossings with the white, bronze or pale-faced peoples who had migrated from the west and the north and with the Dravidians, the Malays and the Hindus who came from the south.

In this manner one deluge was the response to another. As the great waters withdraw from the earth the human flood gains on it and rises in a growing tide. The repopulating of the globe goes on by wave after wave which push forward, jostle one another, intermingle and pass one another in the race, rolling one upon the other and flowing in all directions, sometimes returning on their tracks, sometimes warlike, sometimes peaceful, more often in small groups, sporadic and insinuating, than violently and in great mass.

Their form, their weight, their volume and direction, their speed varied doubtless with the temperament and the faculties of the men who made up the groups; but the variation was caused especially by the necessity, whatever it was in each individual case, which drove them on and set them in motion—the pole of coldness changed its position and the desert belt as a result of the growing dryness widened and stretched out from Senegal to Korea; the wild animals migrated, famine and plague ranged through the world; the inundation spread ceaselessly and the population became too dense for its social condition, for the land which it occupied and the means it possessed of cultivating the soil.

There were also quarrels, ambitions, rivalries; covetousness, politics; wretchedness and poverty; faith, superstitions, oracles; the mirages which caused panics, or legends, or the irresistible appeal of the ancient instincts which in a sedentary posterity awoke the vagabond soul of their ancestors, hunters or shepherds of flocks.

And it was thus that the Caravan grew in numbers and subdued the earth.

III

THE FIRST KINGDOMS: EGYPT, WESTERN ASIA, CHINA

The organization of tribes into peoples and the foundation of States cannot be thought of otherwise than in this limitless Babel which endures even in our times. It is within such a Babel that the first local and national unities are formed, the first cities and the first kingdoms. The book of Genesis gives a list of them under the genealogy of Nimrod and in that list dates them from the third generation of men after the Flood; but it is silent on the question whether those generations are to be counted from father to son.

That "valiant hunter before God" built, we are told, eight cities: we understand their importance and the measure of their size when we consider that much later on in history, in the time of Moses and of the Thothmes, Megiddo and Jericho were still called great cities—they covered perhaps an area one half the size of the Place de la Concorde. Babylon itself, the city empire of antiquity, never covered more than 6,000 acres. It does not seem that Kheops and Hammurabi reigned over any wider area of inhabited country than the king of the Belgians to-day, with the Congo excluded; and they had only one half or one third as many subjects.

The three generations from Nimrod with his eight tribes and their eight capitals scarcely require more than a century for development. Let us multiply the figure by three, or even ten: it is not a matter of importance. The most ancient royalties we know of through historic evidences, inscriptions, palaces and tombs date only from the second half of the fourth millenary before Christ. Let us suppose that history some day advances its conquests a thousand years further; there will still remain plenty of time beyond that length of years back to the Deluge to satisfy the most exacting critics. In that period we shall be able to place, along with our Azilians, Magdalenians, Aurignacians, all the families, languages and nations of the East enumerated in the tenth chapter of Genesis; all the kings, or tribal chieftains, to whom tradition gives the sceptre in Accad, in Sumer and in Elam during this period; all the heroes that traditions make famous, precursors of Rama, of Hercules and Theseus.

The Shemsu-Hor, the companions of Horus who were the first to bring civilization into Egypt, have room in that period to display themselves at their ease. Without any difficulty in that great lapse of time, there can be accommodated the thirty princes of Tao, the thirty stages which the Chinese advanced before Fu-Hi, to emerge from the state of savagery, as they made their way from Turania towards the Yellow River; thirty epochs of progress which taught them, as they penetrated through the forests, to construct huts of tree branches in order to escape the attacks of wild beasts; to make fire by swiftly turning tinder wood in holes drilled for the purpose in hard wood, instead of striking sparks from flint; to smoke their venison; to cook their food; to clothe themselves, to count by means of pins or round counters and to make knots in small ropes to aid their memories.

Let us not then bother overmuch with regard to the remote ages where there is very little that we can know certainly. Let us rather place ourselves in the centre of those regions whence all seems to have been derived; and when the veil begins to become more transparent, sixty or seventy centuries ago, let us see what is to be seen.

From the south-west to the north and north-east, there is no sign of any monarchy. The Cretans of Miamu like the Rephaim of the Jordan, and the Azilians of the west like the first occupants of Macedonia and Thrace, or the peoples ever in motion between the Caucasus Mountains and the Altaï ridge, and between the Volga and the Danube, all this scattered world, either nomadic or partly nomadic, certainly still existed in families and tribes. Fu-hi whom the Chinese make an emperor—much as Raphael paints the Mother of Christ dressed in an Italian costume, seated upon a Renascence chair—was clearly only the illustrious chief of a more active clan, better governed and endowed with more native genius than the others.

From the east to the south and to the south-west, on the contrary, royalty everywhere either makes an actual beginning or at any rate gives evidence of its approach. If we must not take as genuine the Babylonian chronologies, nor perhaps date from so far back the most ancient remains which give us a glimpse of monarchy on both sides of Persia, it is none the less certain that the Sumerians and the Elamites, if not the Accadians and the Egyptians, were organized at the time into tiny States which disputed the overlordship and sovereignty one with the other.

A thousand years, twelve hundred years flash by. The sceptre passes from hand to hand continuously. There are kings in Sumer. There are kings in Elam. There are kings at Mari on the Euphrates half-way to the Armenian mountains. Everywhere in these regions, social order, like the cultivation of the soil, has already advanced very far from the primitive simplicity. The goldsmith works marvels. The weavers of cloth attain perfection. The potter's wheel and the chariot wheel are known. This last, indeed, China was not to have— by independent invention and importation—until much later. And Egypt was either ignorant of the invention of the wheel

I

or scorned it for twice as long a period, being satisfied with the
hand-drawn sledge for all uses.

Egypt awoke and outstripped Chaldaea. Ka and Narmer,
his successor, chief of Thinis towards the year 3300 B.C.,
rallied or subjugated the tribes scattered along the banks of
the Nile, bringing into being at the first stroke, between Nubia
and the Mediterranean, the royal unity which the princes of
Asia along the borders of the Tigris and the Euphrates had
never been able to accomplish, though they had been striving
for centuries to make their empire complete and durable. The
plain which lay open to all comers early became a field of
battle. Languages and peoples—Sumerians, Elamites; Semites
from Accad, from Amurru, from Assur; Hittites from Asia
Minor and Aryan Kassites—fiercely struggled on that plain
for power. But along the Nile, a narrow valley which runs
between two deserts, " a moving road", a veritable king's
way, the task was notably easier. Boundaries were contiguous:
races penetrated into one another's territory: their clashes
were less complex, if not less violent, and ended sooner. Less
avid or more docile, or simply closer in blood and manners
one to the other and trained by the all-powerful rhythm of
the Nile waters which overflow each year and then withdraw,
regulating and making fruitful the toil by which they live,
the Egyptians, as soon as they became the subjects of civilization, easily became one people under one monarch. Ka
and Narmer threaded these human pearls on the long ribbon of
the Nile. Aha, who succeeded Narmer; Atoti, the successor of
Aha, without trouble or difficulty placed the diadem upon their
heads. For more than 900 years it was not to be divided.

About the same time (3000—2500 B.C.) between the Blue
River and the Yellow River the Chinese nomads settled down.
They had perhaps a common chief. Later they would call
him Shin-Nung and would describe his "empire": each
clan with its domain, or fief; each king with his land and his
kingdom. Actually it was a feeble power over less than a
million subjects, the scattered neighbours of savage tribes
in a country as vast and as varied as that where so many

nations and kings moved about under the same parallels from Egypt to the Caspian Sea. But the State that was born in this manner and under these conditions was to see the end of others, was to outstrip them all, up to our own day, in its numbers and extent. Ten times conquered, twenty times dismembered and broken piecemeal, it always absorbed its conquerors and always found men to rebuild its ample edifice from the ruins. The roof of the world is its shelter. Girt by mountains and by deserts, far separated from all, firmly knit together by the social instinct, reinforcing traditions which have developed and become stereotyped into routine, and a family discipline untouched by all the upheavals which were to assail it during the course of 5,000 years; it suffered long periods of anarchy, the most terrible hecatombs: wars and famines, infanticide and misery, plagues and revolutions; and it did not perish. It has not dominated the earth. But what is the world's debt to China? Great vessels of the sea know where they are going and what they bear. They steer their courses, navigate and founder. But this immense raft, which is China, floats patient of all things—of the currents which carry it away, the waves that wash over it, the cyclones which devastate and threaten to overwhelm it. It floats on and waits until such things have passed over it, scornfully regarding the great ships of the sea as they pass it by, struggle and founder in the storms which assail them. As the day declines will the hour come that shall see it set up its masts, hoist its sails, rig a helm and rudder and steer a course for the "Islands of the Spirits"—Ying-Chou, Peng-Lai, Fang-Chang—countries of immortality where man frees himself from the burdens of the material and in his turn leads the Caravan on board his vessels to the conquest of joy?

Some time after Shin-Nung, Hwang-Ti (towards 2300 B.C.) continued and completed his work. At this period nomads no longer existed amongst the Chinese. The king alone came and went unceasingly from one end to another of his kingdom to caulk the joints or strengthen them. It is probably then that writing was invented. Money, the wheel, silk, known more or less for a long time, gradually entered into use. The government seemed more powerful. If one is to believe the traditions, no doubt echoes of those of ancient times, the government introduced a limitation of the fiefs, created the public register of lands, organised the salt tax and forced labour, instituted civil servants, built temples and schools and, in the north of China, led a campaign against the Huns—and provided itself with historians. Rites and customs invaded all departments of life. There was a mania for formalities, forms and uniformity. Houses, furniture, clothing, head-dress, weapons, tools, boats, road-carriages, as well as procedure and politeness, contracts, dances, music, painting and ceremonies became stylized and never differed from the official type, minutely elaborated, according to a system of symbols which bind and subordinate, term by term, all the series which brains devoted to minute details, observers and reasoners, establish for the purpose of introducing classification and order into the world—men and beasts, spirits and things, elements and phenomena, in fact all the creatures and changes of the universe.

Towards this epoch, doubtless for several centuries, the Aryans had been spreading from the Caspian Sea to the Hindu-Kush mountains and along them to the north of the desert. Perhaps they had already begun the descent of the other slope into the higher valleys of the Indus.

Some 500 years earlier (2850 B.C.), Sargon the Ancient, king of Accad, was the first in the world to try to reduce to unity under his dominion all the kingdoms, tongues, tribes and nations which surrounded him, disturbed and threatened him, harassed the merchants of his kingdom, or had in their mountains the wood, the stone and the metal he needed.

His plans and actions were in advance of their times. A thousand years had to elapse before the coming of empires. For a little time the edifice seemed to have been solidly built, but it soon cracked and fell to pieces. Sargon bequeathed nothing to his successors but war.

In the next century came his grandson Naram-Sin (towards

2756 B.C.) still more powerful and glorious; then Shulgi in the twenty-fifth century B.C. Hammurabi, the wise and great king of Babylon in the twenty-first century B.C. (2123—2080), for a score of years and more attempted to achieve an empire of this new type. It was far in advance of the age and like former attempts was doomed to a similar failure.

But the kings of Memphis brought to completion in Egypt what had been begun by the Thinites four hundred years before them. They established a centralized power in Egypt which they organized into districts, the chiefs of which were selected by Pharaoh himself. Snufru, Kheops, Chephron, Menkaura, the builders of the Pyramids and the Pepi and Teti were monarchs of magnificent aspect. They placed themselves at the head of the Human Caravan, whilst on the Euphrates all was still in dispute and on the Hwang-Ho, Hwang-Ti was only just holding in leading-strings a people almost entirely new to civilization. Soon, it is true—at the end of the third millenary—Yao, Shun and Yu the Great proceeded to legislate wisely, to carry out great works, to achieve the organization of the nine provinces, to expel or incorporate amongst their own people the barbarians who had entered the country—I, Man, Yung and Ti; to restrain the Hiung-Nu; and to ensure the happiness on a rich territory— some 450,000 square miles—of two million Chinese cultivators of the soil whom an aristocracy of clan chieftains ruled, exploited and protected. This is China's early history in outline. Try to visualize it. Picture to your minds something like the Far West of America in the time of the Natchez Indians; the immensity, the solitude; the never-ending savannahs and forests. In this territory a few tribes with the manners and customs of the reindeer age, wandering here and there; a few peasants in their settlements, wearing clothes, though primitive, scattered about in the ocean of the prairie like so many islets and archipelagos around feudal houses: a few thousand nobles or petty aristocracy, rustic police, captains of war and of peace in their great or little fiefs; and above them all, in his magnificence, the good king Dagobert!—or Clothair, or Chilperic: for the Hia (roughly 2200–1700 B.C.), the dynasty of Yu the Great, and the Shang-Yin (roughly 1700–1100 B.C.) who succeeded them, are not without resemblance to the history of the Merovingians in France. The Chinese dynasties spread over a longer period, in newer lands, vaster and emptier, but, in spite of the varnish of politeness which Chinese letters without exception paint over all pictures, it is the history of a monarchy still in a semi-barbarous condition. Its princes are not comparable to those of Egypt or Chaldaea. Of ancient origin, indigenous, isolated and distant, they resemble rather the petty kings and principalities which the cycle of Memphis during its last thousand years began to see in numbers.

Kings appeared in Crete as early as the twenty-ninth century B.C. They grew in power and made themselves strong. They spread their dominion over the isles, the shores and the waves of the Aegean Sea; they traded with the Egyptians, sent to them artisans and artists; coasted along Palestine and Phœnicia and perhaps taught the Sidonians the ways of the sea. Their palaces, which to-day are the ruins of ruins, proclaim, in spite of everything, their riches and their grandeur.

Kings appeared in Syria and in Assyria; in Asia Minor where the power of the Hittites was already growing and threatening Babylon; in northern Mesopotamia and in the country of the sea which had but recently emerged from the slimy waters. In Argolis, too, a monarchy was born. The Achaean clans descended towards the Peloponnesus. The Iberians and the Ligurians emigrated towards the west. Abraham made his way with his tribe from Ur to Haran, to Sichem and into Egypt, then towards the kings of the Pentapolis from Gerara to Salem.

It was the time when Thebes in Egypt had just replaced Memphis, deprived for ever of its power and sovereignty after 200 years of decadence. Soon the monarchs of the twelfth dynasty arose and shone on the southern horizon: Amenemhat the First who restored the kingdom and put an end to private wars; Senousrit the First, the conqueror of Nubia; Senousrit II and Senousrit III who completed his work, developed the arts and summoned into Misraim artists and artisans from Crete and drove back into the desert the Bedouins of Idumaea and of Sinai; Amenemhat III finally, the greatest of them all, a beneficent and peaceful king for nearly half a century, inspirer of famous works—Lake Moeris and the Labyrinth—which rank with the Pyramids amongst the wonders of antiquity.

But what a rapid decline there was after so much magnificence! These five great men filled two centuries with their deeds and their glory: 200 years afterwards their works were level with the ground and the Shepherd Kings were reigning in their stead. What a revenge for those Hyksos, "the princes of the desert"! They were to hold Egypt until the eighteenth dynasty which opened up "the succession of empires".

IV

DEIFICATION OF THE KINGS

The cycle of royalty is about to come to an end. It is the moment for us to turn our gaze backwards, towards Memphis and Babel, to see the route travelled over and to understand the nature of kings.

It was an affair which lasted but a brief instant. And the fact of facts about it is that these kings, since they began to exist in the world, whatever were their names, their titles, the forms of their power, in every clime, amongst all peoples—except in China—these kings were gods.

How could that happen? We do not know. Yet there are witnesses and indications to give us a glimpse of its working.

The First Being who gives Life, the supreme and universal sovereign who rules over everything with wisdom, and rewards and punishes human beings according to the principles of justice in this world and the next, He it is alone who at first was God. The civilised Chinese kept this initial faith relatively pure until the eighth century before our era; and the last survivors of primitive races in a savage state still attest under our very eyes this original tradition, by preserving it intact in its most simple form.

To this God different names were given. Those names used to express His essence or His splendour, His providence or His power. People did their best to know and to do what He desired; they prayed to Him and offered Him sacrifices. Those men who were like Him in this world, being wise, strong and worthy of admiration in the eyes of those whom they were ruling, were recognized in their persons as His representatives in this world. Their authority and dignity participated in His. The father was at the same time both priest and king.

When he became chief of his tribe, then king of his people and his kingdom, he did not cease to be both father and priest, interpreting for his people before God and God to his people. He might have remained on these heights, fixed their souls there; at providential moments he might have raised them up and himself mounted with them, higher still. But now there came the beginning and the image of usurpation over the whole earth: his people wanted to come down from the heights and the king did not know how to keep them there. Often he had no desire to keep them there. He was himself the first to come down, bringing his people in his wake. Why? How? History does not tell us, but all imaginable things were in it—fears, lusts, ambitions, jealousies, revenges, delusions, madness.

The deification of kings could sometimes be avoided, for a time at any rate, as the Aryans of Europe and of Asia avoided it in the course of the fourth stage in which we are about to follow the Caravan. And sometimes by the use of the intelligence, men would someday succeed in rediscovering the initial verities under the mass of fables and in developing them, for the initiated at least, into harmonious systems. But in the interval countless idols had been raised up which could not easily be got rid of.

Whether he be father or chieftain, the knowledge that a man holds the place of God in this world merely gives him an exact understanding of himself, according to the Socratic injunction; but for the impure heart there is no difference between holding and usurping this place. The adoration of Him from whom one has received life undoubtedly leads to God, but leads to Him by passing through the father: a great risk is incurred by allowing the tradition to be obscured and the intelligence to think it has attained its goal in the shadow thus arising, when we have in fact merely reached half-way along the path to our goal. This increases the authority of the human being there reigning; its growth is too great and leads to its ruin; but human beings do not see so far.

Between the feeling of love for ancestors and the adoration of ancestors there intervenes but the breadth of a hand-rail. Half, or three-quarters, or indeed almost the whole of antiquity climbed over it and bridged the gap. Religion and superstition grew up quite separately in the mind and heart of man. They engaged in a struggle for possession of his soul. If he chooses ill, or stays indifferent and makes no choice, then earth usurps the rank of heaven.

There is not always to be found a King Shun of energetic hand, wise and prompt to "break the communications" as said the Shu-Ching; a Moses or an Abraham to impose the necessary distinctions. Those who were most enlightened built up for truth the profound refuge of symbolism; but powerless to make these depths accessible to the multitudes, or clear enough for them to understand, all they succeeded in doing was to multiply by myth the forms of idolatry. Along this path also it is an easy thing to halt half-way.

Thus unity is changed into confusion and at the same stroke dominion into tyranny. Paganism, magic and slavery go side by side. With the Sumerians, the Cretans, the Semites of Chaldaea, the Aryans of Elam and of Mitanni the local god is not king for long without the local king becoming a god. Shall he not keep his royalty in another life?

In order that he should lack nothing, they used to enclose in his tomb everything which in this life had been the distinguishing mark of his dignity as a sovereign and served his grandeur and majesty. To-day we find in such tombs the golden mask in which his features were moulded and made immortal and imperishable; his weapons, his jewels, his seal, whether stamp or cylinder; his furniture, his vessels; his chariot drawn by oxen to revictual his house; shops for his clothing and goods for his court; his slaves and his wives put to sleep, eternally on the day of his obsequies in the funeral edifice, by the sword, or choked, or poisoned.

To whom shall we give the name of god, if not to those who are kings in the other world? Dead and deified, the king still fights for his people and watches over his kingdom: why then when he watches and fights during his lifetime should we refuse him the name he will have beyond the tomb? He is already accepted as the son of the local god, or of the supreme god. It is altogether natural that Naram-Sin should call himself "God of Agade", that Gudea should have his altars and the kings of Ur their temples; that Pharaoh in his lifetime should be called the "good god".

All this does not mean that no differences were made between gods and kings; there were in fact many distinctions drawn between the gods themselves. The fusion of the two was not complete and varied from people to people; but the deification of kings obtained everywhere, except in China and amongst savage races.

The Chinese would probably not have escaped, in spite of their isolation, if, like other peoples, they had had a taste for mythical transpositions, intellectual speculations and philosophic and religious esotericism. There was nothing of such movements and systems amongst them for more than 3,000 years. Their positive minds, their formalism and narrowness of ideas, their contempt for the "Barbarians"; the rigorous and vigorous system of exclusion which the best kings of their first three dynasties practised against superstition, maintained their own traditions intact and kept their distinctions sharp and clear. The "Son of Heaven", priest and king, did not become a god. Their ancestors remained human souls, as did those of everyone else, glorious genii, or wandering spirits

whose existence even became uncertain, in proportion as time
went on and their memory became dull in the distance of past
years.

Such, then, is the balance-sheet of this third stage in the
journey of the Caravan: a type of political and social organization more complex; of civilizations more brilliant; of manners
less brutish; the arts of the beautiful and the useful in full
development; writing, the wheel, copper, bronze everywhere
in use, except on the confines of uninhabited lands; iron known;
animals domesticated; the soil in cultivation; the wandering
life of the shepherd become almost the equal in adventure
to that of the hunter; a great step has indeed been taken
towards unity and dominion; but the whole process was corrupted in its roots by pagan confusion.

Earth and heaven, spirit and body, man and god, religion
and kingship, all is confused in practice and in faith. With
material and political progress there spreads a growing spiritual
and social decadence. How far will it go?

V

RELIGION AND SUPERSTITION

We must not be surprised to see the traditions of Misraim
becoming the more profoundly degenerate the further its
empire extended. Despite its activities in making the deep
excavations in the valley of the kings, in building the temple
of Karnak for Amon-Ra; in advancing over the desert to
the annexation of Canaan and Amurru; in imposing on the
kings of the north—Hittites, Mitannians and Assyrians—the
respect of its power by a number of brilliant victories; by
founding and in this fashion maintaining during four centuries
(1550–1150 B.C.) from Ethiopia to the Euphrates the first
amongst the empires of the world which exercised influence
and had enduring stability; all this did not prevent it from
being invaded by the divinities who reigned over the lands it

conquered. All the Baals, all the Astartes of Syria became installed on the banks of the Nile until later, after the fall of the empire, all the beasts of the valley—ibis, serpents, cats, rams, fish and crocodiles—the Olympians from over the sea and Serapis the upstart god, the little provincial god whose fortune was made by the Ptolemies, received the adoration of the most religious of men.

There was even a Pharaoh of the great epoch, Amenophis IV, Akhnaton, son of the Syrian woman Ti, anti-clerical in politics and an innovator it seems by temperament not less than by education, who dethroned Amon-Ra, changed his name, abandoned Thebes, constructed another capital and made of the whole of Egypt the kingdom of Aton who "made the earth at his will when he was still alone, men and animals", who rules over the whole world here below by his good providence and allows his glory to shine forth in the sun's disk.

In this manner "everything is god", including "God Himself" and the multiplication of the gods accentuates the need that is felt of bringing them together into a unity; but one god would not give way to another and Ikhnaton the reformer, whom many historians are pleased to describe as a prophet of that unity—a Mahomet before Mahomet himself—did in fact have statues of himself set up as a king-God; on his forehead he wore the menacing aspic.

Yet men like Thothmes, Amenophis and Rameses were none the less very great princes, cultured, wise, magnificent, energetic and powerful. They succeeded in doing, far away from their own borders, that which neither Sargon the Ancient, nor Shulgi, nor Hammurabi had been able to accomplish at their own door: they succeeded in founding an empire. But it is clear that had they overwhelmed Israel with benefits, instead of treating the Hebrews as slaves, Moses would still have led the Children of Israel out of their power.

He saw too clearly the direction of events in Egypt and towards what excesses 400 years of sojourn in the bosom of idolatry were leading the children of Jacob, Isaac and

Abraham. I do not think that any man, at any time, ever, so loved his own people. How prompt he was to feel and to revenge the injustice which had been done them! The tyranny which overwhelmed them in vain made an exception of Moses; he suffered in soul and cried out against it, as much and more than they in the flesh. His heart rose fiercely against it when he saw an Egyptian strike an Israelite. He killed the aggressor. He was a patriot.

He was a leader. Alone and a fugitive he commanded at the well of Madian the obedience of the primitive shepherds of the desert and, later on, he never abandoned the people whom he led, that people with hard hearts, unbowed heads, who caused him so much labour, so much unrest, anxiety and disappointment. He defended them and he protected them against Jehovah Himself. He insisted on God's pardon for the people and asked to be wiped out from the divine book of life rather than exist as the father of a great nation, without Israel.

Humble, moreover, and without ambitious aims; possessing the faith which dares and acts, nothing delayed or stopped him in his progress. He was a believer united to God by all that is rarest and deepest in the mystic life; a genius of thought and of action such as is not found in more than two or three men in the whole Human Caravan; one of those extraordinary men —like Gautama, Paul of Tarsus and Mahomet—who lived on to mould and fashion the human race for centuries, to regulate its movements and its spiritual life and to train it like a flame and a light for innumerable multitudes towards unity and dominion in the end.

His successors—Joshua, the Judges, Samuel, David, Solomon, Elijah, Elisha and the other prophets—workers at the same task during a thousand years in most wonderful agreement, made use of their powers in the same struggles. For his own triumph and theirs, it was necessary that the Twelve Tribes should become a great kingdom; that those who were most attached to his law and its doctrine, the guardians of the Ark and of the Temple, should remain in isolation on the borders

of the desert and the Dead Sea, a tiny little State in the mountains of the south; that the sufferings of exile and persecutions
should indeed sift the Jews, purify their faith and forge amongst
them the necessary number of faithful souls.

Elsewhere other methods were used; but everywhere the
Hebrews reacted, as by instinct, against the perils which the
confusions of paganism produce as snares for the intelligence
and the destinies of men. Everywhere writings fix doctrines
which have been slowly put together in the course of the third
and second millenaries before Christ, on the foundation of
original traditions. Spiritual and sacerdotal groups devote
themselves to these traditions to make a profound study of
their meanings, preserve them, develop them and transmit
them intact under verbal forms which had been carefully
elaborated. They assembled these formulas; and their books—
Avesta of Persia, Vedic Mantras—amongst the Oriental Aryans,
just as the Pentateuch amongst the Semites and the Shu-Ching
amongst the Chinese attest the reaction which is working.
The reaction continues in the sequel, through all kinds of
vicissitudes and under varied forms, often contradictory
amongst themselves, by the agency of men of letters in China,
the mages of Persia, some of them disciples of Zoroaster, some
not, the Brahmins of India and the schools, Jainas and others,
who at the very beginning of the nineteenth century B.C.
began to spread in different directions and to develop their
teachings.

This reaction was not, I know, merely the reaction of tradition against paganism. Its appearance is manifested in many
places and very early under the form of the attack of a proud
and rationalizing mind upon all types of faith. This I believe
is as old as reason itself, at least as the first delight felt by Eve
at the first speech made by the Serpent; but it was a force
which did not play the principal part in the reaction against
paganism. Beyond all others this duel was the struggle of
religion against superstition. The destiny of civilization was
at stake, that royal and imperial civilization of which Assyria
took the lead, as the Rameses in their decadence lost Phœnicia,

then Palestine, then the north of Egypt and the mastery of the sea.

The galleys of Tyre deprived the Cretans and the Tanites of the supremacy in the Mediterranean. They retained it for 800 years (1140–340 B.C.). On all its shores, as far as the distant west, amongst Africans, Iberians, Ligurians, with whom the Celtic new-comers had begun to mingle, they spread their riches, scattered their colonies, their culture and the gods of the Orient.

In Israel Saul rose to the kingdom. In the valley of the Orontes and on the ruins of the great kingdom of the Hittites, little monarchies grew in abundance. For a long time the Achaeans and the Aeolians had established themselves in Asia Minor. Troy, the guardian of the Hellespont, scarcely stirred to life again from its ashes, whilst the city of its conquerors, Mycenae, already queen of the Aegean world and the throne of Agamemnon, the king of kings, sank and disappeared.

The Dorians came on the scene and invaded the Peloponnesus, as other Aryans, further away, invaded first Persia then the plains of the Indus and the Ganges and rolled back in a mob towards the Deccan, the civilized Dravidians and the uncivilised primitives of India.

In China the aristocracy triumphed over the Yin Kings and were masters for 800 years with Fa, Duke of Chou, who killed the last king of the dynasty and put himself in his place; he was the suzerain of 300 fiefs, the sovereign of 9 provinces, the founder of the Chou dynasty (1050–250 B.C.), under the title of the emperor Wu-Wang.

VI

THE EMPIRES OF POWER

Assyria arose. It was the typical Empire of Power; yet to become an empire at all cost it a vast struggle. Later it was to say: "My hand has seized upon the riches of the nations as upon a nest. Just as one gathers eggs which have been abandoned, I have gathered the whole earth without anyone having moved a wing, opened a beak, or uttered a cry." In fact it exalted itself only by warfare, by devastation, by terror, and it was always struggling against the nations whom it trampled "under foot like a mad bull". It makes the avowal itself and glories in the ruins it piles one upon another, the prisoners it impales or flays alive, and the severed heads which it heaps into pyramids or with which it decorates the ramparts of conquered cities. Yet it had to start its campaigns three times over, to establish an empire which lasted for 270 years.

Shalmaneser I and his son Tukulti-Inurta (1290–1240 B.C.) reduced to their overlordship about sixty kings, from the Persian Gulf to the sources of the Tigris and from the country of the Medes to that of the Hittites, bordered by the two branches of the Euphrates. Their territory almost equalled that of France to-day. It lasted seven years. Then Babylon freed herself and the rest followed suit. A second attempt a century and a half later (towards 1100 B.C.) extended the dominion of Tiglath-Pileser I over Mesopotamia, Armenia, and the Commagene, as far as the frontiers of Damascus and Sidon, to the doors of Cilicia: it covered the area of Napoleon's France from the Alps and Rhine to the sea. When Tiglath-Pileser died, his empire crumbled. That is all for 200 years.

Only then Tukulti-Inurta II and his successors, Assurnazirpal, the Shalmanesers, the Samsi-Hadads, and the Hadad-Niraris were destined to reconstitute and consolidate the empire by a century and a half of almost continuous, atrocious wars. When this had been effected the empire had to grow and extend, all that had not been destroyed had to be reduced to powerlessness. Tiglath-Pileser III (745–727 B.C.) inaugurated the system of transporting populations which the Chinese in their turn practised later on. Before him all gave way. He was king "of Accad and of Sumer". The Medes and the Arabs of Sheba and of the Western desert and the kings of Israel, all had to pay him tribute. His armies burned Damascus and sacked Gaza in the land of the Philistines on the last stage of the march towards Egypt.

And now the Sargonides (722–612 B.C.): Sargon the Great, Sennacherib, Esar-Haddon, Assurbanipal; the splendour and the power of Nineveh, the great palaces, the libraries, the distant expeditions, Cyprus subjugated, Midas conquered. Lydia become a vassal state, the king of Tyre a fugitive, Judah a tributary State, Egypt four times attacked and ravaged. Thebes sacked, Elam invaded by land and by sea, Susa reduced to ruins; Babylon ten times in revolt, ten times beaten down, blow on blow, in less than ten years (689–680) levelled to the ground, burned, and flooded and then rebuilt only to be crushed anew thirty-two years later (648 B.C.); an unparalleled collection of riches, the spoils of war and numberless bloody victories; then suddenly the collapse.

The Medes grew in strength. They extended their dominion, subdued the Persians and attacked Assurbanipal. He beat them (towards 640 B.C.), but taught them how to beat him. Soon the Medes defeated his armies and attacked Nineveh. An invasion by the Scythians caused them to raise the siege (towards 634 B.C.) by ravaging Media, but this they did not out of love for the Assyrians. Thrust back by Sargon 100 years earlier (towards 720 B.C.), this time the Scythians broke through all defences. They laid waste the territories of Assurbanipal, just as they did those of Cyaxares, the Median King. Calah and Assur, royal towns, were reduced to ashes. They spread beyond as far as Egypt.

Nabopolassar, the governor of Babylon, profited by this to recover the throne of the Chaldees, to make an alliance with Cyaxares, to assist him in driving out the Scythians and in destroying Nineveh (612 B.C.). The two monarchs divided the empire between them. Pharaoh Necho, of Egypt, his mind haunted by the memory of Rameses, strove to dispute with them. He conquered the Jews at Megiddo (608 B.C.), he advanced as far as the Euphrates; but Babylon needed Syria, its stone, its metals, its woods and its ports. Nebuchadnezzar

K

defeated Necho at Carchemish (604 B.C.), crushed the revolt
of the Jews whom he deported into Babylonia, destroyed
Jerusalem, destroyed Tyre, crossed the Egyptian frontier or,
at least, by his victories over Amasis, removed from that
prince's mind all desire to pass beyond his own boundaries
henceforth.

The conqueror was a magnificent sovereign. Babylon owed
to him its advance into the first rank of capitals, eclipsing
Susa, Nineveh, Thebes, Memphis in extent, in riches and in
knowledge. The multitude of its houses was spread over both
banks of the great river with its markets, its palaces, its temples,
forming a huge square girt by double ramparts, built round
the city by Nebuchadnezzar who had also created hanging
gardens to embellish the city. It was indeed the symbol of
the *Empires of Power* the cycle of which was unrolled between
that of the kingdoms and that of the *Empires of Government*.
Thus it was that the prophets of Israel and St. John the
Evangelist saw Babylon, the Persians who feared it and the
Greeks whom it fascinated. Alexander made Babylon the Queen
City of Asia.

The development of a growth which lasted for four centuries,
so much success, so much grandeur accumulated in 100
years on the old country of Assur and of Sennaar, seemed
to promise an eternal domination to the Chaldaeans who
had seized the heritage. They were in fact to rule for more
than 300 years, but in the sphere of culture only: just as they
had already ruled over Assyria in the time even when Assyria
had crushed them at her feet. For in the sphere of politics,
the Chaldaeans were like a wave which has been gathering
force and then suddenly displays its overwhelming power.
Only seventy-seven years elapsed between the destruction of
Babylon by Sennacherib (689 B.C.) and the fall of Assyria;
there were only seventy-three between the destruction of
Nineveh and Belshazzar's feast.

Between the Persian Gulf, the Euxine and the Mediterranean
a hundred masters could find room; but could two? Now
Astyages, son of Cyaxares, ruled the Median Empire from

Ecbatana on the frontier of Elam and was the neighbour of
the King of Lydia and of a number of kingdoms which border
the course of the Indus. If he made no conquests it was because
his attention was occupied at home. His vassals of Anshan in
Elam began an agitation which led to a revolt against him.
They drove him from the throne and put their chief in his
place: this chief was a Persian, Cyrus, who set the Persian
empire on the way to being the greatest in the world.

Croesus, King of Lydia, saw the peril. He tried to stem
the menacing flood. They took his kingdom from him. Babylon
was taken (539 B.C.), Memphis was taken, Thebes taken, the
Hellespont and the Oxus were crossed and the Danube reached.
The Arabs paid tribute. The Persian tide submerged everything, from the Tian-Shan to Nubia and from Olympus to
the plains of Sind. Cyrus, Cambyses, Darius and Xerxes were
indeed "Great Kings", the only ones in the world. It became
their turn to promise themselves an eternity of power.

Their empire, however, was doomed to pass away more
quickly than those of Egypt and Assyria. And what similar
eternities there had been, one after another, in the depths of
the obscurity from which they had emerged into light and
power!

In the midst of the anarchy of the war lords who had disturbed the peace of China for more than 100 years, the Ch'in,
princes of the age of blood, seized hold upon power.

The kings of Magadha achieved for themselves a predominant
position amongst the thousand kings of India.

In the Occident the Greek victors of Marathon (490 B.C.),
of Salamis (480 B.C.), of Plataea (479 B.C.) and of Mycale (479
B.C.) cleared the way for Alexander the Great (336 B.C.); just
as the establishment of the little republic on the seven hills
by the Tiber (509 B.C.) with its consuls, tribunes and dictators,
opened up the Roman road along which Caesar and his
legions were to pass to empire.

THE GREAT RISE IN CULTURE DURING THE SIXTH AND
FIFTH CENTURIES BEFORE CHRIST

The advent of the Persian monarchs who were fervent worshippers of Auramazda, "Spirit Knowledge", marks a new
movement against the confusions of paganism and the unceasing attacks of superstition. This does not mean that paganism
and superstition were opposed by deliberate policy: the
policy of the Persian rulers was indeed to humour all gods, to
leave all cults in the enjoyment of their freedom and not to
harass beliefs with persecution. Their empire merely participated in the remarkable flight of development, that soaring
into the upper air and light which rendered the sixth and fifth
centuries before Christ one of the grandest and most wonderful
epochs in the order of the intelligence and the sphere of
religion.

Whence came this universal development and who ordained
it? That is a secret that remains hidden. In each country,
however, its particular causes can be discerned and studied.
Amidst the nations we can observe a kind of reciprocal preparation of the chosen spirits, a kind of spiritual contagion
which everywhere awakes; a fire of ideas and aspirations of a
kindred nature which runs through the world. We can distinguish its sources along the banks of the Nile and the Ganges.
It is conceivable that the expansion of the Persian empire was
the occasion for this movement of the spirit since it brought
Egypt and Greece into touch with India which had already
established relations with the élite of China. In this way
it gave pre-eminence in the Caravan to those races best
endowed for spiritual speculation: but for this wonderful
concert Providence itself is the only possible leader of the
orchestra.

How, without appealing to the depth of the divine wisdom
and to the irresistible designs of Him who rules the hearts of

kings and the thoughts of the wise, can we fully account for such an accumulation of spiritual progress, within so short a period and in countries and circumstances so diverse, amongst men, works and events of such a scope, so wide a spread, so far apart and so decisive? Two hundred years only: and their action still endures; it has become world-wide and is not yet near the end of its influence.

Two hundred years or even more (600–350 B.C.).

The last prophets and the priesthood of the Jews renewed the Alliance, with a precise statement of the faith in the one God and the expectation of the Messiah; they built the temple where they announced that He was to come, fixed the time of His coming and sang His universal reign.

The Seven Sages, the initiates of Orphism and the Mysteries, the poets—Pindar, Aeschylus, Sophocles, and Euripides; the historians—Herodotus and Thucydides; the philosophers— Pythagoras, Heraclitus, Parmenides, Anaxagoras, Socrates, Plato and Aristotle—arose amongst the Greeks so that the subtle genius of their race should not be lost in the profusion of its mythical inventions, in its cult for beauty of form, its athletic prowess, the heroes whom it deified and the gods whom it brought down to the level of the worst of humanity. The poets, the historians and the philosophers of Greece came to save the life of the soul, the reason, the sense of reality and the taste for the truth.

Amongst the Aryans of Persia, the disciples of Zoroaster rendered definitive in writing, in the twenty-one books of the Avesta, his already ancient teachings: a coherent doctrine, a clear dualism which preserved an élite from the popular confusions and ranged them on the side of the wise god who is both beneficent and true against the maleficent god of ignorance and falsehood.

Amongst the Aryans of India the doctrine of the Vedas succeeded in spreading like a tree with many trunks. Its schools of metaphysics, of mysticism and of ascesis,—Mimansa, Vedanta, Sankya, Yoga—its disciplines in monastic or solitary life—Sramana, Sannyasin, Yati—grew to full blossom. The

Upanishads in which it was to find expression in its Brahminical development were then being compiled. It taught the identity of knowledge and of happiness and the necessity to withdraw oneself from the world to reach, by the contemplation of Brahma, the universal being. "Even the happiness of the gods does not, in the supremacy of knowledge, equal the felicity of the man who has found *The Being*." Mahavira gave to the Jains light and new rules. Gautama preached to men.

By spoken word and example, he preached to those who were tormented by the problem of evil and of suffering; to those whose hearts remained hungry in intellectual contemplation and the peace of ecstasy—or hypnosis; to those disheartened by the *samsara*, the transmigration of souls through an indefinite series of illusory joyless existences to a scarcely attainable state of repose; to them all he preached a way of "deliverance".

It is a middle way between the aberrations of the world and the frightful fastings and macerations of the anchorites. It is possible for all men to follow that road whatever be their caste or their sect. Let them follow it and spread their sympathy amongst all beings. After their next death or a few more, perhaps before, in the depths of their souls, if they understand how to withdraw themselves completely, their thirst will be quenched and they will attain "refreshment," "immortality" and an "abode" which cannot be disturbed, in a word "the island" which is surrounded by change, sin, grief and death none of which have any access to it. In that island there is no more desire, nothing which resembles thought, conscience, life, existence, such, at least, as are possessed by human beings here below or conceived by them: it is *nirvana*, the supreme end, and Gautama refuses to define it.

With what prodigious success he preached! How many mendicant monks, under obedience to him, were vowed to detachment, to chastity, to the inner life! What a crowd of devotees to follow him! Let us give every possible credit in these marvels to the part played by the epoch and the clime, by the race who followed him, enthusiastic in its nature, easily captured by an ideal and passionately religious, to the prestige enjoyed by the ascetic of the Sakyas by reason of his birth and noble origin, his renunciations, his knowledge, his lengthy austerities, his eloquence, his very look, perhaps to his voice which is described as having been grave, penetrating and seductive of hearts. Yet these things do not explain everything.

Indeed they explain nothing unless it be the comparatively prompt extinction of this fire of straws in India. The qualities of lastingness and depth which existed in the initial movement of souls towards the Buddha; the echo of his words through the ages, his spiritual conquests towards the north and the east; the fact that he did not—like Moses, Zoroaster and the Brahmins before him—merely build into a national cult beliefs which have no frontiers, but that, on the contrary, like Christ and Mahomet, he disengaged them from such national limitations and in this wise founded a universal religion, of which after his death he remained the Prophet and the Lord; at the source of all this there must be a powerful soul, an ardent heart and a profound genius at whose touch all human cords vibrate.

The doctrines of India which his monks were to sow later on as far as the shores of the Pacific, Lao-Tseu was already adapting to Chinese life and conditions for the realm of the Chou. Being the royal archivist he found in his archives a few things written by the Brahmins. Other men had already commented on these writings and taught the contents to their pupils. In his turn he made a study of them, adapted them to his own mentality, co-ordinated them into a system and published the Tao-Tei-King, or *Book of the Principle and its Virtue.*

Perhaps he hoped in this way to replace by a new culture the old traditions which the seignorial dissensions were in the course of destroying. He did not succeed. His contemporary, Confucius, made a collection of them, praised them and wrote a commentary on them. Being a politician and not a theologian or philosopher, he converted them into the everlasting, unchangeable foundation of order and prosperity in the State.

He rescued them from oblivion and degeneration. In return the men of letters whom he attached to their cult made Confucius a sort of God. This no doubt was too great an honour; for if he preached, as did Gautama, a middle way, it was not for the purpose of arriving at the same end as Gautama; and what a difference there was between the lessons of Buddha and the worldly prudence, the suppleness of opportunism, the interested beneficence and the astute routine which Confucius praised!

But there is a place for everything in the mind and politics of the Chinese. All the figurative wheels of the perpetual mutations of being and the indefinite unrolling of facts—*yinn* and *yang*, giving birth to one another and succeeding one another in perpetuity—can find room to exist in the Chinese mind, can dovetail in it with perfect ease. The sectarians of the Tao-Tei were to have their revenge. When the Duke of Ch'in annihilated the seignorial régime and inaugurated the empire, its power was theirs. They dominated him by the most chimerical conclusions which they logically deduced from the speculations of their master.

Five centuries passed away before Confucius emerged from the shadows of the obscurity to which he had been relegated, and before Buddha, the new-comer in China, had gained enough favour to lay claim to any power amongst the races of the land. The rivalry which then followed between Confucius and Buddha was destined to be fierce and relentless. Each one of the three extant doctrines was destined to suffer a metamorphosis. From time to time Buddha attained to a period of influence and glory, and Lao-Tseu, though deified, was doomed to suffer a corresponding era of decline. Victory was, at last, to be the guerdon of Confucius, but of a Confucius who seemed to have passed, since the time of Darius the Mede, through about thirty different forms of existence as a philosopher in innumerable schools, Chinese, Hindu and Greek, beginning with those of Buddha and of Lao-Tseu.

When weighed in the scales of these great phenomena and events, what is the true value of the "Great Kings"? The epoch of such *Empires of Power* was undoubtedly at an end. They were in point of fact empires in which the sole bond of unity, outside the metropolis, was the domination of the monarch himself, and as an inevitable result they gave rise to nothing but the payment of tribute by subject races and nations. In their common submission, cities and kingdoms remained far too separated and distinct from one another ever to become part of a whole. The time had come when they must be more mightily "pulverized in order to be kneaded together", as Joseph de Maistre was to say of Modern Europe; for coming as they did from all quarters of the compass, in their variety, men exhibited with startling clearness the unity of their nature, their needs, their thoughts and their early traditions. The cycle of Babylon drew near its end. Let us place it under the standard of that Xerxes who was vanquished by the Greeks at Salamis: and all is now ripe for Alexander the Great to appear on the scene of action.

CHAPTER IV

ROME AND JERUSALEM

I

ALEXANDER

ASIA is the earth. She is massive, towering, heavy, primitive and remote. She is the great destroyer; she immobilizes, dissolves, transforms and brings all things to a new birth. She drags everything along with her into that immutable movement in which and by which all things change and begin again. Everything that is turns about in its orbit and upon its axis, even that which on the surface seems neither to change, nor to move.

Until our own times the fate of Asia was decided upon the land: in Sumer and in Accad, at Babylon, Nineveh, Carchemish and Jericho; in the plains of Sennaar, along the valley of the Nile, of the Indus and of the Ganges, the Hwang-Ho, the Yang-Tse-Kiang, the Kipchak, and Manchuria. The sea is not propitious to Asia, though Sennacherib owed one of his victories to an attack he made by sea. To the cities of Tyre, Sidon and Carthage the sea brought the riches of the earth, but it also brought death. Xerxes, in a fit of ridiculous anger, had the sea whipped to show his displeasure when it wrecked his ships, but though a "Great King" he was a foolish puppet of fate. The Athenian gadfly was too strong for the Persian lion. On the other hand it was the sea that opened up a way for the West to Malaya, Australasia, to India and even to Indo-China. Japan, who has embarked her fortunes on the sea, is no longer held as one of her children by Asia: she treats Japan as she treats the Western nations.

Until the epoch of "the Great Kings" it was in Asia and

136

through Asia that the Caravan marched. They led it there along the sea-shore. They tried to pass over the sea to the other side of the straits: for the Caravan urged them on; it had to pass over. Henceforth it was necessary that it should march towards the West, through the West. In that direction its future beckoned it.

The "Great Kings" were not able to lead the Caravan across the sea. And so it passed over without them; and the Greeks, victors on the sea, took the place of the kings. The West is the sea.

The whole soul of the West is in the cry uttered by Xenophon's soldiers. Perils, fatigue, sufferings, miseries, all disappear, all is forgotten as soon as they perceive in the far distance the white crests of the waves. When they gaze on them, they see again and they greet with shouts their home: "The Sea! The Sea!" It is the sea that is sovereign of the West, of the isles which it surrounds, of the peninsulas which it embraces, of its isthmuses, broad or narrow, of the continents which it at once divides and joins.

To that distant limit to which the West is able to push its advance in the wake of the sun, to cross the vastest of the oceans, the West belongs to the sea. Its destiny is on the great waters. On the day when the Cretans seized as theirs the mastery of the Mediterranean from the Nile to the Hellespont, the West made its début in history. It put its hand to the victorious helm on the day of Salamis when Themistocles and the Greeks in their triremes drove Asia from the sea.

Throughout the ages it is on the sea that the fortune of the West is played for; at Salamis against the Asiatics of Susa; at Myles and the Egatean Islands against the Carthaginians; at Lepanto against the Turks; on board the caravels of Columbus who led the West to the New World; at Trafalgar when England and France fought for the mastery of Europe and the world; in the English Channel and the North Sea when the Great War sounded the hour of America's destiny.

"Our future is on the sea": that was a truth for Germany

when she was ambitious to supplant England and to march side by side with America at the head of the Caravan. And it was on the sea at the straits of Tsou-Shima that European Russia received her death-blow. Asia then threw the grappling-irons upon her and drove the hatchet into the keel which three centuries before had been well and truly laid by Peter the Great at Saardam. Would to heaven that this were all and that a day may never come when Asia will be able to speak of Tsou-Shima as the setting of the sun that rose at Salamis.

On that day Themistocles perhaps thought that all he had done was to guard the liberty of his own country. Now of course we know full well that the struggle carried within itself the independence of the West and for Hellas the mastery over thought. Neither Persian gold, nor the envious barbarism of the Dorians, nor the treasons of Alcibiades, nor the everlasting incompetence and the vacillations of Demos were successful in defrauding the intelligence of Attica and Ionia of this splendid triumph. They alone, in spite of their frivolity and their internecine discords, understood and performed what was good and beautiful. Whilst Asia was becoming degenerate through her very riches Attica and Ionia were civilizing Macedonia, educating her princes and spreading over the whole East the illumination of their genius.

As soon as it was constructed, the Greek empire began to split up into parcels. It would have been nothing without this genius which gave it unity and duration in time as in space; and the three centuries (470—140 B.C.) which were the period of its duration were stamped with the names of Attica and Ionia when they bore those of Pericles, of Alexander and the Ptolemies.

It is easy for the scholar from the giddy height of his pile of useless paper to belittle the young demigod Alexander, the son of Philip of Macedon, as a madman who stabbed Clitus, imprisoned Callisthenes in a cage, overran Asia with fire and sword merely to satisfy his vile appetite for conquests, without rhyme or reason, wandered about aimlessly from place to place in India, had altars set up to himself and almost died as a result of a cold bath—he was to meet his death at thirty-three years of age as a result of his excesses—because in spite of all the philosophy of his preceptor, Aristotle, he did not possess the patience to endure heat. It is easy to see him as a dazzling meteor which shot across the sky, leaving behind him a trail of ashes amongst the ancient things whose end he hastened, or as the leader of a band of armed young ruffians, gluttonous for honour and pillage and the collecting of kingdoms, the vain and ill-tempered understudy of the genius his father, who was assassinated under suspicious circumstances at the very moment of starting out upon an expedition he had prepared—an expedition which the son accomplished blindly without taking any thought for the morrow.

All this, I say, is easy, and not without its truth. Alexander was lettered, generous, elegant and handsome, but there was nothing in him of Scudéry's Great Cyrus. I make no excuse for his crimes. I would not even swear that either he or his mother Olympias was absolutely innocent of the murder of his father; and assuredly if Philip had not done what he did and Alexander himself had had to make the preparations, instead of conquering the world, he would have taken as long to cross the Hellespont. His orgies were on a grand scale yet scarcely went beyond the ordinary usages of the upper classes amongst the Greeks; they were in fact the most undiluted of Atticisms. And if he was in fact guilty (the question remains doubtful) of the assassination of his father, in order to accelerate his own accession to the throne of Macedonia, we may with justice ask how many kings had set him the example. The Sons of Heaven themselves, the greatest of moralists amongst princes, had small hesitation in committing this crime of parricide which they cleared of moral obloquy by two declarations on the subject of filial piety carved and framed in sculptured relief!

Alexander's deification was quite in the royal tradition of the East and was desired by him not out of foolish pride but out of political expediency. And in any event Alexander was the equal of the Greek deities, in the breadth of his thought, the rapidity with which he acted, his power, his vices, his beauty, his anger and even his orgies. Hellas was incarnate in them: was he not in truth the incarnation of Hellas?

His father, assuredly, was a monarch of genius. Demosthenes, the good Athenian watchdog, would not have raised so loud a voice at any king that came along. A long time before the reign of Philip of Macedon, Sparta had already attempted the conquest of Asia. At Philip's death everything was prepared for another expedition. It was the dream of Greece. Be it so, but consider, if at twenty-five years of age you were only the pupil of Michelangelo, even the best of his pupils, and you had to paint the Sistine Chapel after his death with no other guide but the confidences of the master with regard to his project and ideas: and you succeeded. That, in its way, is what Alexander did. And that took genius.

This conqueror was the first "citizen of the world" to attain power, no more and no less. Before him, philosophers and prophets—Aristotle, Plato, Gautama, Lao-Tseu, Zoroaster or Isaiah—the Brahmins assuredly, the Chinese perhaps, had conceived in their minds the idea of the unity of the human race and dreamed—or even tried to bring into being somewhere with a chosen people—an ideal republic. Before his time, kings and emperors had assembled under their power many peoples and immense territories and we have watched them pass. How different were his ideas and his work! The domination of the kings created a national unity between families, clans and tribes, whom it subjugated, uniting them by narrow personal bonds: a single chief, a single people, one domain, as far as race and common interests were accessory; that was the objective. The imperial dominion of power united the nations which it subjugated in communities by their chains, formal bonds whose symbol was tribute, without destroying them or administering their territories, often without civilizing them, sometimes even receiving civilization and culture from a conquered people. The imperial ambition was to achieve riches in perpetuity and predominance without rivalry.

Alexander's dominion was a new thing. It civilized and administered the lands of which it took possession. It organized its conquests, caring less to grind the nations into dust than to knead and fashion the human paste and to put into it its own leaven, to unite those whom it had under its dominion by a common culture in the same political life. To shine in splendour, to excel, to endure were not its ideals and objectives. What that dominion aimed at was the whole world—the whole world made Greek.

Yet the Greek dominion did not desire to annihilate the heritage of other races. Persian, Hindu, Egyptian, Chaldaean or Jew, "nothing which is human is foreign to it". All men and all nations were to find existence and peace within its bosom. Alexander did not listen to those who advised him, says Plutarch, "to act as a prince with the Greeks, and as a despot with the Barbarians. On the contrary he thought himself sent by God to protect both Barbarians and Greeks. His desire was that the whole world should be a common fatherland for all men"[1].

Such was his conception, the empire was a city and the city universal. These then were two great novelties in the universe. It is better to grasp their meaning than to sketch their outline by his victories, in lines of fire. He laid the foundation of this human city. In thirteen years he gave it strength. When he died at Babylon in 323 B.C. from an attack of malignant fever, whose malignity, it is said, was helped by Antipater, his dominion was already so well founded on the earth and settled in the souls of the hero's successors that, though they disputed amongst themselves the inheritance that came to them by escheat, they were still able, without destroying it, to carve it up by warfare and by policy and retain it for the next 200 years. There existed from ten to twelve of such kingdoms under the banner of the Greek spirit and the brilliant renown of Alexander.

When the real heirs were to come along, at the head of the sovereign people, to unite the whole of the west into one great

[1] Plutarch's first discourse on Alexander.

domain and to extend it by adding to it their own conquests beyond the columns of Hercules and the English Channel, "Greece, though in captivity, was to take captive her fierce conqueror". The world saw once again the prosperity of Alexander's city. He was the first of the Caesars.

II

THE WORLD IN TRAVAIL IN THE FOURTH AND THIRD CENTURIES BEFORE CHRIST

Around his strange empire which broke in pieces almost as soon as it was erected yet did not perish—and continued to prosper, although constituted of ten turbulent States which clashed together, fell into and out of alliances, conspired together, absorbed one another, betrayed one another—the wind of domination which blows over all races of men arose from all quarters of the compass and threw the new powers one against the other.

The Celts who peopled the whole of the two Gauls and the centre of Europe clashed with the Romans (390–222 B.C.), then with the Greeks (279 B.C.); the Romans with the Samnites (343–280 B.C.) and with Pyrrhus (284–274 B.C.); the Carthaginians with the Romans in Sicily (264 B.C.), in Spain (219 B.C.), in Italy, where by a prodigy of hate, of patriotism and of genius Hannibal maintained himself for fifteen years (218–203 B.C.), always the conqueror and never making any error in his politics, his tactics and his strategy, except on the morrow of Cannae, the decisive day.

The Hindus, whom their divisions amongst themselves had made a ready prey for Alexander, formed under the Mauryas (322–210 B.C.) a vast and prosperous empire which, up to the time of Antiochus the Great (222–187 B.C.) held the Seleucides in check. For forty years the greatest man of this dynasty was to reign over almost the whole of India, from the Brahmaputra to the Hindu-Kush and from the plateau of Persia to that of Mysore. Of the three types—kingdom, empire of power, empire of government—this was an empire of government rather than an empire of power; but the unity of the human race in the universal city did not enter into its aims and vision. It had no other purpose than to weld together in a single nation all the Aryans of India; and in that way it was rather a kingdom than an empire of government.

Chandraguptra (321 B.C.), a rough soldier of fortune, the usurper of Maghada, and his son Bindusara who succeeded him, enlarged their frontiers foot by foot by every possible method of acquisition. Asoka, Bindusara's son (273–232 B.C.), received his inheritance from them in peace and was desirous of imitating them. A cruel war made him master of the kingdom of Kalinga between the rivers Mahanadi and Godavery, but he became disgusted with a career of such harsh conquests. He declared "war upon war"—there is nothing new under the sun—became a convert to Buddhism which he encouraged and protected yet without interfering with other faiths; he gave it premier rank in India, extended its influence towards Thibet and Burmah and assured it of its domination through his own prestige. He became a monk himself without abdicating, and he engraved on the rocks and pillars at the crossways of his kingdom the fundamental rules of the Buddhist doctrines as edicts having the status of law in his kingdom.

He was a Constantine, then, or shall we say a Charlemagne? Perhaps. The resemblance is there but the contrast is as striking. The son of St. Helena, and the father of Louis the Pious (who was deposed by the bishops) were both made what they were by the Church, they were the instruments of its power, its temporal vicars, its "bishops outside the church". On the other hand, Buddhism owed everything to Asoka in the sphere of power; he owed nothing to Buddhism. In that respect he was like Mahomet—but a Mahomet who preached a holy peace and founded the reign of a "prophet" who had died three centuries before without saying what he thought

L

about God! Let us praise the monk-emperor for his kindness his pity, for his remorse at the carnage he had wrought and the destruction of the conquered. Let us admire his faith which proved itself superior to the intoxications of success and o power; and his fidelity to peace from the day when he cursed war. All this is good; but there were other peaceful kings in history. There were indeed some who had neither weapons nor armies. There were even some who surrendered the property and possessions acquired in evil fashion by their fathers, though no one had besought them so to do. This great impulse of fruitful pity reveals a human heart. But such remorse surely is the confession of an unjust war, and many restitutions should have followed. And would this fidelity have been possible if the monarch had had enemies capable of compelling him to go to war? Carthage and Serbia, though twenty-two centuries divided them, in vain strove to preserve peace before fighting against the argument of the stronger.

When all is taken into account, the kings and peoples who have been beaten by force form a list much longer than the list of their assailants who were moved by lust of vengeance or of conquest, of pillage or of combat. We are liable to forget those who were beaten, however, because they are small, feeble and vanquished. Fortunate and great most certainly are those who cherish peace and keep it; but greater still those who preserve their love of peace in misfortune and persist in the service of peace by repulsing heroically the violence which they are constrained to suffer. War is one of the scourges of humanity. This statement does not mean that there can be no just war, no necessary, holy war, though even in them ambitious, unscrupulous men seize the opportunity of hoisting themselves into power. Even those wars which are neither just, nor necessary, wars which cannot be expiated because they were fought in bad causes and their methods were stained by inhuman atrocities, are sometimes the avenging limits of excesses which have been carried to the highest point. The road is often terrible to follow, but peace and order are to be found at its end.

The dukes and kings of Ch'in, for example, the contemporaries of Alexander, of Asoka and Hamilcar, heaped massacre upon massacre. Beneath their feet it was the literal truth that blood ran in streams. From the high lands of the Wei, the first home of the Chinese in China, where they had built their eyrie—amongst barbarous and ferocious mountaineers, these vultures for two hundred years, without respite, attacked, domineered, pillaged, ravaged and destroyed to raise their power upon the ruins of six kingdoms and to restore to their own advantage, by making it absolute, the monarchy of the Chou. These great lords were freebooters worse than their neighbours, perchance, whom they crushed and constrained to obey their discipline under the penalty of feeling the sharp edge of their steel. Yet their crimes spared their country several centuries of disorder and misery.

Cheng, the last but one of the dynasty, at last attained his goal and held it at the price of a labour from which there was no relaxation throughout his long reign (247–209 B.C.). Under the title of Shih-Huang-Ti (221 B.C.) he became emperor at the end of thirty-eight years of warfare. He crushed the politicians whose policy was to sow dissension that they might live upon it, burned the books which they made use of, built the Great Wall to keep out the barbarians, organized everything and endowed the State with stable institutions, a real administrative system which was never shaken or abandoned in the course of the twenty centuries which followed without the whole of China being convulsed and menaced with ruin.

Was this an empire of government? No; that came later on. For the moment it was the greatest of kingdoms in its vastness, soon it was an empire of power. In this manner the hour seemed to have arrived for which the great upward flight of the sixth century had prepared the way.

III

ROME AN EMPIRE OF GOVERNMENT

Now came the hurricane.

Rome triumphed over Hannibal and broke him at Zama (201). The last obstacle had been surmounted. At length the force was unchained, the force of arms, of laws, of a tenacious policy, profound and continuous; of a boldness which nothing could stop, of a will which nothing could turn aside, of an ambition without bounds or limits and a pitiless avarice; the force of a clear intelligence, exact, precise, methodical, penetrating men and things, in love with justice and might rather than loftiness; obedient to facts and actuality, rebellious to the seductive power of ideas; the force of a race of builders and constructors made for kneading, modelling, cementing together all others, establishing discipline amongst them, ruling over them and accomplishing what Alexander had merely sketched out, namely constructing *and governing* for all men a common and supreme fatherland, the *Imperial State*.

For seventy-two years there was universal war: in Macedonia (199–142 B.C.), in Spain (196–146 B.C.), in Achaea (196–146 B.C.), in Syria (192–164 B.C.), in Cisalpine Gaul (194–101 B.C.), in Lydia and Galatia (189–188 B.C.), in Istria (178–176 B.C.), in Sardinia and Corsica (177, 174, 163 B.C.), in Illyria (168 B.C.), in Dalmatia (156–154 B.C.), at Carthage (149–146 B.C.) which but yesterday had been reduced and was now destroyed; in Pergamos (114–106 B.C.), in Asia Minor and in Greece (180–47 B.C.), in Thrace (114–106 B.C.), in Numidia (111–46 B.C.), in Armenia (71–34 B.C.), in Judaea (63–38 B.C.), in Gaul (60–58 B.C.), in Great Britain (55–54 B.C.), in Germany (55, 53, 37 B.C.), in Egypt (55–48 B.C.), on the confines of the Far East, where the Parthians threatened Rome; on all the shores of the Mediterranean, where the pirates (77–67 B.C.) interfered with her food supplies and her commerce; in Italy and at Rome itself, where her own subjects and her slaves coveting the citizenship, her common people envious to possess or rather to live at the expense of the City, her tribunes and her generals longing to become masters of Rome, warred upon one another in the midst of so many foreign wars.

Such was, however, the strength of Rome that she grew in spite of such waste. Nothing beat her down, nothing lessened her courage, nothing wore her out, neither the incursions of the Germans (113, 105, 101 B.C.) and the Scythians (80 B.C.), nor the revolts and intrigues of peoples and kings she had recently subdued, nor the venality of the electors and the elected of the Republic, nor the exactions of proconsuls and tax-farmers, nor the revolutionary agitation of the Greeks (133, 123–121 B.C.), nor the violent acts and vices of Marius, nor the cruelties of Sulla, nor the massacres by which both made themselves famous, one an aristocrat and the other a demagogue, both of them victors over the foreigner and tyrants over their own country; nor the series of wars which their struggle caused (88–86 B.C.), and their followers continued after their deaths (82–78, 72 B.C.), wars which Caesar and Pompey relit (49, 48, 45 B.C.) and which were only brought to an end by the victories of Octavius at Philippi (42 B.C.) and at Naulochus (36 B.C.).

Destiny was to be fulfilled. The hour of the *Pax Romana* had arrived. The whole of the Western world was conquered, from the Ocean to the Euphrates and the Caspian Sea, from the African desert to the forests of Germania; the conquered States and peoples were not mere tributaries, they were incorporated within the Empire. The world was administered and governed. It breathed and lived under the yoke that gave it freedom.

The few kings who still remained in the world did not forget the road to Rome. For so long had they been accustomed to follow it, that they began to go there to solicit from the Senate permission to reign. In 42 B.C. both Brutus and Cassius committed suicide. Antony fell a victim to the charms of Cleopatra; and in the tranquil atmosphere of a world at peace after long years of war, over the great tranquil surge of the tides, hovered the might and the name of Augustus who, by decree of the Senate, had become heir to the power and name of Caesar.

Adored in the capital and the provinces as a father and venerated as a god, the emperor imposed his rule beyond his own frontiers on the barbarians by his armies, and on civilized States by his prestige. For a period of 400 years the work of Force maintained itself, proud and successful against the enemies who threatened it and occasionally shook it, both from outside and from within. Invasion and anarchy remained equally powerless to overthrow it.

But all around the peaceful closed world of the Roman dominion, the ancient vicissitudes continued to disturb mankind.

Always either struggling or bargaining with its neighbours to the west and north—Huns and Scythians, Mongols, Siberians, Turanians, husbandmen in the valleys and shepherds on the steppes, all of them combative and quarrelsome by nature, caravan-pillagers, mercenaries with swords for sale—China in her turn was both their lord and their slave. Liu-Pang, a former brigand chieftain, after four years of warfare succeeded to Shih-Huang-Ti and founded the Han dynasty. His second successor, Wenn-Ti (179–157 B.C.), a wise and popular king—a kind of Haroun-al-Rashid, or Solomon—was able to organize a kingdom. Wu-Ti transformed it once more into an empire of power by his conquests in the Altaï, Tarim, Sogdiana and Korea; but very soon all this empire was overthrown.

Disorders, palace revolutions and rebellions in the provinces succeeded one another without interruption for nearly fifty years (40 B.C.–A.D. 25) reducing the number of inhabitants of China from 60 to 20 millions. A perpetual scourge in the East, secret societies, always ready here as elsewhere to blossom out into factions, upset the country and terrorized it. The "Red-Eyebrows" (18–27), crushed by the advent of the Later Han dynasty and the "Yellow-Turbans" (184–194) who precipitated its end, were then what the Boxers were in our days.

The 150 years which elapsed between the two insurrections

renewed and surpassed the age of Wu-Ti. Confucius, who had been treated with scorn for a long time, recovered favour and the national tradition with him, although the same princes who busied themselves in preserving and re-editing the ancient books also became adepts and protectors of other doctrines, giving them in this way the force which up to that point had been lacking to enable them to grow and spread their influence. The emperor Ming (58–75), who procured for the cult of Buddha a first success at his court, won decisive victories over all his neighbours, and his successors completed them.

These victories were due to three things. They were due first to Chinese civilization, which first fascinated and absorbed the barbarians and only later found in them its masters. They were due in the second place to a diplomacy which by turns united its enemies, divided them, appealed to them, repulsed them, fixed them or mobilized them, winning over some, disgusting others, in the evening enrolling in its ranks the enemy of the morning, overwhelming with favours those who bent before it and giving to those whom it did not feel capable of reducing the investiture of the very powers they had usurped; always crafty, supple, elusive, clever at the game of saving its face, and, like a very virtuoso, playing with the two great political forces: appearance and inertia. And in the third place they were due to the armies which swept and cleared up the edges and frontiers of the desert and the valleys of the mountains, pushing back the frontier as far as the Pamirs, Tian-Shan, the Altaï and Saiansk; thrusting back the Huns from the north and west towards the setting sun, the Scythians towards the south; incorporating within the empire new hordes and tribes which swelled by their arrival in China the traditional number of the 10,000 peoples who were the subjects of the Sons of Heaven.

One would have thought to see ascending towards Rome a rival ready either to dispute with the Romans, or freely to share with them the mastery of the world; but what the tide brings in, the ebb carries out. The Chinese empire at this period resembled rather the Greek empire: scarcely was it

constructed, when it began to break up. Those whom it had
conquered, conquered it and carved for themselves kingdoms
out of its inert body. For 400 years China was a prey to
anarchy.

The Chang, the first authors of this destruction, have been
compared to what the Popes were to become later for the
Church and for Europe. In fact there is no resemblance. An
adept in the magic and the superstitions which the Chinese
owed to the barbarians established before them in China,
Chang-Ling introduced these heady absurdities into the
system of Lao-Tseu. He made use of them, as did his son after
him, to recruit followers whom he turned into fanatics. In this
way came into being the "Five Bushels", the "Perfect Peace",
the "Diabolical Soldiers", the "Makers of Libations", and a
whole swarm of sects, thanks to which Chang-Kiao, his
grandson, exercised in his provincial corner of China powers
which were quasi-royal. A little later (c. 180 A.D.), Chang-Kiao
let loose over the whole State the revolt of the "Yellow Turbans".

These abettors of revolution lasted on from father to son and
remained, at least in name, at the head of their sects; but in
vain: neither they nor their sects were ever anything but
fomentors of trouble. They built nothing, they organized
nothing, they civilized nobody. They perpetuated and propagated the ancient errors which amongst savages corrupted the
primitive traditions of humanity for the benefit of fetishes and
sorcerers. They were only fitted to disorganize and destroy.

The times of their origin were remarkably propitious to
their activities. Around imbecile emperors, the eunuchs and
the men of letters fought for power with a ferocious bitterness.
and almost at once, though there were no invaders from outside,
ruin followed. The Han were dethroned (c. 220). The empire
split up into three kingdoms (not to regain unity till the advent
of the Sui and the T'ang nearly 400 years later). Its advance
towards Persia merely served to throw the Scythians against
the Parthians and the Parthians and Scythians upon India,
and to awake the ambition of Rome.

Trajan (117), Marcus Aurelius (162), Septimus Severus

(198), Caracalla (216), made themselves masters of Mesopotamia whilst the Yueh-Chih extended their domain as far as
the plains of the Ganges (42–225). Then all these conquests
simultaneously broke away from the victors. India suffered
a new partition into numerous States which the dynasty of the
Guptas in the fourth century reduced only in part, and for a
short time, to unity. The Persians, the victors over the Parthians (226), disputed with the Caesars (258, 282, 338–367) over
the ancient empire of Darius which they aimed at rebuilding,
but they were soon compelled to defend it desperately against
the Arabs and the Turks. Alaric the Goth (395) at length
broke through the gates of the West.

The end had come to the *Pax Romana*. Theodosius, it is true,
renewed the splendours of Augustus, merely to bring to a close
the Augustan era. Everything sank into chaos. The human
sea, released from all control, hurled its wild waves against one
another. The spray of the nations in struggle rose from their
crests from all points of the compass.

Nothing great arose that was not ephemeral. Barbarians or
civilized, destroyers or conservers of what once existed, founders
of what was to be—Vikramaditya (375–413), Attila (432–453),
Clovis (481–511), Theodoric the Great (482–526), Justinian
(527–565), Chrosroes the Great (531–579), Harsha-Siladitya
(606–647), whether they marched as devastators across the
world, or established themselves to last in their power in
the Indies, Gaul, Italy, Byzantium, or in Persia, none of them
ever seemed to build a solid Empire. Those who sowed,
scattered the seed merely into the abyss. That which they
sowed came slowly to germination, invisible, beneath the confused waves where all traces of their work vanished.

IV

THE ORIGINS OF CHRISTIANITY

It was under this confusion of human life that for two
centuries the whole continuity of history lay buried. It would

there have remained hidden but for a few threads which bind
men one to another and create for them a soul in common
by creating in them ideas, interests and feelings in common.
These threads held good on the surface against all the
violence of the storm. *The Cycle of the Empires of Government* in
its turn reached its close. Rome, the city which symbolised
that cycle and in the tongue of the Greeks signified Force, was
sacked. The emperors left it for Constantinople. Everywhere
there seemed general ruin; but for some time previously the
Caravan had moved on and directed its way towards another
stage.

The age was past when domination engendered unity and
surpassed it in influence, or marched step by step with it.
Henceforth unity is to take precedence of everything and itself
engenders domination. It is established without rulers or lords
of dominion, sometimes in face of their attacks, in spite of their
multiplication and of the dislocations of the anarchy which
follows hotfoot in the wake of their fall. That we may bestow
its real name upon the power which holds Rome we must
reverse the city's name, just as that unarmed power brought
about a literal conversion of the souls of men.

Roma, Amor : Love against Force. The new city which is
built for the whole world is on a spiritual plane: the *Cycle of
Ethnarchy* begins. *Arise, be enlightened O Jerusalem . . . the
Gentiles shall walk in thy light and kings in the brightness of thy
rising. . . . All these are gathered together, they are come to thee
. . . the multitude of the sea shall be converted to thee . . . And thy
gates shall be open continually : they shall not be shut day nor night.
. . . And the days of thy mourning shall be ended.*"[1]

In this besides there is no sudden change, nor anything
peculiar to the West. It is a phase which has slowly emerged
from another phase in the life of humanity. Amongst so many
royalties that pass, that of the spirit remains. Lao-Tseu became
the official sage of the Celestial Empire; but the disciples of
Confucius did not forget their master. There were not always
enough of them and sometimes they were persecuted: holding

[1]Isaiah lx, 1, 3–5, 11, 20.

fast to tradition the power of which they had experienced, they rescued their master from oblivion and tenaciously laid the foundation of a renewal of his prestige. Zoroaster ascended once again the Persian throne with the dynasty of the Sassanids (223). The Brahmins and Buddha at one time disputed and at another time shared the empire of the Indies.

Buddha who proved victorious under Kanishka (78), as formerly under Asoka, and who was introduced into China towards the same time, there achieved popularity a century later under the form of A-Mi-T'Ouo—or Amitabha on the banks of the Ganges—the luminous symbol of divine mercy and redeeming faith. A Parthian, An-Cheu-Kao, and an Indo-Scythian, Leu-Kiatch'an, popularised this doctrine. By the tenth century it had conquered the whole of the "Continent of Ancestors".

By the instrumentality of this doctrine and the Tao, the wisdom of India and its mysticism overflowed upon the Far East. It sowed there both its tares and its good grain which brought forth the future harvests of unity: the unity of Asia, both an obstacle and a way leading to the unity of the whole world. It established itself alongside national as well as foreign philosophies, without destroying them and often without disturbing them. Confucius, Lao-Tseu, Gautama, Zoroaster, the Vedanta, the Tantras, Manes, Nestorius, Mahomet and a thousand other ancient or recent superstitions and doctrines were its neighbours—amongst them, from the thirteenth century, the materialistic Chu-Hi. Occasionally, but in a few places only, it supplanted them.

From the fifteenth century especially, Confucius (551–478 B.C.) took the highest rank amongst them all; as early as the seventh century he had made an entry into Japan which Buddha had removed from its allegiance to the traditional cult of heroes more than a thousand years before.

Though the scattered people of Israel as a political entity had received their death-blow, the lawgiver of the Hebrews and the Prophets of Israel still preserved their crowns. The people of Israel are indeed a remarkable race. Nothing like or equal to them has ever been seen in any place or at any time in the history of the world. They are unique.

This little people stands out in the world both with regard to its religion and its destiny. There exists not its like among the nations, for it has ever worshipped and adored the one God who is pure spirit, holy and perfect, creator of all things and the lawgiver of the human conscience. What other race has ever prided itself on being chosen, in the person of its ancestors, by such a God to preserve in virtue of the terms of an historic alliance with God the original traditions entrusted to it, being the revelation of the Law and the Promise of Salvation for all the nations of the earth? What other nation survives in a similar state of persecution and dispersion?

Scattered throughout the world, it carries to the four quarters of the globe those prophecies on which for the Jews everything is based, but it will not recognize them either as already fulfilled or as false: yet according to its own confession, all the conditions have been performed which the prophecies fixed for the advent of its Messiah.

What meaning then can there still be in such prophecies? The Jews make no effort to find out. With all the fixity of their indomitable hearts and minds they adhere to the letter of those Writings which are henceforth a dead letter to them. Slowly they have come to read into the prophecies about the Messiah, the Oriental dress of universal despotism which their proud hearts cherish even in the very depths of the worst ignominy; and deprived of everything which could give them the appearance of a State or even of a nation or people, without a head, without a country, without history, for twenty centuries they have bided their time. They are multiplying and spreading; they possess themselves of money and credit; they bend before hostile forces and little by little they monopolize them or destroy them. Nineteen hundred years after their dispersion, they are found everywhere at the sluices of wealth, at the points where they can control the springs which move opinion, in secret places where revolutions are planned, in all the labyrinthine ways that lead to power.

But there are facts more astounding still. Thirty-eight years before the dispersion, a Jew of Galilee, Jesus, the only son of the widow of a carpenter, Joseph of Nazareth, gave Himself out as being the Holy One of Israel, the Desired of the Nations, the Christ who had been so often announced, the Saviour promised to humanity from the time of His First Father. Generally He referred to Himself as "The Son of Man". "I am," He said, "the Lamb of God, the Light of the World, the Bread of Life." He declared that He had been sent to confirm the Law of Sinai by a new alliance, to transfigure it, to complete it and to fulfil the prophecies. His disciples looked upon Him on Mount Thabor at the Transfiguration, standing between Elias and Moses in the rays of eternal light; and His words reaching beyond the confines of Palestine opened up to His apostles all centuries and the whole earth: "Go ye and teach all nations to the ends of the earth."

What He thus founded, mingling in its treasure both tradition and novelty, was not merely a philosophy, or a political system, or a religion, as was the work of Lao-Tseu, Confucius, Buddha, Zoroaster or the Brahmins: it was at the same time like the work of Alexander or Caesar, an empire which claimed to be without limits and without end. His Church is a city; His doctrine the "Gospel of the Kingdom". As Son of David He announced these all-prevailing forces, the universality, the eternity and the divinity of His power. "All power has been given to me in heaven and on earth. Even hell shall not prevail against what I build. I am the Son of God. My father and I are one."

It sounded like madness, for where were His dominions? During the three years of His teaching He had not "a stone on which to lay his head". He lived on alms and when He was in the agony of death in the torture which He suffered as a punishment for these rash words, His work, scarcely begun, had already fallen into ruins. His followers, "a little flock" as He Himself said, hid themselves in doubt and fear. Neither Caiaphas nor Pilate nor Herod had lost any of their authority or of their domains. For the Scribes and Pharisees it was a

triumph. Moreover, what did they all amount to in their little
corner of the earth, in comparison with Tiberius and his
empire and the rest of the nations? A stone has fallen into the
sea, the waters swallow it and it disappears. There is not a
wrinkle on the calm surface of the ocean.

"And we who were hoping. . . . " The challenge which He
threw to the world, to hell and if He were only a man, at God
Himself, Jesus also threw at common sense and the everyday
life of the world. When in life, He who forced the tempests and
death to obey Him had not willed to permit or to do anything
which might realize His ambitions. He had shut Himself up
in His own country—and what a country!—overwhelming the
rich and the great with His anathemas, consorting with humble
people and preaching to the poor, who allowed themselves to
be taken by the enchantment of His discourses, a paradoxical
doctrine which they scarcely understood and which the
Jews looked upon as "scandalous and the Gentiles as
folly".

It was after His death that He said He would act and upon
His suffering that He counted to attract to Himself the people
who were ignorant of Him, scorned Him, or repulsed Him.
He compared Himself to the grain of wheat which produces
nothing until it is in dissolution. He will rise again; but He
will not remain on earth to derive any advantage from His
resurrection. He must go away. The conquests that He had
dreamed of are for His friends to carry out.

Did He give them the means to do this work? "Imitate me,"
He said to them. "Be gentle, humble, patient, compassionate,
unselfish and peaceful. My kingdom belongs to those who suffer
for justice and love poverty. Rejoice then when they despise
you and speak evil of you. Offer your cheek to those who smite
you. Pardon those who injure you. You will be persecuted.
You will be arrested, put in prison and beaten, you will be put
to death as criminals: do not resist! Flee away, but, if you are
taken, confess me boldly before all men. I shall send to
you the Holy Spirit; and until the last day as far as the
most distant countries of the earth you shall be the witnesses

of my life and of my words, of my death on the cross and
resurrection."

Soldiers, diplomats, financiers and politicians were demanded: He sent witnesses—and what witnesses!—*like lambs
in the midst of wolves.*

Moreover His kingdom, as He announced it, was in the
future. A "Kingdom of Heaven", "Kingdom of God", He
is about to develop in this world, without ever being of this
world; without relying on force, or cunning, or money; without dispossessing by warfare or sedition the smallest princelet.
He stands apart.

His growth is to be pacific. He is like the leaven which rises
and imperceptibly transforms the paste; the wheat which
germinates and ripens without the tares being rooted up; the
marriage feast prepared for long, at which, up till the stroke of
midnight, the royal bridegroom keeps the guests waiting;
lastly, He is like the grain of mustard seed which in the course
of centuries grows into a tall tree wherein the birds of heaven
build their nests.

It is the sheepfold of the good shepherd. Within the fold as
outside, humility, charity, self-denial, will be its base, the sign
and the rule. "If anyone wishes to come after me, let him deny
himself, take up his cross and follow me." "They have said
to you: 'love your neighbour and hate your enemies,' but I
say unto you: that you must love your enemies and do good
to those who persecute you. You know that the princes of the
nations have dominion over them and that the great men make
their authority to be a burden upon them: it shall not be so
amongst you. The greatest amongst you shall be the servant
of all, according to the example of the Son of Man who came
not to be served, but to serve."

Jesus pointed out this leader amongst them. He was a fisher
of Bethsaida, poor and ignorant, with a generous heart but
remarkably simple-minded and open to the impulse of the
moment. To him He said: "Feed my lambs, feed my sheep."
Here we see the shepherd, the monarch, the support of the
whole Church: "Thou art Peter and on this rock will I build

my church." Peter is angry because a servant stares him out of countenance. He swears that he knows not "this man" and afterwards hides himself to weep.

Two months later the followers of Jesus are counted by thousands, "*fideles*" who adhere to a God and His cult, a Shepherd and His flock. There was no school. There were disciples it is true; but they did not judge the doctrine before attaching themselves to the Master because of it. On the contrary, they believed in it because of Him. "When I shall be raised above the earth," He said, "I shall draw all men to me." That prophecy was realized to the letter; and since then all has happened according to the promises, the prophecies and the commands of Christ.

V

THE CATHOLIC ETHNARCHY

The new unity was cemented in blood, as was the unity of the great empires; but it was the blood of its martyrs and not of its enemies. It extended in all directions without destroying anything, by the sole virtue of the Spirit, of the Apostolate and of the Testimony.

When Peter and Paul, less than forty years after Jesus, died to be witnesses to the facts related by the Gospels, the Church had its faithful and its communities everywhere, in Judaea, in Palestine, in Syria, in Asia Minor, in Macedonia, in Epirus, in Greece, in Italy, in Egypt and in Ethiopia; perhaps also in Persia, Gaul and Spain; and it was Rome which they consecrated by their sacrifice as capital in this world of the "Kingdom of God".

Nero persecuted them, and other emperors after him; but they did not exhaust the number nor the constancy of the imitators of Jesus Christ. All the efforts made by persecutors for 250 years ended finally and inevitably in the conversion of the empire.

Love won the day over Force. The subtlety, the fantasy and

the cunning of the Orient had no greater success against its vigilance. Far from falling asleep in its victory, it reacted vigorously against the new perils which came with the fruits of victory.

Its kingdom won peace, numbers, extent and duration; and these are gifts that have brought death to the most firmly founded States—whether, gradually sinking under their own weight, they wallowed in the refinement of their own decadence; or whether discord seized upon them and split them into pieces, or delivered them over to those very enemies whom they had formerly vanquished. But no development weighed down the Kingdom of God, no prosperity corrupted it, no disturbance divided it against itself. It became consolidated, organized, enlightened and disciplined in the measure of its elevation and the extent of its dominion.

The Kingdom of God on earth itself cured its sores and its maladies. What the martyrs had commenced, learned men, councils and popes continued. They unmasked and drove out those who were sowers of dissension. They gave precision both to the object and the sense of the Testimony; the hierarchy, the doctrine, and the methods of the Apostolate; the order and the signs which preside over the outpourings of the Holy Ghost.

In this manner the Catholic Church at home preserves intact and brings to fruition for the human race its treasures and those of the synagogue. It was, moreover the Church which preserved for the Kingdom of God from the fifth century onwards, those treasures of Greek and Latin antiquity which the fertile and overabundant slime of barbarism threatened to swallow up. The new world of the West was born of its womb and had the Church as its teacher. As Jesus continues, transfigures and completes Moses, so this New Jerusalem continues, transfigures and completes Rome. It is a family of souls open to all the sons of Adam, it unifies them without doing violence to their nature or enslaving their will; on the contrary, it throws upon them its light and gives them peace.

By the Church the weak are protected, helped and loved. Work becomes a noble thing; suffering and poverty divine;

M

virginity glorious and fertile. Numbered amongst the sacraments of the Church, marriage, henceforth one, becomes indissoluble and holy and clothes husband and wife with a dignity without example outside of her. The wife, however humble the home may be, possesses what the old Roman law reserved for a small number of its matrons. "She became a partner in everything which is human and divine in the house." She sits down alongside the father in a majesty which is rendered higher and nobler by all those attributes and advantages which the living God possesses over the Manes and the Lares of the Latins, the family gods. The ancestor preserves his prestige; but it is no longer towards him that his lineage gravitates: it is towards the child, the model of perfection, the companion of angels, the temple of grace and the immortal seed of paradise.

If the rich man wishes to use his riches for his own salvation, he must become heaven's almoner. Gradually the workmen and the peasants cease to be slaves. The divinely human notion of the Christian power—"the servant of the servants of God, the helper and the defender of the Holy Church, the representative of Jesus Christ, the peacemaker" in all discord, the guardian of the customs and liberties which save its kingdom from excess—shone through the passing clouds upon the thrones of St. Peter, of Charlemagne, of St. Stephen and St. Louis; and the grain of seed sowed on Calvary blossomed out in the beautiful springtime of the Middle Ages into a society of nations.

"Christ triumphs, reigns and governs." The Gospel parables are translated into realities. The Kingdom of God and of His Saints has made its appearance amongst men. Born at Rheims, Western Christendom in 300 years emerged from the chaos in which Rome foundered; and for seven centuries more (800–1500) the whole of the Western world at peace under the guardianship of the priesthood and the Empire would have developed without hindrance a civilization which would have been the most equitable, the most fraternal, the richest in liberties, the most open to the breath of the Holy Spirit and altogether the best ordered that the world has ever seen, if the Empire had only known how to understand and accomplish the mission given to it by the supreme Pontiff when he created it to serve charity, justice and reason.

Alas, this noble bond was heavy upon it! The lower instinct for domination blinded it to that mission. It did not understand unity. New-born from barbarism, dominated by the cult of force, it did not see that force is only noble and great in the service of love.

The princes of the Frankenwald and of Hohenstauffen did not choose for their model St. Henry or Charlemagne or even Theodosius or Constantine; it was Cæsar whom they desired to imitate. Him who made them what they were, their lord by all right and title, they wished to make a vassal. And they made him their vassal. They went much further. They brought him down so low that he was merely their subject and, sometimes, even their creature. Their duty was to defend, to maintain and complete his work: instead of that they put him in chains, corrupted his work and divided it.

Mathan, priest of Baal, against Joad the High Priest of Israel, Guelph against Ghibelline, the Priesthood and the Empire at enmity, such was, from Otto the Great (962) to Frederick (1254), with little exception, the whole course of the history of the Germanic protectorate. It was necessary for the great popes of the thirteenth century to break it, in order that the kingdom of Christ should clothe itself once again in all its splendour on the eve of evil days.

Even then, this kingdom bore scarcely any resemblance to that which the childlike hearts of men, always in love with unreality, had looked for. The golden age? The leaven works and is savoury, but the paste is heavy and coarse. The wheat puts forth its blade and increases a hundredfold, but the field is full of tares. The Church built upon the rock is not a temple of clouds, nor the centuries of its empire an ideal millennium. Everything is real in that earthly edifice built by the hands of men to shelter humanity. The work does not progress without sudden stops, trickery, changes and adulterations. Deformed

from day to day by those who build it, it would have suffered
the fate of everything which passes, if He who conceived it
and abides with it, did not reform it, in proportion to its needs,
by the agency of the heroes of His Spirit—Benedict, Gregory,
Wilfrid, Hildebrand, Francis and Dominic, Thomas Aquinas
and Catherine of Siena!

Peoples, cities, states, families, leagues, crowds, social classes,
all dash against one another restlessly and without truce,
blown about by the fierce winds of desire and opinion. How
many storms must be endured and how many centuries must
elapse to civilize the barbarian, stabilize his vagabond spirit,
discipline his turbulence, master in him the instinct of pillage
and the taste for blood, purify his morals, enlighten him, instruct him, bring together his hostile tribes, melt them into a
body of nations and give to those very nations the sense of their
mutual brotherhood?

Each individual, each group, desires to have a place in the
sun. In the general confusion, fortuitous inequalities engender
hierarchies. The weak look for protectors; the strong, faithful
followers to reinforce them; but the mob of inferior kings, dukes
and barons has a tendency to remain in a condition of anarchy.
Wars, law-suits, conventions, successions, marriages, keep on
producing clusters of vassaldoms, carry over seeds from one to
the other and form new clusters. Carried away in the feudal
whirlwind, the authority of the sovereigns who are themselves
both suzerains and vassals is but slow in its action. At every
moment it is resisted and often it is not of long duration. For
one State which rises, or is restored to power, how many
crumble to pieces never to be rebuilt?

From what source came order into this tumult, unity into
this chaos?

"One king, one law, one faith." Jesus, the Pope and the
Gospel; and that is all one. As they opened out, the Church
gathered under its wings the nations of the future, united them
by this triple bond and breathed into them a Christian soul.
"As the bees make their hive", her pontiffs, her monks, her
priests fashioned them little by little: first France, the eldest

daughter (496), then Spain (587), England (597–680), Germany in the south and west (755–843), Serbia (ninth century), Bulgaria (865), Bohemia (894), Poland (964), Denmark (965), Russia (989), Hungary (996), Sweden (1001), Prussia (1142–1233).

The débris of the ancient Roman empire—the cities and the little ultramontane States, in turn monarchies and republics, grouped together, divided, invaded, independent and subject to the Pope, to the emperor, to princes of every race—achieved in Italy the assimilation of all its languages into one, unified its great memories and its character into a miniature in the great world which it illumined. Venice, queen of gold and of the sea; Genoa, the rival of Venice; Florence, the springing fountain of intelligence and of beauty; Bologna, the mistress of science; Milan, the vigilant warder of the road from the north; Umbria, the new Galilee; Naples and Sicily, lands of soft climate and sunshine, disputed for by Greeks, Normans, Germans, French and Spaniards, surrounded the domain of St. Peter like a glittering crown.

Rome brought back under her authority lands as far away as Asia Minor, Syria and Palestine. The Franks, knights of the deeds of God, hewed for themselves with their swords a number of kingdoms (1099–1244). Their valour and their charity, whatever may have been the fortune of their arms, shone forth in their achievements with incomparable brilliance and, in the glorious aureole promised and awarded at Christ's tomb, nothing equalled the splendour of their crusades. Still further, even to the extremities of the world, Christ's Vicar on earth extended his power over souls. There was a Catholic archbishop of Pekin in the thirteenth century and numerous bishops in several Chinese provinces. The Roman Church, the New Sion, was like a holy mountain in the midst of the human sea. In universal agitation the Church grew stronger. The sun covered it with its rays. The waters of heaven fertilized it. It possessed promises that it would endure. Where shall we see anything like it?

Byzantium even, for long delivered over to the Arians, the

Manicheans and the Iconoclasts, came back for a short period to the fold. She, the advanced sentinel of Christianity on the very confines of Islam and the barbarians, how beautiful was her magnificence and heroism in her stubborn struggles to defend, or raise up from its ruins, the empire of Theodosius. For a thousand years, against the Huns, against the West, the Slavs, the Arabs, the Hungarians and the Turks she waged war; she was often vanquished, never subdued until the day when this last *épopée* was consummated in a final flame of glory through the heroic death of the twelfth Constantine in the mêlée at the breach in the rampart of Byzantium.

During a thousand years this daughter of Greek genius and of the first Christian Cæsar watched over and enriched the heritage of antiquity. She set her mark upon it. She shared that heritage with peoples who were newcomers, whom she incorporated in her faith and in her civilization as in her empire. Her beauty and her destiny would have been immeasurable if she had been able to preserve in the Church of Christ the rank assigned to her under the crook of Rome, a tradition of 800 years, consecrated by unanimous consent and many times recognized by her as universal and primordial and founded on the Gospel. Perhaps she was too Greek to remain Roman. The Promised Land of theological, philosophical, political and ritual quibbling, jealous of her imperial title, vexed by the primacy of Peter and of Rome, intoxicated with subtleties and luxury, early imprisoned within the formalism in which a Church of civil servants and a State of sacristans enclosed themselves as in a cloister, for a long period isolated by her haughty self-sufficiency, separated at last by the schisms of Photius (857) and of Cerularius (1054), she passed for a time under the dominion of the Latins (1204–1261) and attached herself twice to the centre of unity in 1274 and 1439, but too late: exhausted and at the end of her strength she fell under the blows of Mahomet II (1453).

VI

ISLAM

The sound of this fall echoes yet in the West though five centuries have passed. It marked, it is said, the end of a world, the world of the Middle Ages; the beginning of a new world, that which still endures: it marks the apogee of a race, the Turks: that of a religion which resembles at once a Church and an Empire, Islam. This talk of ends and beginnings is, perhaps, a little grandiose. Worlds neither begin nor come to an end on a fixed day. If we had to give our own age a birth certificate it might indeed be dated from the fourteenth century —the age of Wyclif, John Huss, Petrarch, Boccaccio, Giotto, the age of the earliest cannon and the mariner's compass, or from the sixteenth at its dawn—the age of Luther, Calvin, Leonardo, Raphael and Michelangelo; but the middle of the fifteenth century marks nothing more than the barren days of its infancy or the last weary hours of expectation before the nativity of a new age. As for the rest—the apogee of the Turkish race and of Islam—it depends what you mean by a race; and if the Turks are a race; and what Mahomet II did for the Turks and for Islam more than Suliman II (1520–1566) or Mahomet IV (1648–1683) or Tamerlane (1370–1405).

In truth the din of the 29th May, 1453, is only one of those innumerable crashes or shocks, like cannoning billiard balls, which take place every hundred years or so. On the steppes, or the desert, to the north of Nan-Shan, of the Himalayas, of the Hindu-Kush Mountains, of Kopet-Dagh and the Caucasus, from all time in the history of humanity there have come and gone—clashing together, thrusting and resisting, flung back by one another or by the mountain-barriers of the Carpathians or the In-Shan—thousands of clans, hordes, marauding and pillaging bands, tribes and nations. Sometimes scattered almost at hazard or linked in federations, or bound together from one end to the other and included in

a network of reciprocal vassalage under some distant suzerain
—the Emperor of China, the King of the Huns, or the Khan
of the Mongols—they were scarcely ever at rest. After having
turned about, veered and wandered for a long period, some
of them made their way over the mountains which bordered
this closed field; descended towards the lands where wheat
grew and riches abounded, and there established industrious
cities under climates more favourable to human life.

In this wise came, in ancient times, the Chinese into China,
the Aryans into Aryiana and India, the Greeks into Greece,
the Celts into ancient Gaul and the Germans into Germany.
Thus, more recently, the Yueh–Chih poured out over
Turania, Iran and the plains of the Indus and the Ganges;
and the Goths, the Burgundians, the Franks, the Alamanni,
the Avars, the Vandals, the Huns, the Normans and the
Magyars to the west; then the Mongols over the whole of Asia.
It was enough for an adventurer to give the signal to begin; for
a powerful horde to quarrel or covet another's property. Thus,
for instance, a yellow Duguesclin like the famous Pan-Chao
in order to rid Ming-Ti, Chang-Ti and Wu-Ti of the Great
Companies, the Flayers, the brigands, bandits, cut-throats,
highwaymen and thieves great and small whom they did
not know what to do with, led these mercenary encumbrances
against the Hiung-Nu, the Huns of the north whom he dispersed; he drove these nomads back towards the west, installed
himself on the banks of the Tarim and then pushed on to the
very shores of the Caspian Sea into contact with the Romans,
in this manner exalting his prestige and widening the field
of his influence (73–113).

The Turks—Tou-Kiue—were the sons of those Huns of the
north whom Pan-Chao defeated. They had the same customs
and morals. Primitive, unlettered, superstitious, they venerated
the four elements, supported and listened to soothsayers,
practised ancestor worship. They neither named nor adored
any god except the Author of the Universe. In addition they
were nomads with the souls of warriors, men of the horde,
ready to face peril, knowing no law but the will of their chief.

The Altaï range which saved their fathers became too narrow for their numbers and their power, their love of raids and battles. In their turn they overflowed and descended from the mountains. At one time victors, at another time vanquished, at another time mercenaries according as the wheel of fortune to which they clung raised them up or flung them down and crushed them; to-day in the service of China which but yesterday had driven them out and which on the morrow they themselves would invade; the allies, then the enemies, of the Persians, the Greeks and the barbarians; united, divided, federated, they warred at random from the Crimea to Liao-Tung, during the whole of the sixth century. Under Mokan (died 573) they had for a moment the elements of an empire.

Defeated and driven off and then absorbed in the Orient by the Celestial empire they moved towards the west, towards the Oxus and the Caspian Sea. They went on to Ispahan, to Baghdad, to Ghazni and to Kanauj, to Jerusalem and to Stamboul. They were won to the faith of that Islam whose lands they had invaded and they carried the banner of Moslemism as far west as Hungary, as the Arabs had already borne it to the limits of China. Bedouins of the north, they first clashed with the Bedouins of the south, then sold themselves to them. They served them and then ruled them. Under the guise of a new civilization they received from them the ancient heritage of Greece and Persia.

It has been said that their warrior's soul accepted as a military command or password the faith of the Caliph and that when they put themselves in his service for pay they had sworn to obey him. It is very possible. He who sells his warrior hand sells more than he thinks. He sells himself body and soul; and so many other people who were neither soldiers nor nomads have adopted the gods of their masters even when their masters deified themselves. Man is born to follow a leader. Such is indeed nature's law and the justification, the glory, the responsibility of those who within the Human Caravan are its leaders. They must as in duty bound lead their followers towards the true God; but the Turkish troop, when it met the Arab troop (707, 712), was in all sorts of profound ways like the Arab troop had been ninety years before when the Prophet rallied it. So it was natural for the Turks to come under the spell of Mahomet.

They possessed the same instincts as the Arabs had had for pillage, the same warlike ambitions, the same spirit of liberty and adventure, they had the same abundance of men to inundate and submerge immense extents of land without exhausting their numbers; the same rough simplicity, uncultured, and yet ready for civilization, ready to fit themselves into it; the same aspirations for unity in the scattering of tribes; the same passion for justice and honour, added to all the vices which are engendered by sensuality, love of gambling, drunkenness and cupidity; the same leaning towards fatalism, the same religious indifference, the same vague and sterile faith in a sole God under a similar mass of superstitions and idolatries.

Of what use would the contemplative ascesis of a Buddha have been to raise the Arabs out of their condition of wretchedness, or the metaphysical speculations of a Lao-Tseu or of a Zoroaster, or the political ratiocinations of a Confucius? The whole of such systems would have been far too complicated for their simple matter-of-fact souls. What they were in need of was a chief, a leader, whose simple, clear-cut command should draw them on, unite them, take them away from the clan spirit and open their souls to the winds that come from the Most High; a Moses; and God gave them: Mohammed-ben-Abdallah.

He was a genius. A sick man? Perhaps; but if he was, it was in spite of his sickness, not because of it, that he took possession of Arabia and forged for so many nations, brown, white, black, yellow, the enchanter's chains of Islam. The disease served his purpose—I state this deliberately and that he made use of it: genius draws advantage from everything. And afterwards? It is childish to explain such things by saying they are due to epilepsy or imposture. Consider the facts.

The dealer's nephew who married the elderly Kadija at an early age, was by no means a scatter-brained fool. Whilst still a young man, he excelled as a caravan leader: think of the qualities of leadership, of the *savoir-faire* of the merchant, soldier and diplomat that such an accomplishment supposes. He was certainly reflective, judicious, energetic and brave. He knew what he wanted; he knew what he was doing. If at times he suffered from hallucinations and nervous crises, he made no more of them than Pascal of the abyss which hallucination made him see yawning to swallow him up.

He is described as sociable and frank in disposition, a man of his word, a charming conversationalist, likeable, sensual. And his writings give us the same picture of him. Assuredly they are the expression of a religious, passionate and dominating soul, in love with the absolute; a powerful imagination, a trained intelligence, skill in action. Neither theologian nor philosopher, nor even a poet; but a man of faith and action, expert in the rhythms of eloquence. The author of the Koran neither demonstrates, nor discusses, nor instructs. His thoughts are what he wishes to be so; his affirmations are commands. All these characteristics and the foundation of Islam reveal alongside his natural gifts, acquisitions more or less laborious, the profits of the whole of his youth. Such a man was not formed merely in his ripe age and in the course of the accomplishment of his work. He prepared himself for it. He began his mission when he felt himself ready for it: if he began late, it was because the period of preparation had been long.

He was a poor orphan. He was already twenty-four when important business was entrusted to him for the first time. He was twenty-five when as the result of his marriage he entered into the rich circle of his tribe—people who had been raised by refinements, as a result of their commercial relations with Egypt and Syria both Jewish and Christian, above the semi-barbarous paganism which surrounded them and which they could hardly do other than accept though it could not satisfy them.

Like the Hanifs to whom they rejoiced to listen, they were looking for God. And God was looking for them. In this way came Mahomet. Solitude was distasteful to him. He was too sensitive to physical suffering to follow very far into their ascesis the spiritual men whose influence enveloped him as it penetrated those about him; but the echoes of the Bible and the Gospel which were in their discourses caused fountains of flame to gush forth from his eager brain.

"Jehovah, Jehovah. Merciful and compassionate God! Listen, Israel! Jehovah thy God, is Jehovah alone, God of gods, Lord of lords, the great, strong and dread God. His is the heaven; His is the earth!" He gives the earth to him who seems good to Him. The nations are in his hands. "Thou shalt adore no other god. Thou shalt have no other gods before me. Thou shalt not make unto thee any graven image or any likeness of anything that is in heaven above, or that is in the earth beneath, or that is in the water under the earth. Thou shalt be for me a kingly priesthood and a holy nation."

Eyes of fire! A revelation of light! Allah is unique. He is the *master of the universe* and the king of all men. At the Last Day He shall restore all to life and shall judge them for eternity; those who believe and do good shall be destined for perfect joy, the others to the flames of hell. He must reign.

God of Israel, but also the God of Isaac and Abraham. Now the Hedjaz tribes and those of Nedjed and all the Children of Ishmael who trafficked, gathered and harvested and pastured their flocks on all the confines of the desert, had Abraham for an ancestor. How then could his first-born son, the child of Agar and the father of the twelve chiefs of the tribe whose dwelling was between Hevileh and Sour which fronted Egypt, not have his day and his hour? Ishmael and Isaac together buried Abraham in the field of Ephron, the son of Zohar of the children of Heth. Before Isaac, the son of Agar had been included in the pact with Jehovah.

More than Isaac, almost as often as Abraham, he had his share in the divine promises: promises of strength and of multitude at the "well of him that liveth and seeth me";

promises of greatness and of benediction, when he received "in his flesh the mark of alliance"; promises confirmed in the agony of thirst when God, hearing the voice of the lad, opened Agar's eyes that she might save her son from death. Others received "the Torah, the judgment of God; the Gospel, the guide and light"; Moses and the Prophets and the son of Mary, Jesus, the greatest of them all, the Messiah, the worker of miracles on whom were poured out Grace, Wisdom and the Holy Spirit. What in his turn shall Mahomet receive?

Thus, little by little, in conversations, prayer, the workings of his own thoughts and his waking dreams the son of Abdallah felt his race become incarnate in him, the traditions of his faith palpitating and, at the same time as this call from God, rising from the depths of his being, the temptation which it aroused. "Take this and read," said the voice. "Seach the Scriptures." He trembled; he hid himself under his cloak. "Arise," said the voice within him, "flee from the abomination of idols. Wait for the Lord with patience. What you are to do will be told you. Do not kick against the goad. You are the chosen instrument, the prophet of the Lord." It was the same call that St. Augustine heard and Paul when lying on the ground in darkness; "the truth which speaks within the soul, without the sound of words, the true light which enlighteneth every man that cometh into the world."

And here too we have the temptation of Christ Jesus: to change the stones of the desert into bread, the conceptions of genius into revelations from the Highest, and the spirits of God into idols; from the spiritual pinnacle to cast oneself down towards the earth ; to covet from the heights the power and the glory of this world.

What an apostle he would have become if he had known how to conquer himself, not to give way to the opportunities of the moment and to the solicitations of those who surrounded him; to listen, to read, to obey, to draw from pure sources every thing of which he was ignorant and in the Catholic Church whose light shone upon his horizon to find the kingdom which Moses and the Prophets and Jesus had established! He might have done all this: on a day that was to come, in the bosom of Islam and by ways remarkably more difficult and toilsome, Al-Hallaj, the crucified of Baghdad, was to join the Son of Man who was crucified on Calvary. God holds to our freedom of choice. His grace is sufficient. It was for Mahomet to make his choice.

He spoke, he wrote, he retouched the Scriptures, he took and he rejected, as he thought fit, made and unmade, gave and withdrew according to the interest of the moment. He leaped from the temple to the ground. For him the kingdom of God is of this world: a State and not a Church. He had to establish it by war. Outside Islam there was no neighbour in Samaria.

If the faith and all his past life of faith had not dominated Mahomet, the sons of Ishmael would have found in him their Alexander. As he was a believer, he became their Moses; but a Moses who bound his empire to Jehovah's: "There is no God but God and Mahomet is his Messiah"—the conquering Messiah, the dream of Jewish blindness. Hence he allowed himself from day to day to see more darkly. The light of his genius fell from the spiritual to the temporal plane, from unity to domination. It was always a light made to spread afar the brightness of Jerusalem, but henceforth vacillating and wavering in the wind of politics.

Of three idols he made angels to cajole the people of Mecca; then, whether through deception or scruple, he retracted. The devil, he said, had deceived him. This might quite well have happened; but what of the revelations of the Prophet, who could henceforth attest for us their origin? Did they come from the goodness of God, from a Satanic ruse, or from the tactics of Mahomet? If he speaks of the Christians as brothers; if he talks in their manner of the Word and the Holy Ghost who proceed from God; if he reproves his followers for having infringed Nakhla the sacred month, was it Allah who inspired him? And was it Iblis, the Devil, a little later, when he expressed his approval of what they did; when he falsely accused the Christians of adoring three gods; when he treated them as "liars, imitators of idolatries, falsifiers of the Scriptures", and wished them to be exterminated?

In proportion as he achieved success, the political statesman gained the upper hand over the prophet, the man of God. He rose amongst the grandeurs of the flesh and of pride; but he was to experience temptations, falls, and the base actions which are in wait for those who are all-powerful. After his flight to Yatreb, too often the end became for him a justification of the means he employed. Soon he obeyed with impatience the laws which he had quite recently dictated as being from God. The four wives that the laws allowed, besides amours with serving-maids, were not enough for him; he wanted twelve or fourteen; convenient revelations authorized him to marry them. He coveted the wife of Zaïd his adopted son: another revelation made this incest legitimate.

Allah or Iblis? God or the Devil? Or imposture? None of the three, probably, in his first days; but "the Holy Spirit flees away from the astute man. It withdraws at the approach of iniquity. The vertigo of passion then perverts a soul which is otherwise without malice". Because that soul has once felt God, and no longer desires to know itself, it persuades itself easily that the thoughts, the wishes, the lusts that move it come from God; that God frees it from the laws that bind other men, and that sin is impossible for it.

VII

THE MONGOLS

This then is the source of that river of fire which in less than one hundred years covered with its shining flames a third of the civilized world. Two years after Mahomet's death it submerged Syria (634); soon Egypt (640), Iran (642–644), the whole of northern Africa, Sicily, Sardinia, Spain (647–711), it overflowed over Gaul (720). What was going to happen to

the West? Would the victory of the Franks at Poitiers be sufficient to defend it? Would Antioch, Byzantium and Rome
meet with the same fate as Jerusalem, Alexandria and Carthage? Would Christianity everywhere be consumed?

That was a question which depended upon Asia. The
height of the river was almost at its greatest. If it dug itself
out a bed and strengthened its source with strong dykes, then
its waters rolling all in one body might engulf Christianity.
If it divided, if it continued in its efforts to flood the East,
then Charlemagne's moment had come. And this precisely
was what it did. It poured out over Sind and Ferghana (707–
712); it grew in bulk with the addition in Turania of hordes
of Turks, impatient for conquest; it broke out into new ways
towards Thibet, China and India. At the same time its dykes
began to crack and give way, then they broke, undermined
by politics. There were many rebellions. The Abassides
overthrew the Omayyades (750). Cordova proclaimed its
independence (756). The Edrissites (788), the Aglabites (800),
the Fatimites detached Africa from Baghdad and cut it into
pieces. It is possible that the splendours of Abd-el-Melik
(683–705), the glory of Haroun-al-Raschid (786–809), the magnificence of Abdur-Rahman II in Spain (822–852), the victories
of Obeid-el-Mahdi in the Magreb (909–934), and those of
Saladin (1171–1200) in Palestine and Syria extended, enriched,
embellished and consolidated Islam; but they did not prevent
its overflow being stopped on the shores of the European sea,
nor the power of Ishmael, like that of Israel his nephew, being
handed over to the Barbarians of the North.

Kotaiba-ben-Moslim scarcely suspected when he took possession of Samarcand in 712 that he was transferring to the
vanquished Turks the conquering Califate and so opened up
to them, as also to their cousins the Mongols, ways which led
towards the domination of Asia. Three centuries were sufficient
to bring forth the harvest as a result of this ploughing of the
soil and planting of the seed.

At the end of the tenth century, Subaktagin (977–997)
and his son Mahmud (997–1028), converts to Mahomet,

invaded India which the fall of the Guptas (535) in spite
of the transitory unity which Harsha-Siladitya there established
(606–647) had replunged into chaos. Togrul-Beg took possession of Persia (1051), and under the mask of the Abassides set
up as ruler of Baghdad the sons of Seldjuk (1055). Mohamed-
Shihab-ud-Din conquered Delhi, Kanauj, Benares, Bihar,
Bengal (1193–1206).

Then arose in China, connected with the Seldjuks on the
female side and Christian in its maternal origin, the family of
Budantsar to give their autonomy to the Mongols, to join
them to the Turks of the north and east, to ally themselves
successively with the Chinese of the south, then to the Man-
chus who had become Chinese in their lives and were masters
of ancient China, at length to dominate them all and restore,
unify and further extend the boundaries of the empire of
Mokan-Khan and that of the T'ang.

Reference has already been made (p. 167) to the sixth-
century Turkish ruler Mokan. Having established a federation
of all the Turks from Mongolia to the Black Sea, he had
conceived the design of using them to bind China to Europe
(568). He saw the world as a balance, with China and
Europe as the two scales: the Turks were to be the cross-
beam, a thinking and acting beam, one which should not
merely sway with the scales but sway them: the real masters of
the world, without unity, or ordered control, but with their
hand on the pivot of politics, and the exchange of goods
and merchandise. This conception was defective, inasmuch
as it did not take into account the weakness and the confusion
of Byzantium, the anarchic inconsistency of China, the fragility
of the edifice he had constructed. He died in 573 and the
whole of his empire tumbled to bits. When the Sui and the
T'ang restored the cohesion and the power of China (581–620)
the Turkish empire was already in fragments and the Arab
deluge came.

T'ai-Tsung (627–650), the second T'ang emperor, was intelligent, gifted with energy and culture; clever, though devoid
of faith and scruples, he saw that his own interests were those

N

of the States over which he ruled and he knew how to make himself beloved of his people, but he was devoured by vaulting ambition. Did he also dream the same dreams as Mokan? His campaigns and those of his successor against the Turks; their relations with Harsha-Siladytia; the extension of their empire towards Turania into the valleys of the Ili and the Yaxarte, might make us think so, if they had not also thrown considerable forces against the Koreans for a period of twenty years (645–668). In any case their conquests were not of long duration. In 670 the Thibetans took Tarim away from them. In 677 Korea became once more independent. As for themselves they fell under the power of the distaff. By intrigue and assassination, Wu-Hou, the Chinese Fredegonde, for half a century (645–705) reigned and governed under the name of the T'ang. This was a prelude to the long decadence (705–907) and the end of the T'ang dynasty, which was followed by 300 years of dislocation and anarchy (907–1205).

Thus we are back at the thirteenth century and the family of Budantsar. There was nothing but chaos over the land of Asia when Temouchin, the son of Yesukai, arose from his misfortunes and, so to speak, from death; he recaptured the heritage of his father; imposed his power over the Turks of the Steppes, rallied the Mongols, got himself proclaimed emperor by all of them under the title of Genghis-Khan (1206); got together powerful armies and, being a politician of genius served by strategists and tacticians of genius—for Sabutai was equal to Hannibal or Alexander—extended his power over the whole of the north of China, raised his standard against Islam, overwhelmed the Kharismian Turks who had just effected the conquest of India, deprived them of Persia in spite of the heroic resistance of Djelal-ed-Din; terrorized and subdued the Slavs of the south, by pushing as far as the Dnieper the 25,000 epic horsemen of Sabutai; hurled at Delhi a still weaker detachment; pacified that immense empire with a high hand and died, bequeathing to his sons the task of consolidating it and completing his work.

They committed a double error; they made the empire too

big and they divided it. Fascinated by the idea of universal dominion and having no superior civilization to bestow upon the peoples whom they mingled together, they went from conquest to conquest, without being able to lay the foundation of anything durable. They invaded Poland, Silesia, Bohemia, Hungary; they went as far as the shores of the Adriatic, into Syria, Thibet, into India and Burmah, as far as Siam, Indo-China, Java and Korea. They attacked Japan. The whole of China was theirs, as also Siberia, Turania and southern Russia: one-third of Europe and three-fifths of Asia (1240–1260). Never have States been seen of greater size, nor more motley, nor weaker. Very soon broken into two, then into four, then into a hundred morsels, in all directions their conquests returned to their origins. What traces remain to-day of the Mongols?

On the soil which they ploughed and drenched with human blood the harvests are Chinese, Hindu, Persian, Greek, Buddhist, Mussulman and Christian. As early as the year 1280, the great Mongol ruler Kubla Khan in his glory was nothing more than the first of the Yuan, one of the most fugitive of the dynasties that ever reigned in China. And Timour, the Genghis of the fourteenth century, who made the great massacres at Delhi and Baghdad—a sultan-cavalier of the Arabian and Persian type—all he did, as just before him Alp-Arslan, son of the Seljuks, and Othman, the founder of Turkey (1288), was to place the Turkish power in the service of Islam.

Jerusalem, first conquered by the Arabs and made an Arab city and then Aryanized, got the upper hand in western Asia over Karakorum and Cambaluc; and in China these were supplanted by Nanking, the Ming capital (1368–1643). The torrent from the North was lost in the torrent from the South. The later torrent, like the earlier, was absorbed in the soil of the East and stopped on the very verge of submerging the West.

VIII

THE DECLINE OF CHRISTENDOM

Against such invaders the defence put up by the West was not characterized by much military ability, or even by much strength. We must not let ourselves be deceived by the noisy jingle of arms which was heard in the West in the Middle Ages, nor by the shouts and commotions of the Crusaders. The age of Charlemagne was far distant.

The feudal lords of western Europe were far too busy with petty brawls and squabbles before they started out on the Crusades to unite into an effective force. On the march to the east they continued these ridiculous personal quarrels. Their objective was the conquest of Syria, Palestine, Cyprus, Rhodes, Sicily, Salonica and Constantinople. On these far-flung expeditions they had no other soldiers than their own men-at-arms and the vassal nobles who had agreed to continue on in their army after the termination of the meagre forty days of military service due from them according to their oaths of fealty and homage. There were as many armies in the field as there were leaders: valiant armies perhaps, but each of them few in numbers and possessing no knowledge of field movements and tactics. They were accustomed, to none but little wars in which they had forgotten—if they had ever known—the strategy and the art of great battles and campaigns.

For centuries the mass of people had forgotten how to fight. They were even forbidden to hunt and to bear arms. The professed defenders of Christianity succeeded in causing divisions and dissensions in the realm of Christendom itself; but it was beyond their powers to defend the realm of Christ against a genius in war, supported by brave and indefatigable soldiers. The courage of the Crusaders saved their honour, compromised by their discords and the diplomacy of Frederick II: that is the best we can say of them.

If the Mongol conqueror did not proceed to the annexation
of the vanquished kingdoms, did not demolish the Holy
Roman Empire, nor conquer France and even Spain and
England, it was only because he preferred first to take possession of that land which for so long had exercised its fascinations
upon him: China, land of immensities, rich, populous and
cultured, and Thibet whence flowed over China the wisdom
of Buddha; Iran, the Indies, Syria, lands where the sun shone
forth in all its brilliance, the highways of mountaineers and
the people of the steppes moving ever towards the sun.

Suppose that the successors of Genghis Khan, with their
massed forces, had rushed upon the West and conquered it.
What would have happened afterwards? Events in China
leave us, indeed, no room for doubt: instead of Asia, Europe
would have absorbed the hordes of Genghis Khan, and in this
way have met her end. As it was, such forces scarcely had any
effect either in hastening or retarding the crisis of the nations
which was near at hand in the middle of the thirteenth century
of our era and was even then ready to attack their Empire
as well as Christendom.

Already, in spite of the conquests of Tamburlaine, the spirit
of Nationalism had broken Islam into pieces. The triumphs
of the Priesthood could not prevent that spirit from dislocating
Europe. Its thrust was irresistible. The Caesars of Germany
were vanquished and could not answer Dante's appeal to put
the bit into the mouth of the Italian horse. The imperial eagle
in Germany, like the papal dove in the Italian peninsula,
hatched a brood of republics and monarchies. The Hundred
Years' War, the Babylonian Captivity of the Popes at Avignon
and the Great Schism shook to its foundations the edifice
erected by Charlemagne, by Innocent III, by the Capetians
and Saint Louis so mightily that the Rock on which everything rested seemed to be broken into three: and it took the
miracle of Joan of Arc, unique in the history of men, to save
the eldest daughter of Rome from the England of Wyclif.

Everywhere, from Gibraltar to the islands of the Levant,
between the Arctic Circle and the tropics, powerful nationali-

ties were coming into existence in the midst of a unity which was disappearing The decadence was general.

Intelligence was on the wane. From the time of Avicenna (1030), Averroes (1198) and Djelal-el-Din-er-Roumi (1273), Islam declined. India had slumbered ever since the great days of Çankara (c. 789–820) and Ramanuja had gone to sleep. Chu-Hi and the Mongols brutalized China. In the Western world scholastic pedantry buried under its dust the synthesis in which St. Thomas Aquinas had gathered together and expressed with sovereign clarity everything that human wisdom and divine revelation had brought into the world as a light by which the sons of Adam might come to a knowledge of God, of the world and themselves; whilst the humanists having abandoned Jerusalem for Athens and Rome went back again to the schools of the sophists and the pagans.

Spirituality was also on the wane. Christian mysticism had caused even the deserts to blossom. It had penetrated to Islam, probably Persia and China and perhaps into India. It had come to a magnificent development in the monasteries, the guilds, the third orders of lay brothers, from St. Benedict to St. Bernard, St. Francis and St. Dominic. It flourished brilliantly amongst such mystics as Suso, Tauler, John of Ruysbroeck, Thomas à Kempis, Gerson and Catherine of Siena. It never failed; but false mystics grew in numbers and, under cover of divine inspiration, the Fraticelli, the Spirituals and the Brothers of the Free Spirit opened up the way for Wyclif and for John Huss who were the fathers of Private Judgment and so of Free Thought.

Furthermore, morals were on the wane. The salt of the earth had lost its savour. Clerics allowed themselves to be spoiled and corrupted by riches and politics. On all sides and amongst all nations they failed in their allotted tasks. The original traditions were obscured and misrepresented. "The faith has perished, because the verities which come from on High have been diminished by the sons of men." The world grew weary of God, weary of His service and hungry to live for itself.

Finally there was a waning in public spirit. Neither the Christian power nor the unity of Christ were any longer understood in the ethnarchy which marched at the head of the Caravan. Men expert in the legalism of the Caesars controlled the minds of the emperor and the kings. The doctors of the Sorbonne rejected the Rock on which Christ declared that His Church was built, proclaimed the supremacy of the general council over the Pope and in that council they proclaimed the supremacy of the theologians whom they claimed to invest with the right of suffrage over the bishops who were less numerous. Thus the University of Paris would have substituted for the Pontifical monarchy a republic in which the university itself would have had sovereign rights, with the Pope at its mercy.

Two hundred years of degeneracy plunged Christianity into this sad state. Both its head and its body became gangrened. It was necessary for it to cut off the hand and pluck out the eye which offended it, effect a profound reform in its head and its members when neither the members nor the head seemed capable of reform; or else in the manner of the Chinese and the Hindus, to widen the boundaries in order to admit into the unity of Christendom all contradictions, heresies and schisms; to exclude therefrom by the same method both dogma and authority, in a word, to abandon the work before its achievement, abandon the road before its end, and allow the Caravan to turn suddenly round and go backwards for one or two stages and to start again on other ways, with other guides and under other chiefs than Christ, after this endless toil.

The best amongst the popes had no eyes for anything but the Ottomans whose conquests they regarded as a new offensive by ancient Islam. They were absorbed in the efforts of the Crusades. This error of judgment meant putting back the clock for at least 300 years. What was now in question along the Bosphorus, and in Thrace, and in the Balkans was not an offensive against Christianity, but a thrust for national expansion. During this time the nations which the Church had both

formed and civilized broke from its influence and control and
engaged in a similar national thrust forward. The pagan tide
began to mount. The wise reforms traced out in plan by
Nicolas of Cusa remained a dead letter. Sinful popes were
chosen, scandalous popes, Innocent VIII and Alexander VI
(1484–1503), worldly popes, Sixtus IV (1471–1484) and
Leo X (1513–1521).

This stage of the Caravan came to an end under heavy
shadows. If the West was falling to pieces and abandoning
itself; if the East, flung back upon itself, was simply letting
itself go adrift, who would assume the leadership of the
Caravan? And if it fell back 2,000 years; if everywhere unity
were broken or relegated to the background and tyrannies
were multiplied, where would the Caravan go?

Never were those wise men nearer to being right who see
nothing in history save evolution without end or goal and
perpetual new beginning.

CHAPTER V

CIRCLING THE GLOBE

I

RENASCENCE AND REFORMATION

HERE then is the funnel of the great crater: a dangerous gulf for such ants as we. Rocks, unseen before, have been torn up by the great explosion from the depths of the earth and piled up on the surface. Historians and philosophers and the rest have a glorious time arguing about the mine, the miner, the explosive and the explosion. But the confusion they discuss is largely their own creation.

The Renascence, the Reformation, the discovery of America, the social revolution in Germany; inspiration and dogma, mysticism and religion, nature and grace; individualism, humanism, paganism, evangelism and I know not how many other —isms; the causes, the effects, the origins, the sequences, the developments, the progress, the retreats, the benefits and the disadvantages: all these things make admirable matter for theorizing.

But the facts in their complexity are simpler, and the obscurities whence they flow are clearer, than the theories advanced to account for them. After all, the great crisis in the West of the sixteenth century was in no way an exception to the customary movements of human affairs. What about the Mine? There were several of varying depths, some short and others long, and of all sorts of outlines and shapes. The miners also were numerous and diverse in origin, means, procedure and objectives. Very often they thought they were working in opposition, which is why their works converge, supplement and reinforce one another, even when the miners knew nothing of

t. What of the explosives? All the detonating mixtures, all the combinations and mixtures of fulminants manufactured by philosophic, religious, economic and social chemistry. And the explosions? The whole gamut in every tone and at every depth and for three centuries and in a score of places.

Anagni (1303) and Nogaret, right-hand man of the worldly-wise Pierre du Bois; Nuremberg (1326) and Marsilius of Padua, the radical democrat; Rome and the dictator Cola di Rienzi; Oxford and John Wyclif (1356), author of many heresies and apostle of free criticism; Florence, where the red flag was hoisted in the name of liberty (1376). These were the explosions of the fourteenth century of our era.

Prague and John Huss, the revolutionary disciple of John Wyclif; Constance (1414), Bale (1432) and Pisa (1511) with their self-styled councils which laid claim to dispense with the Pope and to replace the foundation Rock of the Church by a heap of pebbles; Florence, already mentioned, where by the voice of Savonarola the urgent necessity for the reform of Christianity in its head and in its members was proclaimed openly with brilliant eloquence, only to be spoilt by imprudent ardour by the reformer himself, obscured by violence and crushed in revolt (1490–1498). These were the explosions of the fifteenth century of our era.

At Wittenberg in the sixteenth century Luther broke loose (1517), as a prelude to the social revolution; Westeras and Copenhagen are associated with the apostasy of the northern kings (1527); in England came the schism of Henry VIII (1531); at Munster, "the kingdom of Sion", John Mathis and John of Leyden created a Bedlam centre of illuminism and anarchy (1524); from 1535–1541 Calvin made Geneva his home; Cranmer, Archbishop of Canterbury, was the pioneer of Calvinism in England (1547–1552); and again London comes to the front with Queen Elizabeth forcibly imposing heresy upon a people already forced into schism (1559–1563); Edinburgh is associated with the Puritan reform of John Knox (1559); at Vassy came the first skirmish of the wars of religion in France (1562); at Louvain there was a ferment of Jansenism in the school of Baius (1567); at Donauworth there was in 1606 a riot which was the prelude of the Thirty Years' War and the final collapse of the Holy Roman Empire; Champré was the solitary abode chosen by Jean Duvergier de Hauranne and Cornelius Jansen in 1611 for the making of that bomb which under the name of *Augustinus* they used to torpedo the Council of Trent, St. Thomas Aquinas and the Church of Rome, whilst Angelique Arnaud was unwittingly building their fortress at Port Royal in 1605.

In the tumult of three centuries two main elements are clearly visible—the Renascence and the Reformation. But the relation between these two is altogether misconstrued by many. "On the one hand," they say, "the Renascence of Antiquity and the return to paganism; on the other, the Reformation of Christianity and the return to its primitive fervour: two forces diametrically opposed. The latter must kill the former, or the former the latter. Both cannot survive. All the misfortunes came from the favour which the popes bestowed upon the Renascence; and what the Reformation is in the popes' eyes, they themselves became in the eyes of the supporters of the Reformation: the Beast in the Apocalypse, the Woman clothed round about with purple and scarlet; Babylon the great, the mother of fornications and abominations of the earth, which had to be destroyed.

"When a definite beginning was made of the Counter-Reformation, it was too late. Although the broken union was mended, the division was on two occasions too much for it and caused an interruption in the Great Council. The whole thing very nearly proved abortive. In the end the work accomplished was fine and bore fruit. It saved the Roman Church: but it was another and more difficult matter to return along the stream of time, reverse the flow of things and make up for so many faults and errors and opportunities lost. Christianity was dismembered; the Holy Roman Empire was dying; scholasticism was dead. The era of reason and science, of nationalities and of the State, of revolutions and democracy was opening: and it lay in no man's power to close it. The door was never closed again; the walls, which had been thrown down by the three-hundred-year assault of a world alive with novelties, were not rebuilt."

This indeed is a brilliant explanation; but of what value is the point of departure? There is perhaps much evidence to show that the most fascinating reformations often become deformations. This is a question to be examined. But in all the talk there is of the Holy Spirit, the Scriptures and the Primitive Church, there is no agreement as to what the Holy Spirit has in fact revealed, as to the meaning of Scripture, as to the belief of the Primitive Church. These great phrases become labels to be pinned on any and every contradictory doctrine according to the fancy of each new sect.

How do you recognize the Holy Spirit with which you say you are inspired?—By the voice of my conscience. Why do you attribute this Scripture, rather than any other, to the Holy Spirit?—Because my researches and my thoughts compel me to do so. How do you guarantee that the interpretation which you place upon it is legitimate and true?—By the demonstrations of my reasoning faculty, by my knowledge, the inspiration that enlightens me and the mission which I have received from the Holy Spirit.

These would be strange replies in a Christian mouth, even if one saw in those who made them the peace of Christ; unselfishness, humility, the submissiveness of the apostles; purity of morals, simplicity of soul and life, the spirit of prayer, of tradition and discipline; patience, renunciation of self, forgiveness for injuries suffered, love of God and brotherly charity, the virtues by which the Primitive Church reformed antiquity. But in the leaders at least, one sees little enough of all this: Luther, a man of turbulent soul, obsessed with self, of strong passions, powerless against his flesh; Calvin who consecrated himself as predestined to grace, because he was devoured by the passion to impose everywhere, upon the State, the Church and the human mind his own mind and his own will; Henry VIII, schismatic through personal vanity, ambition, rancour and lust; Elizabeth of England whose public

and private life moved on its way as far from the Gospel as
the life of Queen Semiramis. In the spiritual order not one of
the leaders of the Reformation was equal to Gautama, or
even to Confucius or Mahomet.

It must certainly be admitted that there was need of reform
in Christianity; but see what they made of it. Instead of one
king, the Christ, a thousand kings, born from the individual
conscience of each one as a result of free criticism and
free mysticism. Instead of one faith, that of Peter, as many
faiths as there were believers; opinion, mistress of the world,
annexed the kingdom of God. Instead of one law, the Gospel,
under the ward of a Church, as many laws as there were and
are autonomous individualities, autocephalous churches and
secular masters, kings, princes, dictators, parliaments, theologians and prophets who arrogate to themselves dominion
over the human conscience and arrange, as they think fit,
official relations between men and God.

Did Protestantism attack the Renascence, the philosophies
of antiquity, the unbelief of the humanists, the shamefulness
of their morals and their writings? It did not concern itself
much with such things. The Theses of Wittenberg, the Confession of Augsburg, the book *Concerning the Institution of
Christianity*, Cromwell's five articles, Cranmer's two *Prayer
Books*, Elizabeth's *Thirty-Nine Articles* and the claims of John
Knox wasted no words on such frivolities. The Reformers
of Smalkalde, refusing to lend a hand in the reforms of Trent,
demanded that the decrees arrived at without their consent
should be annulled; that there should be no Pope and no
legates, except in the crowd of bishops; that no decision should
be reached without a text of the Scriptures to warrant it,
and that there should be no interpretation of the texts, except
one by the other and by the light of reason only.

What possible doubt could there be after that, with regard
to the bearing of the facts, the sense of words, the secret
thoughts of hearts, the principle and the spirit common to
so many churches, religious clubs and different sects? They
were not directed against the Farnese family, nor against the

Borgias, nor against the Medici; they were directed against all their predecessors, the Councils, the Fathers, Catholic Tradition, the dogma revealed and the authority which defined it. Render unto Caesar the keys of Peter; to the flock, primacy over the shepherd, to the individual, licence to act according to his free inspiration and to believe according to the freedom of his conscience: that was the final word of the Reformation. In what way did it differ from the Renascence? The Reformation brings us close enough to Rabelais's Thelema: "There is but one clause in their law: Do what you like."

It is of course possible that they started on the road towards the Primitive Church; but at the cross-roads they certainly took the wrong way. They arrived at Mahomet: the spiritual absorbed by the temporal, unity by dominion. They even went further. They outstripped the old paganism, in which religion is indeed something better than a lay worship veneered upon individual opinion; and I think I understand it when the pagans of to-day say to the Anglican missionaries in India: "If Christianity is the religion of 'do as seems good to you', that is all we have to do."

II

REFORMATION AND INDIVIDUALISM

The Reformers of course were not all like Luther, or Calvin, or Elizabeth. Many of them never grasped the reality that lay hidden under the name of Reformation, and would have been horrified if they had. Protestants there are in plenty, separated from the Roman Church by invincible prejudices, who hate qualities they think to be in her not knowing that she hates those same things as much. They love what she loves. By the grace of God they are submissive to the voice of Christ who is the master of their souls within them. The Reformation did not fail to play the great part in the history of Europe which its nature implied. What is that rôle? An enlightened Protestant, M. René Gillouin, quite recently wrote that "Protestantism is neither a form, nor a cause, nor an effect of individualism," but only "a solution of the problem" posed, in the first place, by the tendency of each individual man to make himself the centre of the universe and, in the second, by the periodical predominance in the Human Caravan of this tendency over the social instinct. "This solution," he adds, "was found useful to meet the individualist thrust of the Renascence. It was also found useful to meet the individualist thrust, serious in another way, of the eighteenth century and the Revolution. And for that reason the Protestant nations for 300 years, more especially for the latter half of that period, have taken the lead in world affairs." Let us rather say the Protestant States, Prussia, England and the United States of America. Where, however, and in what manner have they taken the lead? A tree must be judged by its fruit and not by its height. In what way did their Protestantism bring about this hegemony? The hegemony in fact depends upon so many causes and by itself proves so little that we can but congratulate them. The eighteenth century thrust did not differ essentially from the fifteenth. Or why was the Protestant solution of the problem found to be suitable to both? Chronic illness may be a useful remedy for acute illness, but it remains illness and a bar to recovery. We might go on indefinitely discussing these questions, if we did not grasp the deep-rooted identity of the Reformation and the Renascence. The capital facts of the sixteenth century put this identity beyond doubt, and in its light everything becomes clear.

Look back over the march of events from the time when the Church of Jesus Christ and the Holy Roman Empire of the German nation began their associated existence; look more closely at the thousand years that lay between the moment when the West passed under the primacy of the Church and the moment when it thrust that primacy aside.

Rome at first a temporal city, an empire of government and a dominion creative of unity was changed little by little

into a spiritual city, a society of nations and a unity which
bent the powers of this world to her laws. Christendom had
been established. Slowly this unique thing was built amid the
persecutions of the first three centuries of the Christian era.
It was developed during the two succeeding centuries under
the Christian Caesars. It liberated itself and organized
itself in the sixth century, extending its power over the Barbarians who had destroyed the Roman unity. It restored that
unity and consolidated itself in the seventh and eighth
centuries by civilizing the barbarians. Finally, it clothed
itself in its definite form at the beginning of the ninth century,
by associating the Holy Empire with the Papacy. Constantine
(313), Clovis (511), Gregory the Great (590–604), Charlemagne (785–814), mark the stages.

Henceforth the road lay clear. For four more centuries
Christendom continued to climb, not indeed without vicissitudes and failures, struggles and reforms, but victoriously
towards its perfection and its plenitude. The nearer the
Church approached to fullness and perfection, the greater
was the restraint she put upon the workings of individual
instinct. In this way, individual instinct was driven back,
repressed, tamed, disciplined by the Church, even amongst
those who lent themselves to its powers; but amongst those
who denied it all satisfaction, by storing up its explosive forces,
it undermined in a hundred ways the city which was being
built.

Scarcely had the Church strengthened her bases, built
her ramparts and made provision for their defence, when her
assailants were upon her. The Emperor, the very defender
whom she had chosen, marched at the head of her enemies.
He was compelled to obey the Church, he was driven off and
replaced. The walls were rebuilt; but new breaches followed
and the new protector was worse than the last.

It began with Otto the Saxon (962–973), who distinguished
himself by two armed attacks upon Rome, a false Council,
an anti-Pope set up to his own wishes, a legitimate Pope
deposed and deported to Germany. We are already far

enough from Charlemagne. But Conrad of Saxony, the three Henries of Franconia, Barbarossa, Otto of Swabia and Frederick II the Impious, followed the earlier Otto's example and improved upon it. But the hour had not yet arrived. Before Constantine the Church lived, though she did not break the powerful procession of the pagan Caesars: nor did these new Caesars nor the Turkish triumphs prevent the Church from continuing to climb up the rough road of Western primacy.

Nor did interior disorders stop the Church's progress: the plots of the Roman Republic and of the Roman patricians, the scandals of Sergius III, of John XII and of Benedict IX; simony, the incontinence of the clergy, the investiture of lay-men, royal divorces, the heresies of Berengarius, of Abelard, of the Vaudois and of the Albigenses—these things did not thus early produce the effects that similar facts produced in the fifteenth and sixteenth centuries. But the total effect of all these things was to presage, prepare, make unsuccessful attempts at what the legists and humanists of the Renascence and the theologians and princes of the Reformation later succeeded in achieving.

In this manner in the shadow, in the very bosom of the Christian City of the eleventh and twelfth centuries, there were laid the foundations of the city of the future. The foundations rose higher in the two centuries that followed; the new city obtained its charter and organised itself in the sixteenth century on the débris of the Christendom it had broken up; was consolidated, extended and took its definitive form in the seventeenth and eighteenth centuries, separating the nations from the Church and almost everywhere introduc-ing and setting up a culture exclusively worldly in an impersonal and laicized State. Philip the Fair and Marsilius of Padua, Luther and Calvin, Elizabeth of England, Jean–Jacques Rousseau mark different phases of the same thrust forward of an individualism at first royal and national, moral and intellectual. The Reformation in Germany, however (1517–1523), from its very beginning let loose the movement on

o

the world under the pure form of an anarchy "fresh and joyous".

In their fear of this the Reformers naturally enough reversed the engines. They had exalted their "Christian Institution", their Church, their Bible, their doctrinal authority, their princes and their State. I do not think that Luther and Calvin would have felt more indulgence for Voltaire and the Encyclopaedists than for the Church of Rome, nor for the "Feuillants" or the "Jacobins" of the Revolution according to Rousseau than for the papal monks. Port Royal hated the Jesuits, but threw the "libertines" overboard in the same sack. And afterwards what was to happen?

It is not a question of judging either the Reformers or the reformed upon what they aimed at doing. Many other men have had the same reasons as they had for saying: "I did not wish that. That was not what I taught. I both desired and taught the precise opposite." But whatever they may have wanted, we can see what they produced—the effects, foreseen or unforeseen, of their words and acts, the doctrines to which their doctrines opened wide the way and delivered over the West. The smallest loophole is enough for the individual instinct to spread itself and, sooner or later, to commit all its ravages. Declare a single individual to be the final judge of morals or the faith and, even if he were king of England or the dictator of Geneva, the rest follows inevitably.

Individualism does not consist in proclaiming that every individual carries within himself his king, his faith and his law. It consists rather in having as legislator, doctor, or prince, one or several individuals, a minority or a majority who find within themselves, even if they declare it divine, the origin of their right.

The Protestants condemned the Anabaptists and preached revolt against the Pope; yet they preached submission to the orders of the prince. But what right had Doctor Martin Luther more than the baker of Haarlem to define what must be believed and what must be done? Zero is equal to zero. If the individual Luther is the arbiter of the Scriptures and of faith, why not the individual John Mathys, or John of Leyden as well as John Calvin, John Knox, or Jean-Jacques Rousseau, or Kant, Comte, Plato, Voltaire, Montaigne, Epicurus, Mahomet, Rabelais, Confucius, you, or myself? Truth comes to mean opinion, religion to mean philosophy and observance.

The Anabaptists as Protestants are every ·bit as good as the Lutherans, the Spiritualists, the Mormons and the Pious Atheists whose preaching I hear in the open air at Marble Arch in London. But, you say, the Protestants are Christians. Doubtless. You must know some, however, even amongst the Established Church of England, who give to Christ and His Virgin Mother a lower place than was given by Mahomet or Arius. Their opinion is as good as Martin Luther's—or Buddha's, or Anaxagoras's. It is after all merely an opinion. Luther raised the lid of the box and the whole wasps' nest flew out, sect by sect, one philosophy chasing the other.

Sin had spoilt our human nature. Whether we ignore sin or so exaggerate its evil results as to deny man's power against it, the consequence is the same. In the one case we see our nature as absolutely virtuous, in the other as absolutely corrupt, unless something comes from outside of us and independently of us (even in spite of us) to corrupt it or make it well. In this absolute dwells all individualistic usurpation. The two errors lead to the same conclusion: "Do what you please."

All the learned doctors who profess one or the other theory in this way accomplish the same task: they isolate the individual and reduce him to himself by rendering God useless to him, or him useless to God. Thus, intentionally or not, they liberate man's worst instinct and put him in the place he is ambitious to occupy, the centre of the universe. We all know that elementary instinct, the original cause of man's revolt and fall, the agent of division amongst men, of dispersion and of multiplication, the spirit of Babel. Those who are dominated by that instinct, whatever may be their illusions of progress, are swept downward by it towards the primitive anarchy from which their ancestors had toiled upward. Under one form or another this regression is always accompanied by a Renascence. This has been clearly seen as such and acclaimed as such in Italy and in France which are countries of the old Latins. Amongst the Northerners it received the name of Reformation; but the habit does not make the monk, nor the word the thing.

Everywhere the same influence urged the nations with the same power back towards the level they had long left. One such movement—the Renascence—was toward Graeco-Roman Antiquity: Caesar's order looked for in a unity through politics; the gods, that is to say nature deified and man in the first rank of the natural order, with his reason to give him light and lead him along his path, his passions to prompt his actions, his works which realize for all ages and in all kinds the type of perfection which his genius has discovered under every conceivable diversity of appearance. The other movement—the Reformation—was towards Germanic Antiquity: the spirit of the barbarous tribe where order is looked for in multiplicity through domination; the primacy of custom over law, of will over reason, of action over the product of action; of ideas, images and sentiments over reality; of becoming over the perfect and the absolute. From the difference of direction arise the differences which placed these two movements in opposition the one to the other, though they were fundamentally alike.

The Renascence had no hatred of Rome. It did not threaten the Roman unity. But it wished to modify the character of that unity and to deprive the Galilean of it, to destroy or transform the Jerusalem which He built on the ruins of the Forum, to restore the City and the Empire. Hence the Renascence did not achieve its goal. Jerusalem is too well built and too rich in virtues. The Council of Trent and a pleiad of saints—popes, bishops, the founders of different orders, clerks both regular and secular and the laity to aid them—effected a real reform, threw down the idols which had just been set up and soon inspired the Renascence itself with the spirit of Catholicism. But the ravages were frightful. At times the pagan wave seemed to have submerged everything even to the destruction of the Christian city. But Christ is the Resurrection and the Life even in the corruption of death. He might for a space suffer luxury, avarice, ambition, vanity, and cowardice to sit on the throne of Peter, but at the worst they never made sin lawful or falsified doctrine. And the moment came when Peter "converted, confirmed his brethren".

The Reformation hated both Rome and Jerusalem. It disrupted Christian unity; it dislocated Roman unity. Force regained its empire; the force of some one man or some few men, despotism; the force of numbers, anarchy. There remained only the débris of Christendom and the remains of the Christian spirit. The pagan spirit knew neither bounds nor barriers. In the divided West these two spirits collided and clashed, tearing the nations between them. Once more man became a ravening wolf against his fellow man; and national egoism towered tyrannously over the egoism of sects, corporations, classes and individuals. Empires once more come on the scene. Social revolutions raged: in Germany (1642–1660), in France (1789, 1848), in Russia (1905, 1917). The crusades were at an end, but national and civil struggles achieved an amplitude, a duration and a bitterness hitherto unknown: the Thirty Years' War (1619–1648), the Napoleonic wars (1789–1815), the Great War of the Nations (1914–1918) —a terrible crescendo, a whirlwind of fire and blood in which conscription, for a thousand years abolished under the rule of the Church, dragged into battle entire peoples—200,000,000 souls and more around the circle of the trenches.

No, against this thrust of individualism the Protestant remedy is of no avail; it is on the side of individualism and against the Catholic Church.

It detached the Germans from the Roman unity and the Latin culture. And even among the Latins the same spirit worked towards unbelief and secularism and the ruin of authority: for their objective logic and their absoluteness made impossible for them the inconsistencies, the contradictions and the subjective relativity which partly save the German in practice from the errors he has committed in speculation. Thus the Latin States were weakened from within; and from the outside they were encumbered with Saxon institutions contrary to their traditions and their temperament. It is not, therefore, the Protestant who takes the lead in world affairs, but the German and the Anglo-Saxon—as a consequence of this disturbed balance of the Latin mind.

III

MODERN CIVILIZATION

The civilization which thus developed on the millenary foundation of the Western world has not lost all the influence of that foundation. One can indeed deny one's own mother, but her blood is in the veins, there is some heritage from her in the nerves, the mind and the heart. Yet we must not see modern civilization either as a renascence of the Graeco-Roman culture or as a reformation and rejuvenation of the Christian culture. It is something quite new, a civilization of apostasy created by the human genius in a sudden impulse of independence, a new paganism, more abstract, more learned, more reasonable, more open and more radical than the paganism of Western antiquity.

It does not adore God. It denies Him, or declares Him unknowable, or relegates Him into a distant perfection, solitary, shut up upon itself and indifferent. It attributes to itself, not as a religion or a faith but as something superior, an immediate knowledge of reality, a science which excludes faith and makes religion a superfluous thing. Far from laying any claim to tradition, any superhuman revelation, it despises and rejects all such things as childish illusions.

Its oracles are observation, experiment and calculation; novelty is its criterion of excellence. It replaces myths and dogmas by the theories of mathematicians and psychologists, the utopias of sociologists, the lucky hits and the hypotheses of biologists, of physicists, of geologists and astronomers. It knows not prayer; and if it preserves as the heritage of centuries of Christianity a remarkably keen sense of human dignity, the equal possession of all men who thereby become brothers, it nevertheless hands them over to a strange and unprecedented slavery. They become serfs of the very forces that men have subdued by their penetration of the secrets of nature, they serve the slaves of steel they have themselves constructed.

But the turning of machines into masters, the subduing of natural forces to human use, the better understanding of nature, the inheritance from a time of faith, the substitution of philosophies for religion, the deification of science, the State, the individual—these things essentially are of all times and all places. It is with them as with the human body which with all the diversity of features and costumes remains universally one thing. The wave of individualism which carries the New West along with it, flows in this manner from ideas, aspirations and ambitions which are universal.

It is true that there is a renewal of nationalism. Every nation violently strives to become a sovereign State, within its frontiers; but what could be less local or national in character than the other intoxications of the modern world—humanism and rationalism, liberalism and laicism, naturalism and materialism, mercantilism and capitalism, State absolutism and socialism, democracy, internationalism and humanitarianism?

Born from the very heart of European Christendom which was in its essence a universality, the Renascence and the Reformation drew their own nature from their opposition to her. Their first effort was to destroy her. They gave a loose rein to the selfishness and egoism of princes, nations and individuals. Individualism was to be universal. Universal individualism first acted as individualism and not as universal. Because it strove to put an end to Roman Catholicism, before putting another in its place, its first action was violently anti-Catholic, particularist, revolutionary and separatist; but as soon as this destructive action attained its end in a certain measure, it passed to the back of the stage.

A constructive action supplanted it. The individual became aware of his universality; the nation of international solidarity; and behind the façade of rival nationalisms, localized democracies, absolutisms with frontiers, a universal form of political organization was developed, adaptable to the human race, as to each part of it: the modern State.

There was the new god: the State, impersonal, absolute, capable of indefinite extension and rejuvenation; divisible, but at all times reducible to unity under the form suitable to the circumstances, from a simple entente to a complete fusion; the same everywhere, whatever its form, and always easily penetrated, worked upon, shaped and led by powers which are either manifest to the world or hidden; powers which for their own objectives and universal ends make use of the ideologies and systems which I have enumerated.

Henceforth it appears that the main struggle is no longer, as in the times of pagan antiquity and in the countries of oriental paganism, between the egoisms of individuals, princes, nations, or empires, but between the Roman Church, the only real Catholic Church, and the modern State which everywhere strives to eliminate and supplant it. The "two cities" of St. Augustine once more stand face to face; but between them local wars are no longer possible: the war can but be worldwide.

IV

NATIONALISM

A powerful yeast is necessary that the paste of humanity may be kneaded into the good bread of unity. Up to the sixteenth century for this great task there sufficed nomadic migrations, barbarian invasions, the raids of conquerors, bringing the evil of domination, the mixtures of races and peoples within empires, the successive wreckage of great structures, the slow, peaceful extension and the mutual penetration of civilizations. But all that was over by the year 1500. After the raids made by the Arabs, the Turks and the Mongols there were no more nomadic or barbarian attacks anywhere which could play a similar part in the march of the Caravan.

And what about the conquerors? In this old world, henceforth compact, governed and civilized almost everywhere, in the heart of which the simple elementary forms of the State—families, clans, tribes and cities—had almost everywhere given way to secondary and complex forms—kingdoms, empires, ethnarchies—conquests of the kind which took place in the ancient world became singularly rare and difficult. What strength, what genius, what luck were necessary if a conqueror was even to make elbow room for himself—and immeasurably more if he was to found a dynasty that should endure. Napoleon himself, mighty in war and one of the subtlest and most penetrating political intelligences the world has ever seen, did not hold his power for twenty years.

It is manifest that great conquests by force of arms will not be effected in the future except over lands which are either empty and unoccupied or inhabited by savages—darkest Africa, the islands of the Pacific, the West Indies, or the small civilized States of the Incas, the Mayas and the Aztecs, weakened by their superstitions and discords and ready to crumble in pieces before the first *conquistador* who presents himself.

If elsewhere there are created great and durable empires, it will come about by the action of politics; and politics will conquer the best armed States or deprive them of the fruit of their victories. Generally speaking, alliances, inheritances, treaties, exploration, commerce and finance will play the principal rôle; behind these come military operations directed by politics; and if these operations are often epic and decisive, they are very different from those which created the empires of former times.

For the fermentation and the kneading of the human paste, war still remains and sometimes assumes colossal amplitude and power; but peace has more notable victories; and organized revolution, united and methodical, is at work from end to end of the world. We have the great movement of the Western world, the awakening of Asia, the advent of world-wide affairs in this stage of the march which is like no other in the history of the Human Caravan.

The things of the ancient world soared up in one last flame, then died out. Christendom had a magnificent finish in the majesty of Charles V; but it was a finish. China's sleep from the epoch of the Mings to the time of the Republic (1668-1911) was beautiful in the pride of a refined civilization and the bosom of a vast empire; but it was a sleep. It was a gorgeous ending of the Mongols to disappear in a cloud of splendour at the time of Baber and Aureng-Zeb, the conquerors of India; but they did disappear.

India, China and Christendom were just so much prey from that time forward for the nations of the Western world. Observe how these nations, the impersonal States of the future in embryo, rise into prominence one after another when the Holy Roman Empire disappears.

In the sixteenth century we have Soliman's Turkey which in its national advance reached the very gates of Vienna, and now similar advances by other peoples have driven the Turks to Angora. The Spain of Philip II on whose dominions the sun never set lost those dominions to twenty nations eager to become States. In South America these small nations shared the empire of Spain amongst themselves. There was the Sweden of Gustavus Vasa; and in the France of Henry IV, the efforts and accomplishment of Charles VII and Louis XI reached a climax in the powerful unity which Richelieu, Louis XIV and Napoleon succeeded in perfecting and, perhaps, carried to excess.

By the seventeenth century there were Elizabeth's England, the Russia of Peter the Great and Frederick the First's Prussia. In the eighteenth century appeared on the stage the American Republic; and in the nineteenth a swarming of independent States in the New World and the Near East.

But the West did not crumble to pieces and return to the chaos of the fifth century. New unities appeared: Cavour's Italy, Bismarck's Germany. Turn by turn, the nations which marched at the head of the Caravan—the Portuguese, the Dutch, the Spaniards, the French, the English—developed into empires of a new type, neither of power, nor of government, but of prestige, influence, protection, authority, economic dominion: colonial empires in whose bosom the component peoples, whether they were barbarians or civilized races, gradually took to themselves the modern form and spirit and moved towards emancipation in the unity of the human race; rival empires which destroyed and supplanted one another and finished by dividing up the earth amongst them.

At the same time came the development of successive national hegemonies; soon they were transformed into Western hegemonies, then became world-wide hegemonies, and thus took a fresh step towards unity. These hegemonies were European and American in the sixteenth and seventeenth centuries; those of Spain and of France gave way slowly, beginning from 1750, to the hegemony of England. The Victorian era (1837–1901) gave to the English throughout the globe a preponderance which the Germans disputed with them in vain from 1870 to 1918. The United States of America since that date have begun to take the lead and have also imposed their prestige on all the States of the two Americas.

These nations—colonial empires, hegemonies, preponderating influences, all the particularisms which collide with and jostle one another—are interpenetrant and uniform in their manners and style of life. Currents carry them all towards unity, universal currents which overtake, submerge and bear on their waters the peoples of the Occidental world. Currents of commercial exchange, of scientific research, of political or financial interests; and more especially democratic and revolutionary currents. The democratic current is in no sense the democracy of the tribe, with its strongly marked hierarchy, such as existed in the cities of the ancient classical world, but an egalitarian democracy which is the political and social expression of theories worked out and elaborated for man in himself, with no regard paid to times, places, traditions, history; and the revolutionary current does not mean palace revolutions, revolutions originating in the harem or in coteries, the result of individual ambitions and intrigues, but revolutions national in character, international, humanitarian, passionate explosions of these same theories.

The Peasants' Revolt and the excesses of the Anabaptists in Germany were the first of these explosions. Cromwell and the English revolution of 1688 finally opened the gates. Locke, Montesquieu, Rousseau, Marx reduced the doctrine into formulas for the use of mankind; the parliamentary system, the sovereignty of the people, the sovereignty of the State and finally the sovereignty of the proletariat.

The natural tendencies of peoples and individuals are erected into rights; the principle of nationality—the right of every nation to constitute itself an independent State, as soon as it thinks well to do so; the right of the State to its natural frontiers; the right of nations to dispose of themselves; the rights of man; the rights of children; the right of the individual to live his own life, and the right of the mob to dictate its own laws. As if a tendency, even a natural tendency, or an interest, even a pressing interest, were enough to found a right and establish its measure. No more radical denial could be given of the very nature of a right, nor could the ideas which are essential to anarchic individualism be more faithfully translated into its language.

Carried on the waves of this formidable current the Orient at length awoke. Japan was the first to become modernized, and at a single stroke (1868). China followed its example and adopted democracy as a form of government. India has obtained a parliamentary constitution and like Egypt has made efforts to throw off the yoke of England. Turkey abolished the Caliphate in order to transform herself into a republic under a dictator. The whole world was seized upon, embraced in their clutches and broken into bits by the great "internationals"—

moderate socialism, thorough socialism (called also communism), mercantile capitalism, freemasonry or humanitarian Messianism.

Nor let us forget the League of Nations. In its origin it was a mere sketch of a great unity. England played perhaps too great a part in its deliberations and decrees, whilst the United States of America stood aloof from it. China, Japan, Italy and Germany and many other States either have or had seats in its councils. Laws were elaborated for world acceptance, and most of its members accepted them. The conception of a new State superior to all the others, to which all the others have surrendered some portion of their own sovereignty so that they form some kind of universal republic, can no longer be regarded as outside the real order.

If Christendom no longer exists as a political unity, nevertheless the Church still possesses as much importance in world affairs as it ever did. Pius IX, Leo XIII, Pius X, and Pius XI are in no way inferior to the greatest popes of the Middle Ages. Their power is somewhat different in its nature; they no longer dispose of thrones; but everywhere they are respected as amongst the greatest authorities of the world.

The reforms of the Council of Trent were confirmed at the Vatican (1870). Saint Thomas Aquinas became once more the undisputed teacher of the Catholic intellect and his influence is constantly becoming greater outside the Church. From the time of Columbus Catholic missions received a great and progressive impetus which Pius IX and Leo XIII have increased tenfold. The methods of the Apostles have returned and Benedict XV and Pius XI have fixed them as normal for the future by establishing everywhere, at the earliest possible moment, a native episcopate attached to the centre of Catholicism without any intermediary.

By now the leaders of the Caravan are to be found scattered in the four quarters of the globe: Washington, London, Paris, Moscow, Rome, Berlin, Nanking and Tokio: among them they ring the globe.

The whole earth has been exploited and occupied. Obviously it can feed many more human beings than the population of the globe to-day; but could humanity double its present numbers without exhausting its resources? Even if only the usual catastrophes afflict the world, would such an increase require many centuries more? At the same time and to an ever-increasing extent the trappings of civilization—costumes, artificial needs, new commercial methods, industry, agriculture, mechanical equipment, the methods of publicity, civil laws and political systems—everywhere have a tendency to become identical. Everything is amplified, accelerated in pace and made universal. Not without reason does the expectation of some new and monstrous development weigh upon the human spirit.

On the threshold of this future, after traversing with rapid steps the times that are no more, we feel as we face the mystery of the ages something of the thrill which Pascal experienced when he gazed upon the immensity of the heavens. "The eternal silence of these infinite spaces terrifies me." Yet neither this silence, nor this eternity, nor this infinity have anything real in them. The heavens sing and they pass; and though our hypothesis may push far back from us the boundaries of the space we contemplate, nevertheless, our minds, themselves limited, embrace and penetrate without difficulty beyond this multitude of worlds. They conceive a multitude of other worlds and times, of ages without end.

But what does all this amount to in face of the Spirit who has revealed Himself to us, and whom we have contemplated outside time and space; what are those measures which the creature attempts to apply to the Creator who Himself alone is the measure of Himself? He is Thought, infinite in its substance, complete in the least point of His work, and for Him His entire work is itself but a point.

Whilst I have been writing these words, three cockchafers attracted and dazzled by my little lamp have dashed against the glass and have fallen dazed upon the sill. Here is our analogy. With aeroplanes, dirigibles, wireless telephony and television, we have abolished time and space: and thereby have but transformed the vast world of former ages into a narrow cage against whose walls we beat at every instant. That is the result of the mirage of domination which hurls us fascinated towards the light of what we call progress which is too dazzling for our weak eyes. Of a truth if Providence is making use of us: "we are unprofitable servants."

FOURTH PART

THE LEADERS OF THE CARAVAN

P

CHAPTER I

THE EAST AND THE WEST

I

THE PROBLEM OF GOD IN HISTORY

WHEN the Caravan started on its march it was small in an immense world: a family in the midst of a solitude; and for thousands of years, at the pace of man who was compelled to get a living forcibly from the hostile earth, the Caravan made its way never emerging from its desert, always in the middle of it, since men never saw the end of the desert beyond their horizon.

Now the desert no longer exists. The Caravan has filled it with its own multitude of beings swarming in a world which has shrunk to smallness: in a few paces at modern speed the tour of the world is made, and from end to end of the world men speak to one another without raising their voices.

We have followed the stages of the journey, but is the end any nearer? Unity, perhaps; Domination, undoubtedly; Joy? . . . Now is the moment to apply our touchstone.

These prodigious changes, this magnificent development, imply a certain progress; but progress in the full sense of the word, absolute progress, as we have defined it, what of that? If it is to be found, is it a constant, if not everywhere at least in some part of the world? If it is a constant, does it date from the very beginning of the journey? It reveals God; but that revelation comes whilst the Caravan is on the move; and everything in the Caravan passes and then dies. God lives. He lives beyond time—in the present, without beginning or end of His being. If the Caravan is on the march towards God, how could this eternal *Living Being* be absent from its origins? If He is the Principle and the End, how is it possible for Him not to be its guide and leader?

We can of course think of God as the creator of everything who yet mingles with nothing, isolated by His transcendence. But that is to misconceive Him; and indeed men misconceive Him all too easily. The "God of the wise and learned" is too often merely an abstraction, a kind of algebraical symbol, an idea which is scarcely of greater value than an idol or a fetish of painted wood. In truth it is quite impossible that He Who Is should not penetrate and dominate all things with His life. It is the true expression of His essence that He should diffuse Himself, in order to give Himself and to draw everything after Him. Henceforth we must find His traces everywhere mingled in the passage of the Caravan—yet deeper, more visible amongst those who are at the head, among the leaders. Whoever claims to be a god, promises us divinity, or claims it for himself, must show us this mark or sign of his transcendence—permanence in progress.

To be an agent of progress; to have been so from the beginning of history; to have remained constantly, ever since, such an agent of progress; to carry within oneself in the same way, not the human mark of death, but the divine mark of life without wear or decrease: these are the signs which cannot deceive.

Let Naram-Sin, Alexander, Caesar and Rome, the State, Humanity each in their turn declare: "I am God, the God of gods, the supreme God; there is no god but me"; the historian has no need to examine one after another the title of each to divinity; nor to sift the reasons alleged for recognizing as the interpreters of God the College of the Brahmins, Zoroaster, Lao-Tseu, Gautama, Apollonius of Tyana, Plotinus, Mahomet, Luther, Kardec, Rudolf Steiner or Annie Besant.

Of necessity divinity is unique and universal in the multitude of its manifestations: where divinity is in operation there will be this double mark of uniqueness and universality. If then there is discovered amongst all the facts of history one unique and universal fact, marked also with the sign of transcendence —permanence in progress—that fact is assuredly divine. Nor should it be difficult to discover. If among all the systems claiming to be of God there is one whose claim is well founded, it must be able to justify our faith and show that all things which do not contradict it strengthen it, whilst all others fall to pieces.

II

THE CONTRAST BETWEEN THE EAST AND THE WEST IS A UNIQUE FACT IN UNIVERSAL HISTORY

History does not develop in the same way in every region of the globe. There is one contrast almost violent. What commonplace is more hackneyed than to put them in opposition one to the other? "Oh, East is East and West is West, and never the twain shall meet."

Yet the terms East and West are very inexact. It would be rather summary to divide the earth and its inhabitants into halves by the meridian of Damascus, to show us on either side of that line people who about the time of the flood turned their backs on one another and moved off, some towards the rising sun and others towards the setting sun, until they met again in the sixteenth century of our era on the plateaux of Mexico and Peru.

Without mentioning those who make their way from north to south and those from south to north, there is Africa which, in its character, is less occidental than Asia though it is situated right in the West. Savages, you will say—— Not everywhere in Africa; and why should we exclaim in scorn at savages? The finest civilizations, colossi with heads of gold, have their feet of this same clay, or, to change the metaphor, plunge their roots down into this same earth of savagery just as the forest roots plunge down into the decomposition of grasses, creepers, vines, brushwood, dead wood and fallen leaves while the tree itself rises upwards in its beauty.

The savage takes his place in the Caravan. He is a straggler if you wish; yet he follows the Caravan. He plays his part in universal history. You distort it if you exclude him from it.

But, you say, there are savages everywhere, to-day as in the past; and everywhere they are like one another. Exactly. If this contrast has not always existed between the East and Europe or America; if it is not less perceptible between Africa and Europe than between Europe and the East; if it does not exist between the East and Africa, in spite of everything which distinguishes them, the reason lies in the fact that in its essence the contrasts do not result from primitive separations and divergent migrations. It had its origin and growth at an epoch not very far distant from us; for some 3,000 years or so, it has set, not one half of the globe in opposition against the other, but two fractions of mankind, the less and apparently more insignificant of which was at first lost to view in a corner of the Arabian deserts but has grown unceasingly for the last twenty centuries at the expense of the greater fraction, gaining ground around the Mediterranean Sea, then turning towards the north and finally penetrating the whole world.

The Western World owes its origin to this smaller fraction of humanity, which at the beginning was but a mere point in the immensity of the East. To-day continents, seas, islands, all have come within its power, all perhaps save China, Thibet and India; and even their absorption is going on apace. They are being Westernised.

How do these worlds differ from one another, the West which is in ceaseless growth and the East which wanes? To answer this question we must thrust beyond surface things —clothes, parliaments, machinery, academies and share-values on the stock exchange.

Travellers, historians, sociologists are almost in agreement with regard to the key-point in the contrast. The East, they say, bears the mark of Immobility: and that word is true. Not that it remains motionless: such movements as changes, progress, decadence it is not unacquainted with. Such movements are not foreign to the most uncouth of savages—Veddas, Papuans—to those of to-day as well as those of prehistoric periods, or to the people of the lowest classes—the fellaheen of Egypt and the pariahs of India—to-day no different from their predecessors of thirty or forty centuries ago. The East moves. At the first view it seems to move as the West. Here and there kingdoms, empires and civilizations rise, fall, succeed one another and pass through similar vicissitudes; but if the East has its agitations, its upheavals and its ruins, it tends constantly and with all its weight towards immobility.

This ocean of States and peoples is crystallizing in spite of the cyclones that rage over it. Its currents move in circles. Its novelties are already old when they come to life and its traditions are never rejuvenated. Up to these days of ours, where shall we find its modern times or its middle ages? The Orient is Antiquity itself, Antiquity which endures; it is contemporary with all men and in their several turns it swallows them up. Life in the East, whether swarming and exuberant in the cities or slackened and diminished in the scattered tribes, remains everywhere subject to the law of death which the East carries always in its own flanks. It is a life whose movement is constantly and perpetually in a circle.

III

PAGANISM AND ORIENTAL TRADITIONS

Of this circling immobility the East makes its glory. Wrongly shall we say? No, rather justly; but in the same way as a picture would get a glory from its lines and its shadows, if it were absolutely void of light and colour; black lines on a dark background. What would their value be and what would the background be? On the other hand how moving and grand is the picture of the East, as it really is, in the full light of day, vibrating with numberless tints and colours.

Everywhere there gleams, more or less developed, veiled, deadened, perverted, or atrophied, the primitive tradition, the tradition of truth, simple and brief yet profound, the key to the mystery, the sacred germ given to man that he may derive from it, according to the times and the standard of

culture, by his own genius but aided by God Himself, all
the verities whose knowledge is necessary to man for the
accomplishment of his destiny.

Amongst the savages or the barbarians of the two Americas,
of Africa, amongst the islands of Oceania and the far distant,
unexplored corners of Asia, primitive tradition is but a live
coal preserved under the ashes. They say: "I believe in God
the Father, all-powerful, who made heaven and earth. I wait
for the life to come"; but all that lies between in our creed
escapes them. With regard to the life to come, most of them
conceive it only as a vague continuation, reduced or darkened
by shadows of this present life; and that supreme God whom
they call "all-powerful Father" and "First" they also often
name "the Unknown, the Forgotten, the Lost God, he who
has been Replaced, He who obliterates, or hides himself."

Many of them say that he has departed, after being ill-
treated by their ancestors and that he has abandoned them
to their resultant wretchedness. It is in this way that the
gods according to some, but according to others, spirits have
usurped his place: spirits and formidable gods whom men
are compelled to appease or to constrain or to reduce to
powerlessness by means empirical and traditional.

Taboos, totems, magic, sorcery, amulets, unchanging rites
to achieve the effect desired without looking for the cause,
take possession of the soul and congeal it, ever preoccupied
with forms and formulas, in the immobility of fatalism and of
fear. Withdrawn from the action of its reasoning faculty—
between the inaccessible true God and the false gods which
thrust their dominion upon its lusts, its ignorance and its fears
by rendering them incapable of any remedy—the soul becomes
torpid and sinks down. Selfishness hardens it. Sadness dis-
courages and shackles its flight. Yet amidst these heavy
shadows and darkness the soul preserves some memory of the
light, some spark of the primitive brightness. Admirable
tenacity, poignant vibrations of its original nobility.

All these are our brothers: the blacks who tremble before
the sorcerer or dance their farandoles of sensuality to the

nerve-racking rhythm of the tom-tom till they are whirled to the point of madness in the damp hot night; the Aztecs who in a single day with their flint knives tore open thousands of human breasts to snatch the hearts out of them and to throw them, smoking and still beating, to the monster crowned with feathers, the "Terrible Humming Bird", Huitzilopochtli; the Egyptians who ended by consecrating their temples and their prayers to all kinds of animals; the Phœnicians who used to burn their children alive in the idol of Moloch; the Chinese who threw theirs into the water (or to dogs when they were daughters) if they saw that there was nothing to be made out of them, saying that neither their Ancestors nor Heaven had any interest in their lives; the Hindus who worship the cow, the elephant and the waters of the Ganges and piously decorate their foreheads with obscene marks, even if they have ceased, since the English ruled in India, to sacrifice to Kali "predestined children".

Amongst the Hindus as amongst the Chinese one finds, however, alongside these aberrations more and better things than false and fragmentary reminiscences of the initial tradition. China has buried this talent in a chiselled casket: to the Son of Heaven the worship of his father; to his subjects the worship of their ancestors and obedience to the Son of Heaven, whilst man waits to pass into the life of shadows. For them it is enough that they know and practise the rites, the discipline, to carry on their agriculture and conduct themselves with courtesy towards their fellows; that they honour the spirits of their ancestors and do nothing to offend other spirits nor to thwart the wishes of the civil servants.

India has entered upon and developed theories and speculations of a religious and philosophical nature; and all Asiatic peoples with the Chinese at their head—to say nothing of the pre-Columbian Americans or the Pythagorians, or the Gnostics of Alexandria or of Islam, or of certain philosophies, theosophies and "occult sciences" of our modern Western world—have received from India, or at least sought from her, something of her riches.

We should not be surprised to find in the confused accumulation of rituals, symbols, myths, legends, poems, dissertations and glosses which fill and surround its sacred books, so many pure verities, so many texts which could not possibly be attributed to Jewish or Christian inspiration, yet which, beneath the polytheism or pantheism of their literal meaning, admit of interpretations which are in harmony with Catholic theology and the Scriptures of Israel.

For the élite of India's sons, amongst those who are not excluded from her temples, the idols are mere symbols, figures on a blackboard which help the intelligence to consider and understand some of the multiple aspects of the one supreme being, the Being of beings—Brahma, Vishnu, Siva, Rama, Krishna and Jesus—the same in each one of these heroic incarnations and under the name of each god.[1]

Here and there on this background of what they call "the eternal religion of sacrifice" there is projected the shadow of the highest mystery.

Their sages speak of a Brahma who is not Brahma, but the Brahma without any fixed quality in his infinite transcendence, of whom it cannot be said, when considering him alone, that he acts, wishes, thinks, knows, knows himself, lives, or even exists in the manner of a person. How can it be possible for us to avoid thinking upon that which we call the divine nature?

The personality in whom and by whom this Brahma manifests himself to himself and to the beings he has created they call Ishwara. They add that his manifestation is triple: "Having the form of Brahma he creates; having a human body he protects: in the nature of Siva, he would destroy. Such are the three appearances or conditions of the Father-God."[2]

Confronted with the producer of beings, Ishwara-Brahma, how can we not think of the Creative Intelligence, of the "Father all-powerful who made heaven and earth and the

[1] Wallace even cites examples of this pantheistic syncretism amongst members of the common people.
[2] Hopkins, *Religions of India*, p. 412.

whole world, visible and invisible"? In face of the protector of beings, Ishwara-Vishnu, must we not think of the supreme knowledge, Wisdom, the Word, "the only begotten Son of the Father, before all ages God of God, Light of Light, true God of true God; begotten not made; consubstantial with the Father, by whom all things were made and who was made man"? And before the transformer and renovator of beings, Ishwara-Siva, must we not think upon the eternal Act, "Charity, Flame, Holy Spirit, Lord and fountain of life who proceedeth from the Father and the Son"?

Assuredly these speculations, this Hindu mystery, are merely shadows. We are ignorant of their origin. We may talk of primitive tradition, of special revelation, with greater truth perchance of Western influences more or less recent: all such statements and ideas remain without proof. Those who see this shadow none the less are on the verge of the divine abyss; and if they have failed to explore its depths, at least they have gathered along its edges magnificent flowers and refreshing fruit.

They know the power of faith, the wisdom of obedience, the fruitfulness of renunciation, of mortification and of sacrifice; the virtue of intellectual ascesis and of intuitive meditation. They aspire to what they term "the silent peace", the "pure state of peace which rises like an aura about the heart which is separated from all the joys of the senses". Samadhi, mahabava, moukti, nirvana, or whatever other name they give it, "there", they say, "is what the sages call salvation."

Shall we regard this as the mystic union, or only as the complete repose of thought in what thought has been able to seize of the eternal? "God lives in us and we in him," writes the Flemish theologian Ruysbroek, called the Admirable. "It is a superior life . . . and as it exists in us by nature, there are some men who can perceive it independently of faith and every practice of virtue: these people devote themselves to natural contemplation above sensible images, in the simplicity of their essence. Then they believe that they are saints and blessed."[1] There, for them in any case, lies the decisive step and the dawn of "deliverance". The soul when it quits the body, freed for ever from that which is merely temporal, will be absorbed and lost in the One Supreme Being.

IV

WHAT IS LACKING IN THE EAST

Desires, impulses, doctrines of holiness—magnificent things but in the depths of what a jungle! For along with the initial tradition, and with the same vigour, confusions developed and spread—confounding spiritual and temporal, supernatural and natural, spirit and matter, eternity and duration in time, God and the world. These confusions produced their effects. Asia civilized contains all the aberrations to be found in all paganisms alike, staying their development. In India we find them as soon as we question, not the pagan animists who are still counted by millions, but even the sages, upon the destiny of man. They believe in "samsara", the transmigration of the soul through a multitude of lives and states, through beasts, plants, stones, men or gods—sometimes higher in the scale of being, sometimes lower—according to its works at the time of each of its deaths—the series continuing until the soul has merited its "deliverance".

This is an ingenious conception, logical and profound, which would require only a little revising and retouching to find a place alongside the conceptions of Dante as truthful symbols of the realities of existence beyond the tomb. Every sin bears within itself for the sinner a diminution of being; every sanctification means a growth which carries us nearer to the one plenitude, the final end: that is certain; but, such as it is, the "samsara" adulterates this truth with concepts

---

[1] *Le Miroir du Salut éternel*, ch. xvii (Works trans. from the Flemish by the Benedictines of Saint-Paul de Wisques. Vol. i, p. 124. Brussels and Paris, 1922). We leave, let it be understood, to the celebrated mystic the responsibility for his text which we have no space to discuss here. It is enough for us that contemplation even when purely natural can be absorbed in a single view of the eternal.

explicable only by a certain spiritual immaturity. The sages
of India are quick to smile when they see the people of the West
so prone to look upon God as a human personage enormously
developed: anthropomorphism.   They themselves are not
exempt from it; nor from a certain subtle materialism, the
reverse of the universal spiritualism which they regard as their
particular glory.

If they were less entangled in these confusions they would
have a better conception of the simplicity of spirits. They
would see this simplicity in its splendour, incompatible
with the modalities of matter—time, space, number and
quality—although subject as far as quality is concerned to
diverse changes. They would draw the conclusion that every
soul as it leaves the body, no matter how bound it may have
been by the joy of the senses and the things of this world, leaves
behind it that which is ephemeral and finds itself in the eternal.
They would have a better concept of eternity, seeing it as
simple with the simplicity of God, an instant in itself and
without end, division or measure, in which there are neither
centuries nor ages and which is distorted, if in order to picture
it we multiply the minutes of this world to infinity.

They would then know that, once in the eternal, the
destiny of every spirit is fixed.

The spirit does not begin its career afresh, for what second
moment is there?   In that you have the testing of the angels:
a single act. There also lies the test for men: a single life.
When life is at an end, our choice has been made; or rather
it is made for eternity, like that of the angels, by a single
eternal act. In this manner our existence on this earth is for
ever summed up. This single act not only truly expresses the
soul's desire, but by the judgment of God assures that the soul
has that desire. If such an act separates us from the final
goal of existence, it results in eternal woe. If, however, the
separation does not imply so fearful a result, but only our
falling away from purity in striving to achieve the purest
End, then the suffering or punishment will be transitory.
The End or Goal we are striving for takes possession of us and

purifies us. If there is nothing within us in opposition to the divine union which this act makes perfect for those alone who in the City of God are perfect, we enter immediately and for eternity into perfect and complete joy.

There is certainly grandeur in the idea of "samsara". The world, a unity with a thousand forms developed illimitably, which has been turning round and round for ever and ever in the abysses of space and time; spirits, souls and gods carried away into this whirlwind, from existence to existence, in the desire, the expectation and the pursuit of "deliverance" which draws nigh only to flee away: yes, that is a great and tragic picture; but in the fashion of humanity, limited and comic.

If all souls inevitably attain deliverance, when do they undergo the necessary testing of their liberty? "Do what you like", for all roads lead to Rome and every series of new lives to consummation in unity. God is merely "King Log": jump upon him, frogs! That is consoling for those who do not find things too bad in this "vale of tears". The perspective of varied experiences may even tempt their dilettantism and incline them to act in such a way that "deliverance" may not come too soon. For those who are wretched and who have in view scarcely anything but a long series of miserable existences, the prospect is a cruel mockery.

If "deliverance", on the contrary, though it be the one goal of all souls, must remain for ever inaccessible for a certain number amongst them, will there then be in the universe always something unachieved? Whether this universe is God, as certain texts declare, or whether God is the universe without it being God, as certain commentaries explain, in either event God is a failure. At the very least, His work is a misfire; and what shall we say of His omnipotence, if its only result is to hurl the world towards an end that it misses? One can imagine the sigh of scepticism breathed forth from the hymn of the Rig-Veda on the creation which is no creation: "And He, the Supreme Being, is the witness of all; but at the moment when we say: he knows, it is possible that he does not know."

This is a very human miscarriage of conceptions which flatter themselves that they are superhuman and make every effort to that end. Everything sinks into a pessimism which despairs of God, or an optimism which makes mock of Him. Discouragement or presumption, there is no middle course for souls if they live according to this doctrine. For some there is joy with sadness at the end, for others, as with savages, the "sadness that brings death"; and always the same God, that God who leaves the world and flees away; for whom substitutes must be found because only the initiated élite amongst men can attain to Him.

And what is the function of this élite? They meditate and contemplate. They withdraw themselves from the illusion of the cosmos to scrutinize the universal being. A prolonged, meticulously planned ascesis controlled by a remarkably acute observation, puts at the service of the soul for this work all the ways in which the body affects the soul and the states and acts of the soul affect the intelligence and thought. The sages who compose the élite have therefore some reason for claiming that Descartes, Leibniz, Spinosa, Malebranche, Kant, Bergson, the re-inventors of old things, have nothing to teach them.

"The philosophy of India," they say, "begins where the philosophy of the West ends." The Church of Rome can say the same thing for its philosophy; only their intuitive speculation is purely intellectual, purely human and untested. For them "salvation does not come to men through justice, it comes through knowledge",[1] as if union with God necessarily followed knowledge whilst in fact a thousand examples, beginning with Lucifer and Adam, cry out that "misfortune comes upon that knowledge which does not turn to love."

The pride of the spirit is there on the watch. What a prey for it is the sage, busy upon delivering himself by his own powers and his own deserts. And if this prey escapes him, if the sage does not believe that he attains a godhead himself, but allows himself to be absorbed by the Divine Being who

[1] Lyall, *Studies*. French trans., Paris, 1908. Vol. ii, p. 137.

is the foundation of his being, how (without even wishing it or even perceiving it perhaps) could his soul avoid being seized upon and devoured by pantheism, since it looks upon itself as an emanation and not a creation of God? "Thou art that. I am thou. We are God."

The "guru", the spiritual master, is on the watch and receives the blind obedience of his disciples. But "who shall watch over him who watches"?—Tradition, the Scripture. And who takes care of tradition and the Scriptures, if it is not some college of the sages? It looks like a vicious circle. By no means, they retort! The doctors of orthodoxy derive nothing from their own resources. They simply transmit without alteration. Prepared by an heredity which has endured for thousands of years and trained from their early years for what is demanded of it, their memory preserves intact what has been entrusted to it both of the letter and of the spirit. How can anyone be sure of this? I know the wonders of the "oral style", but, in this matter, lapses of memory are less to be feared than the weakness of the intelligence and the will. There is absolutely no initiation which results in infallibility. There is absolutely no initiation which can prevent pride, temporal or spiritual, vanity, self-interest, naïvety, zeal, from seizing upon and teaching falsehood as truth, novelty as the "substantial marrow" of the texts and traditional teachings.

In point of fact the traditions of the Hindus and their Scriptures have not merely been developed by transmission. They have absorbed a mass of heterogenous even contradictory elements, which they have assimilated as well as they can by the great efforts of commentaries, symbolic interpretations, hazardous speculations, subtleties, contradictions and distortions, even on essential points.

It is possible that the multiplicity of doctrinal schools corresponds to a convergent division of intellectual labour, such as those collections of temples which make but one temple at Ellora, Madura, Trichinoply and elsewhere; but it is a unity of chaos on which they congratulate themselves.

In God, it is said, all opposition is resolved, all contradiction disappears just as the two parallel sides of the road meet on the horizon; just as the sun and the planets, if we travelled away from them into infinity, would be in our eyes no more than what they are, an atom. But thus to argue is anthropomorphism. God does not look from afar, and no horizon limits His view. He is there, still much nearer than we are to the basis of everything; and His mind perceives more not fewer of the contradictions, the oppositions, the distinctions, and the real distances which our minds perceive and measure.

They accuse us of taking some and rejecting others of the books which bring to us the teachings of Jesus Christ and of Jehovah; whereas they keep everything that comes to them on Krishna, Rama, Siva, Vishnu, Brahma and Indra and all other forms of God, for nothing which gives any light upon such a subject must be lost. But surely with regard to traditions, Scriptures, mysteries, asceses, intuitions, philosophies, revelations, or works miraculous or divine, there must be some criticism to separate true from false. For them there is no use in such criticism, since it is not a question of excluding some, nor of safeguarding others, but of reducing all to a unity. There are a hundred ways, according to times and places, of conceiving the Universal Being, the Supreme One and His manifestations, eternal religion, God, the gods, spirit, matter, mortification, detachment, ecstasy, the cosmic illusion and deliverance—this because souls are different and the degree of their development different and they hold diverse points of view. They see no point in your anathemas. The centuries of their past lives weigh down upon some souls and push them along their road: it is enough to show them a better road, if they feel a desire for it and are capable of walking in it, which are signs indeed that the hour has come.

In this manner a free road is opened for the Spirit which "bloweth where it listeth"; but also, be it noted, for its Calumniator who apes it, as well as for all human aberrations, for all the trickeries and confusions of paganism, civilized as well as savage. It is perhaps proper to observe upon this statement that, if India is the country of religious instincts and metaphysical speculations, it is equally the country of exuberant imaginings and false miracles.

At the very best, we must see that in India pure truth remains an object of luxury, the lot of a few privileged people, the reward of heroic ascetics and of virtuosos in contemplation. There is reserved for such privileged persons, not only that which makes the whole man, but also a life worthy to be lived by him, the unique necessity, the ultimate end, salvation, the rapture of love, deliverance; for the others who are not so privileged, enigmas, images, figures, myths, legends, symbols and distant hopes in the mists of what may be. "*Samadhi, nirvana*," say the disinherited, "*it is not for us. Do you see a dwarf weeping for the moon ? We shall be happy if we arrive there after innumerable existences.*" Until they succeed in reaching down the star, they will put up with something else instead. They fall back upon the gods and the world and they take their enjoyment in them.[1]

"*The middle class adores the great gods of the Hindu pantheon as signs of omnipresent divinity. The superior minds in the holy castes and the students of orthodox Hinduism are absorbed in the discussion of the same problems, the same difficulties, the same metaphysical solutions which were discussed at large in Antioch, Ephesus and Alexandria sixteen centuries ago.*"[2] In other words, Hinduism is where Western Paganism was at the time of Julian the Apostate. For the inferior castes what was left? Idols, superstitions and magic. Even the idols are refused to the people without caste, strangers and pariahs, excluded from the ceremonies and the temples. Let such creatures replace as best they can the Unknowable and the Inaccessible, if they feel the need to do so. Later on, when they have been through innumerable deaths and rebirths, it is possible that they will succeed in finding their way upwards from ignorant superstition to idolatry, from idolatry to symbolism, from symbolism to the initiative mysteries, from ignorance to knowledge. The exceptions—they are extremely rare—prove the rule.

[1] Wallace, op. cit., p. 180. [2] Lyall, op. cit., 2. 128.

Here lies the inhuman blemish: the "religion for the people; a goad and a bunch of carrots hung in front of the donkey's nose". The privileged caste believe in knowledge and as the result of their faith "*they have known God, but they have not glorified Him as God, and they have vanished away into their own thoughts*". They have made of Him the God of philosophers and savants, of the initiated, a light hid behind a bushel and for human reason darkness.

"*As for us, we have believed in charity.*" For us as for them "*to know the only true God is the whole of eternal life*"; but we know that God is love, inaccessible and unknowable assuredly in the abyss of His being, known however and easy of access to all, "*A God who draws nigh*" and bends down, "before whom there is neither Jew nor Greek, nor slave, nor free", "*nor Brahmin nor pariah*", nor man, nor woman, because "*all are one in Christ*".

To the rule of paganism (and of the Reformation): "Do what seems good to you," we add a word, just one word— Augustine's word, "Ama et fac quod vis", "*Love and do what seems good to you*". For as Jesus said: "*If anyone love me, he will keep my word. And my Father will love him: and we will come to him and will make our abode with him.*"[1] Then he shall possess, according to his proper measure, the fullness of knowledge and love. He shall understand, without running into the dangers and perils of pantheism, that every time he cares for or neglects the least of his brothers, he cares for or neglects God Himself. He shall learn by his own experience that good works, when they are done in humility and inspired by love, neither interrupt nor disturb divine contemplation. He shall see with regard to the most profound truths that God, far from desiring that only the initiated should be entrusted with them, "*hides them from the wise and learned and reveals them to the simple*". Not only in the greatest miracles—"*the blind see, the deaf hear, the dead are raised*"—but also in this consist the work and the joy of God, that "*the gospel is preached to the poor*".

But that is the revolutionary poison? On the contrary. It is

[1] John xiv. 23.

not a question of destroying, but of perfecting, straightening out what is twisted, making smooth rough ways, putting love into knowledge and kindness, humility and mutual service into the legitimate requirements of the social order.

V

THE POWERLESSNESS OF THE EAST TO DEFEND ITSELF AGAINST PAGAN CONFUSIONS

India, it is true, is not the whole of the Orient, nor do the Brahmins and the castes constitute the whole of India.

Buddha excludes nobody. He submerges himself and the whole body of his disciples in universal sympathy. Now the Buddha, under diverse forms and names, and either alone or in company with some other, is the leader and the head of 200,000,000 souls in Thibet, China, Japan, Burmah, Indo-China and Malaya. And even in India which is his fatherland he is not altogether lost to view.

Krishna excludes nobody. He offers salvation to whosoever desires it. He describes himself as "*The Way, Immortality, the Source of all things, the True One, the Lord, universal sovereign, incarnate in a human body, the seat of the Supreme*". He loves us. "*He delivers from sin.*" He is "the offering and sacrifice of eternal religion". A stranger come from elsewhere, now, he has acquired by conquest a right to citizenship in Brahminism. The worshippers of Vishnu adore him.

The Tao excludes nobody, though it has its mysteries and its initiations. Lao-Tseu derived it, however, from the sacred books of India for the use of his own country. It still counts a multitude of followers.

Confucius excludes nobody. All are welcome to the veritable heritage which he preserves, defends and transmits. The Son of Heaven is the father of all his people, and the poorest of beggars, despite his poverty, still has his ancestors whom he can honour. By suppressing the Son of Heaven Suenn-Wenn does not reserve, as far as I know, to a caste of initiated the enlightenments of the "triple demism". Now Confucius and Suenn-Wenn between them are the whole of China, the China of long ago, of yesterday and to-day.

The Shintoism which obtains in Japan excludes no one, at least in the bosom of the nation which it deifies in its heroes.

Islam refuses entrance to none. Far from excluding them, it forces them to enter. The majority of its faithful expressed their belief under the shadow of the sword and with no better evidence. The Koran exalts mercy. Within the faith it teaches fraternity. It prescribes alms, hospitality and mutual aid. Now Islam represents the fifth part of India and almost the whole of Malaya, one-fourth of China, the whole of western Asia and the half of Africa.

The Deism of the Turkish and Mongolian hordes excluded no one. For thousands of years the whole of the north belonged to them from the Ukraine to Manchuria.

The list could be lengthened indefinitely—thereby illustrating de Musset's mocking remark: "The god Michapous is a good little god." Yet the items on the list are no more than the links of one chain the two ends of which we drew together just now, when we were discussing one after the other the most savage and the most civilized forms of paganism. The links differ. This is of more value than that, according as you attach more importance to form or to grandeur, to the nature of the metal of which the link is made, or to its solidity. They are none the less part of the same chain. Certain links have reflections of the West: such as Amida, Krishna, the religion of Thibet and, above all others, Islam; they are sparkling reflexions sometimes, but nevertheless reflexions.

The light thus reflected by them seems indeed to come from outside: Jewish importations perhaps or memories of the first Christian apostles, Nestorian aberrations, traces of such men as Montecorvino, or Francis Xavier, or Ricci; even more recent still, spontaneous borrowings from Europeans books. Islam owes to India, in part at least, its mysticism. But who knows what India owes to the Bible and the Gospels, even if only by the medium of Islam? Under these reflexions, however, mingled with the natural light which the Orient has never ceased to discover in itself, the links of the chain remain the links, and if the chain is thereby lengthened it is not always improved. The new link may be better in some respects than the chain it joins, yet something is lost in the soldering.

Fetishism, after all, excludes none, any more than the other religions. Superstition is universal. The principle and practice of non-exclusion proves nothing.

In India, even in our own times, there flourishes after fifty years of elaboration and propaganda a syncretism analogous to that of the old Gnosis. Vivekananda, its best apostle, would no doubt have subscribed to what I said in these pages just now as to charity. The adepts and followers of this system lay claim to renovating paganism by symbolism, by lowering the barriers of caste, uniting all men in mutual benevolence and mutual service, federating, from one end of the world to the other, all the religions which seek God within the depths of the soul by an interior life. In this way they associate the Baghavat-Gita with the Imitation of Jesus Christ, the Yoga with mysticism whether Musulman or Christian, the Vedanta with the Gospels; and from all these mingled together is compounded what is called the Universal Gospel.

Free Spirit, free thought, free symbols; each one chooses the masters who are pleasing to himself, selecting and rejecting according to personal feeling, personal inspiration and "religious experiences"; confusion is taken for the sign and the means of unity. It is, of course, possible that, through their instrumentality, a few Orientals are making their way towards the light; but such enchanting illusions are made rather to lead astray both in East and West those souls who are tormented by the need for God yet find dogma a narrow thing and authority interfering and liable to abuse, since they have neither the power nor the will to comprehend their necessity. Moreover, amongst all the dangers of paganism is there a single one which is driven out by this syncretism? Does it not indeed aggravate some of the perils?

If the disciples of Brahma—those who are modernizers as well as the others—run the risk of falling into pantheism and nihilism or quietism, what shall we say of the disciples of Buddha? It is easy to see how great is this peril; the effusions of Buddhist sympathy have not in practice caused the foundation in the Far East of many hospitals, orphanages, or charitable institutions. It has saved millions of animals, both harmful and useful; but the unfortunate amongst mankind or the degraded do not really owe much to Buddhist professions of sympathy and benevolence.

Read the gospel of Gautama, extracted from the Buddhist canonical scriptures edited by Brewster under the advice of Rhys David, and you will understand why. I know few books more painful to read. Though the gospel is one of smiling tranquillity, neither God nor the Love of God is in it. This is indeed a lamentable absence, for, in spite of the sympathy and the universal detachment the book expresses, it leaves the field free to love of self. It is a gospel of dust and ashes.

Doctrine, ascesis, poetic and sentimental impulses, impressive rites, harmonious liturgies, the whole has in this way but little effect against egoism, superstition, and the confusions of the pagans. It sometimes happens that the light makes its way across the darkness and the shadows to simple souls and upright hearts; but "the shadows have not absorbed the light" and they remain darkness and shadows.

Less dangerous and more beneficent in divers respects, Krishna, Amida and Confucius yet leave an open door for all the aberrations of paganism. Is there more than the breadth of a hair between Shintoism and Atheism or worship of man? And in what respect does the reverence of the northern nomads for the Tengri rise above the things of this world? Ready to tolerate everything—even the truth, like Genghis Khan and Kubla—with an equal indifference, they remain in "*human animality which does not perceive that which comes from God and is pure spirit.*"

As for Islam, it leaves nothing to idols, but does it leave no foothold for superstition and magic and the practices and beliefs of fetishism? Being a political religion, propagated by force, it is far from avoiding the confusions of paganism; and the dogma of Islam that salvation is by faith alone in virtue of an inescapable predestination—like fetishist formalism, Buddhist pessimism, the traditionalism of the Confucian religion and the religious indifference of uncivilized hordes—comes back again to that revolving immobility which is the mark of the Orient.

VI

THE ORIGIN OF THE FACT THAT THE EAST MOVES ROUND AND ROUND WITHOUT ADVANCING—THE CIRCULAR IMMOBILITY OF THE EAST

And that is where this mark originates. Other origins are readily assigned to it: heredity, natural selection, climate, soil, language, ways of communication, different régimes of property, of work and of the family; different governments, diverse laws, needs and increases in the numbers of the people, industry, commerce, science, arts and many other things besides. If these explanations are closely examined—verbal and verbose as too often they are—it is evident that they are derived more or less directly from geographical considerations dominated generally by the idea at the back of men's minds that human races, diverse from their very roots, cannot come from the same stock.

But this explanation leaves out of account several facts of some importance.

In the sense of our present question, the two terms East and West, Occident and Orient, belong to history rather than geography. On the globe, the thing which they express is found everywhere and nowhere. Every man places it where his fancy dictates. As we have defined it, the Orient formerly extended over regions which in our days are completely Occidental in quality. The Occident has despoiled the Orient of a great part of its domain. But, during this time, the face of the earth has neither lost nor taken a wrinkle. There are scarcely any places where it has been either deforested or dried up.

The second fact for consideration is that man is essentially the same everywhere and always, beneath the variety of his features, of his colour, of his manners and morals, of his language and his dress. His physical needs, his instincts, his passions, are the same. He eats, drinks, sleeps, clothes himself, amuses himself, builds, cultivates the soil, manufactures and sells what he makes or acquires, makes discoveries, fights, multiplies, suffers and dies: at all times and in all places, these are his great affairs, all basically identical.

The third fact for consideration is that men of the same race bear, in the same countries, sometimes the marks of the Orient and sometimes the marks of the Occident.

And finally the fourth fact: outside religion, the Western world knows almost nothing which the Orient did not possess before the Occident began to know. India, China, Persia, Chaldaea and Egypt have been through the whole round of wisdom and folly and of human experiences. Among what Western races shall we find more intuitive genius, greater boldness and vigour of speculation, more creative and more penetrating imagination than amongst the people of India? More practical minds, more of reason and refinement than amongst the Chinese?

The Orient knew gunpowder, the mariner's compass, printing, newspapers, bank notes, mechanics, payment by salary, collectivism, America, smoking, drinking-parties and modern philosophies long before the Occident received them or invented them. What does it matter that it did not make the same use or misuse of them? You do not solve the question, you simply push it back when you say "the race, the environment and the moment."

It is a hopeless undertaking to look in this world for the key of man's mystery outside man himself. Such an undertaking yields much interesting data, but no solution of the problem. Accidents do not account for the essence, on the contrary they are explained by it. The great facts of history are dependent on man, especially those which are unique. Man experiences them, but man has first caused them—not necessarily by his will, but by his existence, by his life, by his actions; and these actions may be conscious or not, but they always issue from that interior principle which makes him to be what he is and develops him according to the laws of his being. External things influence him as the banks influence the river which flows between them : they do not make him, he makes them; and his source is beyond, deep down beneath the glacier or the subterranean stratum.

If the Occident escapes the revolving immobility, the mark of the Orient and the fruit of the religions which fashion, move and inspire Oriental souls, we must then find the cause in Western religious beliefs. That cause must be that they first freed the Western mind and then kept it from pagan confusions and superstitions; and these beliefs must be, like the contrast which they engender, unique in history, as much by their own character as by the manner in which they have been established and developed.

VII

DOES THE WEST ESCAPE FROM THIS IMMOBILITY?

Is this the case? Does the Occident in fact escape from the revolving immobility and stagnation of the Orient? It is enough to listen to the voice of the West for a few moments as it gives utterance to its thoughts of life, to arrive at the observation that the ideas which dominate its life are in harmony one with another and are in the tones and rhythms of liberty. The West breaks through the circle of immobility and marches forward along the path of progress.

It speaks of destiny and perhaps believes in it. It extends a welcome to philosophies which make of the universe a machine, moving of its own power, and of man a system of cog-wheels moved by the universe. These are amongst its theories and pronouncements. But when the West passes from theory to action, it behaves as if all things, both within the soul of man and outside it, depended on his free will. If the West changes and wants to change, it is because it is looking out for and expecting to find new and better things. It directs its gaze and its affections more seldom and with less love towards the past and its ancestors than towards the child and the future which is the child's heritage.

Animated in its thoughts and doings by this desire for freedom and the spirit of liberty and conquest, the West has never at any time ceased, since its distant origins, from directing its steps upward towards universal dominion and preponderance. "Let God enlarge Japhet. Let him dwell in the tents of Shem and let Canaan be his slave." That is the horoscope of the West, its mission and its history.

Western man first occupied and civilized the plain which opens towards the west of Sennaar (Gen. xi. 2). In this direction men came up against the frontiers of that vast expanse, the ocean. They crossed the ocean to take possession of the high lands where Oriental humanity had established and brought to a high standard of prosperity the civilizations of Yucatan, of Mexico and of Peru.

They came to the border which lies along the southern extremity of the country of Sennaar: the desert. The Western peoples first rounded, then crossed the desert; and, like North and South America, the black continent of Africa to-day is in their possession.

Western man then reached the frontiers which lie to the east of Sennaar: there they found a region of deserts, oceans and glaciers which were so many closed doors, where entrance was forbidden by nations great in numbers and in the possession of power. The Occidentals broke through these doors. They climbed over the mountains. Westwards, northwards and towards the south they launched their ships across the immensity of the Pacific waters and of the southern ocean. They seized upon the vast extent of Russia and Siberia, India, Burmah, Indo-China, Malaya and Australasia.

Let those who suffer from narrow vision or short sight find fault with this conquering mobility and the spirit of war they say it manifests. Man indeed ceases to be man, in the measure that he ceases to be animated by this spirit of conquest. It is the spirit of our original vocation for development, for ruling the world and for unity. "Increase and multiply and replenish the earth and subdue it and have dominion over the fish of the sea and over the fowl of the air and over every living thing that moveth upon the earth."

If it is true that since the expulsion of man from the Garden of Eden there has been for us no peace without struggle; and that love which longs to serve mankind and sacrifice itself tends none the less invincibly and by its very essence towards unity and domination, how can we possibly find ourselves in opposition to the spirit of love and peace which comes to us from the Lord Jesus Christ? If it is a fact that the men who lived around the Mediterranean had a better and prompter understanding of Christ's message and a readier acceptance of it than other men, it is precisely because they had better preserved the spirit of liberty, of progress, of conquest and of that unity which is proper to human nature.

Warfare did not increase by the coming of the Christian spirit. There are, it is true, men of science and learning who depict the Christian era as one of blood and massacres. They declare that the Western spirit, the spirit of struggle and combat, is opposed to the spirit of inertia, of that passivity of indifference and fatalism which holds sway in the Oriental world, that it has made Universal History into a Universal Homicide and has for a thousand years laid waste the world by war in the name of the religion of peace.[1] But in hard fact, for blood and massacres the East is immeasurably worse. What devastations did the religion of peace bring to the non-Christian world during the 1,480 years of its reign from the age of Constantine to the French Revolution? In that period Christian lands were laid waste by the Germans, the Huns, the Arabs, the Mongols and the Turks. Nowhere do we see

[1] Kidd, *The Science of Power*.

the religion of peace responsible for the devastation of the lands of others.

Even the Crusaders in no way contributed to the falling back of Asia Minor, Syria and Africa, thanks to Islam, into that semi-barbarous condition in which the prophet of Islam had found—and on his deathbed left—Arabia.

If we add up the murders and massacres perpetrated amongst Christians or by Christians outside their own community for the last 1,500 years, we shall be far from the figures recorded in a few years by Shih-Hwang-Ti, the Attilas, the Genghis Khans and Timours, to say nothing of Napoleon I, of William II of Germany and of Lenin, who were as independent as any pagans of the authority of the Pope.

The wars waged in the Catholic middle ages, movements to administer justice, campaigns to enforce law and order or to suppress brigandage were carried on by small armies. When a force of 20,000 men was spoken of, already men began to talk of "the great army". Three thousand men seemed an imposing force. If at the roll-call after a battle 500 men were missing, there was lamentation with regard to the "heavy losses". Only on three occasions during that lengthy period were there massacres "in the name of the religion of peace". A misplaced and ill-conceived zeal which was reproved by the authority of religion inspired Charlemagne to carry out such a massacre in Saxony, Cortez in Mexico, and Pizarro in Peru. Moreover the zeal exhibited by these last two derived its flames much more from those passions which the religion of peace teaches us to conquer and subdue than from that religion itself. The *conquistadors* made no attempt to conceal it.

Thus the contrast between the Orient and the Occident is a reality. It is unique. The growing preponderance of the West is also unique; and also the manner in which it has strengthened, established and defended itself. In it we rediscover—transposed from the spiritual order to the temporal order and mingled with baser features—an image of the conquests of the Church under the Caesars. War plays its part, but in general this growth is carried out under the banner of peace. It is more like the growth of a tall tree than the violent construction of a great empire.

VIII

JUDAISM, THE GRECO-ROMAN CIVILIZATION AND CATHOLICISM, WHICH ARE UNIQUE FACTS IN THE HISTORY OF THE WEST, SEEM TO BE WITHDRAWN FROM THE OPERATION OF THE LAW OF PERPETUAL REBEGINNINGS

The image is unique and the model is unique. The Orient offers to us merely common facts which can be reduced to the grand fact of perpetual rebeginnings, governed by the law of oscillating and circular continuity, which is the universal law of death. But there are three things peculiar to the West which seem to escape from this natural law: the Catholic Church, the Graeco-Roman civilization, and Judaism.

At the beginning of the Occident were the Jews, a nation apart who could never be assimilated by any other race or nation, retaining their identity in spite of servitude in Egypt, transportation into Babylonia, subjection to the Ptolemies and the Seleucidian monarchs, the reduction of Judaea to the status of a Roman province, and the dispersion of Jewry to the four corners of the world. Whether they have been scattered in all directions or gathered together in a small heap, whether they live as free men or as slaves, whether they have been persecuted or held in favour, the Jews have never permitted themselves to be absorbed into another race.

These people with the "stiff necks" do not derive their power and their grandeur from their numbers, nor from their weapons, nor from their science, nor from their civilization, nor from diplomacy or riches, though they are indeed specially endowed with qualities which make them masters of commerce and money. They were a very little and numerically insignificant people on a small territory. Their two great princes, David

and Solomon, were potentates on a small scale: in the political
or military or financial order William of Orange or Leopold II
of Belgium would easily have surpassed them.

But in the historical order, Judaea surpasses the greatest of
empires. The history of the human race cannot be written
without attributing as much importance to the literature of
the Hebrews, their institutions, their doctrines, their morals,
as to the most humane and productive of cultures; and this
is brought about by a single motive. The Scriptures of the
Jews have become for the Occidental world the Book *par
excellence*. The Scriptures offer, without doubt, to every man
capable of thinking, an incomparable treasure of human
wisdom totally exempt from that alloy of worthless matter
which disfigures all other "sacred" books. But the Orient
had not the capacity to discover this treasure. Hidden away
in its own bosom for many centuries, its influence spread
without the help of the Orient, suddenly, quite alone and
unaided, over the coasts and the isles of the sea.

The civilization conquered in this way by the Bible has,
however, nothing Jewish about it. One single thing for the
whole of the West—whereas in the Oriental world there is a
complete lack of unity—this civilization was perfected and the
Jewish nation was scattered at the same time. Born from the
soil of Greece, transplanted to Latin earth, propagated by
the Romans in Mauretania, in Spain, in Gaul, in Britain and
in Germany and all along the course of the Danube, it eliminated in every direction the civilizations which had preceded
it amongst the barbarians. When this civilization had become
Christian it resisted the assaults of barbarism, absorbed within
itself its assailants, endured, grew great, and invaded the whole
world.

The Church which it preserved, maintained, and perfected
is, like this civilization and the Jewish race itself, unique in
history. Where else are we to find a kingdom which is not of
this world, and a society purely spiritual in its nature under
the form of a great power organized, independent of all temporal authority and sovereign in the moral order? Through

the Church it has come about that the "Testament" of the
Jews, completed by the "New Testament" of Jesus Christ,
has become the *Book* of the Occidental nations and civilization.

It is illuminated and at the same time it is transfigured. The
personality of Jesus Christ shines across all its pages. It penetrates the whole Book. The dogma and the morality are of
Jesus Christ. That which the Church brings and preaches to
every creature—the "Gospel", happy message, good news—
is the message, the coming, the reign, the divinity of Jesus
Christ, our adoption by His Father, our participation in His
heritage. And much more than that; He is there Himself, the
rule of what one must believe and do, the living rule of life
for ever present in that Church which was founded by Him.

In the Church are tradition, interpretations of Scripture,
developments, symbols, the Scriptures and the Liturgies; an
infallible authority, the authority of God made Man, perpetuated in this world in the mystical body of Christ and in the
Pope, the visible head of this body, guards and guarantees them
all. None such exists in the Oriental world; they have a
tradition whose origin is lost in the night of time; initiates who
guard it; but to guard these initiates and to guarantee the
tradition there is in the East no authority and no Christ. That
is the reason why—in spite of the possession of traditions—
variations, contradictions and novelties multiply in abundance,
are close neighbours, dwell together and are amalgamated
in Oriental countries, nations and souls.

In the Western world there are to be seen many other
Christian Churches besides the Church of Rome; but all of
them are branches torn away from the trunk at certain dates
known to history. None of them goes back in a direct line to
Christ himself. I do not here and now dispute their titles; but
for history the Church of Christ is the Church of Rome. That
is indisputable. Those who dissent from Rome, when they
treat Rome as a usurper or as a faithless trustee of the faith,
give their testimony that the Church of Rome occupies that
position and has in fact received the trust.

The only Church is Rome and none other. The unique

qualities in the history of the West are not explained without
her, without her action on Graeco-Roman civilization, without the light that she shed on the Bible of Israel, without the
doctrinal and spiritual authority she exercises as a sovereign
power with the daily presence of Jesus Christ.

IX

IS THE CONTRAST BETWEEN THE EAST AND THE WEST IN COURSE
OF DISAPPEARANCE?

Jews, Greeks and Romans, the Church of Christ and of Rome,
such then are the guides and the leaders of the West, which
itself is the guide and the leader of the Caravan. Do they bear
on their brow the mark of God and the sign of transcendence?
Do they in truth display permanence in progress?

The last word is not uttered. What does the future reserve
for them? The outworks, the exterior things of Western
civilization are invading the whole world; but is the new
paganism, which is now invading that civilization, itself of an
essence which differs at all from the paganism of the ancient
and Oriental world? The East is being modernized, the West
being paganized—which is absorbing the other?

We have seen the consummation of the apostasy of the
Western nations. Those amongst them who have not denied
God and His Christ have forged christs for themselves, national
christs, whose divinity is reduced almost to nothing or to myth.
Men who are without Christ and men who are without God
have grown in numbers. They give their adoration to
humanity, the state, the proletarian class, progress, money,
pleasure. For them metaphysics have no existence and
theology is but folly. They believe in science—and in mas-
cots. Their enthusiasm is divided between the heroes of sport
and the cinema and the men whom a cult entirely earthly and
secular has consecrated as national glories.

What of the dead? There is no longer any question of

R

helping them, of praying for them, or, if they have lived
saintly lives, of paying homage to their heroic virtues and
soliciting their aid. They are venerated. Monuments are
erected to them, and if such monuments have not yet become
altars, they are already more than tombs. There are now
pantheons for such men: "To the memory of great men
erected by a grateful fatherland"—and what great men they
are! They are borne in pomp to the pantheon; but these
funeral processions no longer have about them even such
remnants of spirituality as are in pagan ceremonies.

The Great War of the Nations has given a fresh impulse to
this Western Shintoism. On the 14th July, 1919, I marched
in Paris before that catafalque, non-religious from the top to
the bottom, by which it was alleged that the heroes of France
were honoured and their heroism commemorated. The flame
periodically relit in Paris and elsewhere on the completely
secular tomb of the "Unknown Soldier"; the minutes of
silence which take religion even out of the prayers of those
who believe and laicize them in honour of those who died in
the War; the secular processions to secular monuments erected
in memory of those who died, or to commemorate victory—are
all these things characteristic of the West, or rather of Japan,
China, Babylon, or, in one word, the Orient?

I love my country. The War was not necessary to awaken,
nor has peace put to sleep, my love of her. But I have never
taken part in these liturgies without feeling myself enveloped
in paganism and wounded to the quick in my faith.

Doubtless there is no need to attach too much importance
to such signs. They none the less show the drama that is
being played. Suppose that this great fact, unique and of
capital importance—the contrast which exists between the
Oriental and the Occidental worlds—be removed from history.
What will be the result? The effect may be expressed as an
alternative. Either what has happened in the West will also
have happened in the rest of the world: Christ will have conquered everything; or else the East will have conquered and
Oriental uniformity spread its illusory variety over the whole

of the globe. The antiquity of the world will have been indefinitely prolonged—Jesus become merely a Buddha, a
Confucius, a Plato like the others. Men will hold that the
synagogue has given the world nothing new; nothing of a
divine nature has come into the world to transfigure the Graeco-
Roman civilization; the Church means nothing; and human
history is an illusion also—there are stories only. The race of
men will turn round and round, but immobilized as in the
Orient, in confusion and division without progress, subject to
perpetual rebeginnings.[1]

Now, in point of fact, the West, up to the present day, has
remained immune, not indeed from these accidents, but from
their deadly dangers to unity, order and the continuity of
human development. It has broken the circle. It is flowing
over the Eastern world. It is thrusting its preponderance upon
the increased multitude of humanity, a humanity which has
entered into possession of the universe, having the mastery over
beings and forces in the air and under the water, in the soil and
in the depths of the earth. The Occident is bringing the world
back to its primitive unity.

Under the power of the West the Human Caravan lives and
marches on, by stages, towards the end of its journey. There
is such a thing as universal history, but it is not merely the
juxtaposition of all other histories; it is rather the fusion of
them into a single whole. We should be able already to make
a definite statement with regard to the direction that universal
history is taking, if the line of its development had not a constant tendency to move round and round in a hoop like a snake
biting its own tail. In fact the Caravan moves in a circle which
is becoming visibly narrower and narrower every day since the
Jerusalem stage was passed.

The play of the laws of life has brought into predominance
in the Oriental world the law of death which every life carries
within itself because it is bound up in matter; the Western
world has so far not been subject to this predominance and it
looks as though it may never be. On this point the grand

[1] See the second part of the note placed at the end of the volume.

fact—if the contrast of East and West sheds no clear light—is that history has a direction we half-see but without full certainty. And the direction we think we see remains indistinct. So far no clear perception of the sign of transcendence has been vouchsafed to us. However, if the sign is anywhere to be found, it can no longer be doubted that it will be discovered in the West. In this direction there is something, an obstacle which manifests itself by facts which are unique and arrest the law of death. Only by analyzing these facts can we discover the something which is manifested in them. One thing at least is certain: if this obstacle to the law of death is invincible, it will bear the sign that we are looking for.

There lies the whole question and the anguish of the present moment, for to-day the grand fact, the contrast between East and West, is growing feebler. The Western world has been orientalized from within, the East has been occidentalized on the surface. Does this mean that henceforth they will be confounded and fused one with another, carried away in the whirlwind of things—*yinn* and *yang*—for ever and ever?

Jews, Greeks, Romans, the Roman Church, civilizers of the West, the last comers amongst the leaders of the Human Caravan, by them, in them, something has resisted the Law of death. If this something must at last submit to that dread law; if "The Twilight of the White Races"[1] is a prelude to a night that Christ and His Church shall never illuminate; if "The Decline of the West"[2] is the fatal decline in which there will be no return of that "light of the world", all hope for humanity has gone. The dream and the drama have both miscarried. The history never has had, never will have, and never can have any direction. There is nothing for man beyond and above man and the world. Man is then a meaningless being, a caprice of purblind nature, a laughing-stock of chance, a mere abortion cast for a few moments of agitation without any object or purpose upon the earth; for him there is only misery and

---

[1] Title and résumé of a work by M. Maurice Muret.
[2] Title and fundamental thesis of a work by Oswald Spengler.

darkness, chaos, the shadow of death and the abode of everlasting horror.

Or is it not rather that the West is dividing between the two
civilizations, one which for so long a time has made of her sons
the true leaders of the Caravan—the other which threatens to
cast them back, and the Human Caravan with them, into the
whirlpool of endless beginnings? The direction of human
history is revealed. The drama comes to a crisis and we now
catch a glimpse of the dénouement. Dreams become reality.
The road which is followed, the journey, the stages, the Caravan
now show themselves to be real and splendid. The twilight is
the harbinger of dawn; the decline is only in the sapless
branches soon to be replaced by shoots more vigorous.

In the face of the City of this World, of the Orient and the
Occident, of paganism, materialism and Islamism, the Church
of Rome, impoverished by Western apostasy but enriched by
her apostolate amongst all the nations of the earth, remains
erect to lead the human race towards new growth, towards
domination, unity and true happiness. "The words of glory
have been uttered over you, City of God."

CHAPTER II

THE JEWS

I

JUDAISM IS UNIQUE, EXCLUSIVE AND UNIVERSAL

WE have looked at them as they pass and we have observed how different they are from other peoples. Let us take a closer look at them.

They were constituted of twelve tribes formerly nomadic. This taste for a wandering life is in their blood. Canaan where they were born did not hold them. Goshen in Egypt, the land where they increased in numbers, became hateful to them, as soon as Egypt had driven out the Hyksos, the Shepherd Kings, Bedouins like the Children of Israel. They did not submit to the works they were set to perform in the fields and the towns. The civilized governments of the Thothmes, of the Amenophis and the Rameses soon made their rule intolerable to the Israelites. They had to have their liberty.

Their God, "He Who Is", laid claim amongst them to this title before every other: that He had "taken them out of the house of bondage". He had it written at the head of the law which He dictated for them. He knew their nature. Later on they would demand kings and would entertain the dream of subduing all the nations of their world under their empire; imitation, jealousy, national pride, a just sentiment of their superior gifts as a race; but always their restless souls inevitably broke away from order and rule. A sense of nationality was theirs. It was at the basis of the tribe and no other people has ever possessed it to the same extent as they; but they lacked the political sense.

They put all their leaders one after another in difficult positions. What a world of trouble they caused them! To what extremities did they reduce them sooner or later! Jehovah disputed the command of their souls with the Golden Calf, with Baal, with Moloch and all the other false gods of their neighbours. Their judges from Othniel, the son of Kenaz, to Samuel, son of Elkanah, had troubles and to spare from them. Their kings? Scarcely 150 years after the coronation of Saul, the kingdom was broken into two, Israel and Judah. Samaritans and Jews were at daggers drawn. Nothing could ever reconcile them again, neither the disasters of Osee and Sedecias, nor the sorrows of exile, nor the joy of seeing Solomon's temple and the city of David rise again from its ruin. Their prophets? They stoned those whom God sent to them.

The Romans came to the end of their dealings with them only by breaking them into pieces and throwing the débris to the four winds. And yet this very débris made itself felt powerfully. Whether their hosts were pagans or Christians, they were all driven to shut them up in ghettos, drive them out periodically and seize upon their goods.

Left to itself this little people would turn its back on progress, on universality, on permanence, and on everything which in the midst of other peoples could make for it a place apart. Is it, indeed, a people? Certainly its temperament and its origins predestine it to dissolution as a political entity; isolated clans, moving about from place to place, pillagers, hostile amongst themselves and towards their neighbours, eaten up by superstitions and ready at all times to "prostrate themselves before the whole army of heaven". It is in spite of themselves that they have escaped the dissolution which their character seems to make so certain.

With what amazing stubbornness they struggled against those who desired to help them escape it. Moses, the first to make the effort, felt that stubbornness, and so did Jesus, the last. But the struggles were vain. The metal is hard and resistant, but it is on the anvil; and the blacksmiths beat it with their hammers.

Do not look for any parallel to them elsewhere, nor to that astonishing sequence of prophets who followed one after another for 1,250 years, without any exterior bonds, without any common rule to unite them, to form them, to define their mission, to guide them and co-ordinate their successive and diverse actions which yet link them into one chain, complete them and harmonize them through that long period into a miraculous unity.

It might have been expected that they should belong to the same caste, receive the same training, lead the same kind of lives in the same country and prophesy under similar circumstances. But it was nothing of the kind. One of such leaders or prophets came out of the tribe of Levi, others from Judah and from Ephraim. They rose to prominence in the very centre of schism, as well as when the kingdom was faithful and loyal; in the midst of peace and prosperity, as in the midst of misfortunes and war, on the river Chobar and at Babylon as well as in Palestine; shepherds, kings, priests, labourers and warriors, savants, great lords, artisans, magians, hermits, philosophers and unlettered, to say nothing of a handful of famous women. These it was who, being possessed of God, imposed upon a rebellious people and forcibly and finally thrust into their heads and their hearts a desire for three things—a king, a law, and a faith—as unique as themselves in the antique world.

A king who is not of this world, but who chooses, crowns, directs, raises up and puts down, rejects and replaces as He thinks fit the kings of flesh and blood whom He charges to rule over His people according to the orders He issues from day to day. No one sees that king who is not of this world. He does not permit anybody to carve or draw His image. His throne above the Cherubim remains for ever empty. He is a spirit, the God, the Only God, "He Who Is", from whom everything receives its being, the Lord to whom the universe belongs and whom it obeys, who gives both the earth and power to whomsoever seems good to Him, even amongst the Gentiles. He insists, not only upon glory, respect, fear,

obedience and gratitude, but upon confidence and love. He
loves and He wishes to be loved. "Hear, O Israel—thou
shalt love the Lord thy God with thy whole heart and with
thy whole soul and with thy whole strength",[1] for that which
He has done for thee, He has done "because He loveth
thee".

Jehovah's love was strong and jealous; exclusive. He
allowed no division with other gods. This king was a king of
hearts. His authority was not satisfied with being an external
authority. He wanted to reign in the most intimate depths
where no other king had any access whatsoever. Order, peace,
riches, grandeur, numbers, power and well-being, all that
which the nations aspire to possess He meant that His people
should be laden with; and it was He, the All-Powerful, who
preserved the liberty of His people; on condition, however,
that they remained faithful to Him: "I have mercy up to a
thousand generations upon those who love me."

His titles—and that also is a unique quality—do not reside
in the idea that the world forms of Him. He puts forward,
in support of His demands, none of those things which express
the idea outside: symbols, myths, legends, popular fables with
regard to Him, the inventions of poets and the speculations of
philosophers or theologians. His worshippers do not adore
in Him the sun, life, joy, wine, or the force of procreation;
if men tremble before Him, nevertheless thunder and lightning, darkness and death, go for nothing. He lives far above
them. He created them. He is the God of all gods.

His first title to royalty is a statement of fact: "I am who
am," and all His other titles are facts too: the creation of the
world, the fall of man, the promise of redemption, the punishment of the Flood, Noah saved from the waters, the confusion
of tongues at Babel, the dispersion of the nations, and amidst
this chaos of movements, discords, of slavery and errors, the
call of Israel and its wonderful deliverance: "It is I who brought
thee out of Egypt," I "the God of Abraham, of Isaac and
Jacob"; His divinity and royalty go side by side: these titles

[1] Deuteronomy vi. 5.

are historical, manifested and made good in reality, not there simply because the ideal requires them.

The Gentiles made a selection of their gods. If they did not find some of them satisfactory, they took others. If they came across some whom they thought good and redoubtable they added them to their previous choice. They attributed their prosperity and their reverses to all of these gods. They called them either the kings of their ancestors or the ancestors of their kings. They apotheosized their great men: Tammuz, Minos, Rama, Bacchus, Alexander. In this manner their religion and their history became intermingled; but against the grain of history and religion, as these are conceived by the Jews.

Jehovah allowed no choice. He chose first. He called and His servitor answered. He commanded and His servant obeyed the command, often against his own desires, sometimes doing violence to himself, almost always against what human reason and human passions, the temptations of example and the irresistible course of things, seemed to exact. He chose Israel for His people, and He Himself alone settled the terms of the alliance. Who then would dare to attribute to Him a posterity of the flesh, or associate with Him anyone, even amongst the greatest of men, David, Moses, Abraham? Such things could not for a moment be thought of. As for prosperity and reverses, Israel did not attribute them to Jehovah; it was rather Jehovah who announced them, defined the precise epoch when they would arrive and their duration, and stipulated the conditions under which they would come upon the Chosen People.

King of the Jews, but also King of the Gentiles, King of all the kings of the earth. That also is unique. Israel, the chosen people, preferred of all the world, the depository of the true tradition, the guardian of the promise and of the truths concerning the salvation of the world, the "Royal Priesthood" marked out for the primacy of the world, "the holy people" from whom is to be born the Redeemer of the World—Israel did not crush the Gentiles under the weight of its scorn. Amongst the Israelites the word "stranger" was not, as else-

where, synonymous with enemy and barbarian. The Israelites knew quite well that other people in Egypt, in Mesopotamia, in Crete, in Tyre and Sidon were more civilized, more
educated, richer and more powerful than themselves. Their
idols and superstitions, their manners and customs fascinated
them only too much. When the people of Israel did what was
good in the eyes of Jehovah, they held these aberrations in
horror; but they allowed those who had gone astray, they
invited them indeed, to come back to the straight road, and
they showed them the way.

"God is known in Judaea": for the pagans He is the God
of the Jews; for the Jews themselves He is the God of the whole
world. Their tradition does not come so much from their own
ancestors as from primitive humanity. The promise received
by the Jews opens up to humanity of the future the ways of
holiness. The truths entrusted to them as guardians are human
truths. The Redeemer who is the Son of David will also be
the Son of Man; and the liberator of Israel will deliver, will
redeem and will govern the whole of humanity.

One king, one law. The Decalogue is its source and its
résumé. Is it unique? There are very learned men who
deny it. But dare they summarize the code of Hammurabi
or any other lawgiver as Jesus and the Pharisees, the Scribes
and the Doctors of the Law summarized the Jewish law:
"*Thou shalt love thy God: this is the greatest and the first command-
ment. And the second is like unto it: thou shalt love thy neighbour as
thyself. To these two points are related all the law and the prophets*".
Let us admit that this law, however, is not unique in the world
of antiquity merely by being a law. There were others. But
it is unique at least by reason of three characteristics which
are to be observed in it at the first encounter and which we
quickly recognize as the radiation of its essence. It is a divine
law, a spiritual law and a preparatory law. Moses who
was its promulgator, the prophets who were its interpreters and defenders and Christ who confirmed it and gave
it its perfection, all united to declare it divine, spiritual and
preparatory.

When the Gentiles believed in the God of the Universe they adored Him above every other god as being the God of their nation, or of their race. The law which ruled the relations of the people, of the families and the individuals with the nation is merely a law of their tribe, of their city-state, or of their empire. Amongst the Gentiles the civil law embodies within its codes the law with regard to religion. In the case of the Jews the reverse is the fact: it is the law of religion which embodies in its tenets the civil law.

Israel is a Church. If indeed it takes the form of a State, it is necessity which constrains it to take that form. Unless it adopted a political organization, the States amongst which its sons would live would destroy the Church by compelling them to take part as citizens in the national cult. The three young men of the Book of Daniel who were thrown into the fiery furnace of Nebuchadnezzar had that experience, and Daniel himself who was thrown to the lions, and old Eleazar and the Seven Martyrs with their mother, scourged, mutilated and burned by the public executioners of Antiochus. Long after Jesus had uttered the liberating words: *"render unto Caesar the things that are Caesar's and to God the things that are God's"* the emperor Diocletian followed the example given by Antiochus; and Constantine had but a poor understanding, if he had any understanding at all, of the fact that his conversion did not make of him the bishop of bishops nor the legislator of the faith.

Amongst the Gentiles there was no Church: there was the State and no more. Religion was but one of its organs, under the same title as the treasury, the army, the law-courts and the other State departments.

The family is conceived as created for the sole purpose of extending and perpetuating the cult of its ancestors by prolonging and multiplying the numbers of the family: but this does not constitute it a Church. The father, even if he becomes a god, remains the father and is still a member of the family. He does not pass out of the framework of the family in any way, and it remains as it always was: a domestic society, temporal, flesh and blood, into which one enters independently of one's own will and taste.

When the family develops into a political society it does not thereby become either a voluntary or a spiritual society. Despite the statements of Fustel de Coulanges, the city of antiquity bears still less resemblance to a Church than does the family of antiquity; and the empire would not bear any greater resemblance if it did not deify itself by a daring political move, a move to which not the slightest efficacy could be attributed outside the sphere of politics. The net result of such a process was not to spiritualize the State, but merely to secularize religion.

What was seen on Sinai was just the opposite of this process. Elsewhere the father and the king became gods; on Sinai God became a king in human fashion, that He might one day be the Father of the Word made flesh. At His voice, Abraham, Isaac and Jacob prepared this marvel, Moses and the prophets with an incomparable energy advanced, maintained or restored the work; and during more than 600 years amongst the nation of the Jews, and the Jews alone, a real theocracy was carried forward. God reigned and governed, very often by the agency of His priests, often also by means of special messengers or envoys whom He chose for Himself outside the ranks of the sacerdotal tribe and whom He did not always make judges, kings or princes when He gave them the mission to prophesy. Israel is a State, but a State submerged in a Church; a spiritual State which recognizes as its own proselytes of all nations, languages and races who have at their own will and accord rallied to the law of Jehovah.

Hence it follows that this law is, above every other consideration, spiritual, like the king and the kingdom: a law of hearts, promulgated as an edict for the kingdom of hearts. It governs even the desires of the heart: *"thou shalt not covet"*. It is established in the very secret place of the soul: "Love is its fulness." There is no other principle in the law but that, and he who loves observes it in its fullness. It is beyond all doubt that the law fixes what is right; but it is a right which is not merely rooted in morality: it is enveloped and penetrated by it in such a way that it becomes inseparable from it. This law takes a hold upon the human conscience which is beyond the power of any other law. It actually reaches those sins which have done no harm to anybody but the thinker of them, which do not disturb public order and remain hidden in the most secret place of the mind. It is a moral law. It is even the *Moral Law*. No philosopher making a study of that famous law which, though unwritten, is yet inborn in man, has found any precept which the law of the Jews does not make obligatory and has not already brought to perfection.

From this we come to the fact that it is and proclaims itself to be a preparatory law. Just as the Mosaic code continues and completes the law of nature, in similar fashion it is itself to be continued and completed by a third law, perfect and universal as Jehovah Himself. Moses announced the coming of the Prophets. They, in their turn announced the coming of the Messiah, the Gospel, the New Jerusalem and the New Dispensation, the call to the Gentiles, the admission of the whole of humanity to salvation, to justice and to the greater kingdom made beautiful and sanctified by Jehovah.

What other nation has ever believed in such promises, or has made the like promises for itself, several centuries before the events happened ? There stands the Faith of Israel. This chrysalis in its cocoon is not unaware that it was the cater-pillar of yesterday. It was already a prodigy amongst nations when all other peoples, or almost all, were extravagantly embellishing the history of their past. There is a still greater prodigy: the Jewish people knew themselves to be a chrysalis; and they knew the butterfly that was to be. What shall we call that amongst prodigies?

Virgil puts into the mouth of the Jewish Sybil, disguised as the Sybil of Cumae, the words of a chant which announced the near approach and the felicity of a new cosmic cycle "when the stars shall return to the mansions they dwelt in during the golden age". Plato caught sight of "the mar-vellous loves that the truth when contemplated by the eyes of the body would bring to birth for wisdom". India awaits the tenth incarnation of the Supreme God at the end of the present age and a renewal of the Universe. These are vague hopes, dreams, utopias, expectations and confused wishes and there is nothing in them which is comparable to the clear, precise, detailed Promise, many times reiterated, which is the basis, the centre, the key-stone, the reason for their existence and everything else to the Jews.

Law, kingdom, religion, people, nothing has any existence amongst them except towards that Promise and its realization. It dates as far back as humanity itself. Abraham was not chosen, was not separated from the Chaldaeans, did not make his way towards Melchisedech the king of Salem, priest of the Most High, except by virtue of the Promise and to give birth to the nation in which the Promise was to be accomplished in this same corner of the earth.

The benediction, transmitted to Isaac and from him to Jacob, which they regarded as being their most precious heritage, had no other object than the Promise. It was by reason of the Promise that Moses led the Twelve Tribes out of Egypt and brought them into the desert and there organized them into a State.

And what was Joshua's mission? It was to conquer the Promised Land. It was to carry on the Promise that Samuel crowned David king of Israel at God's special command. Judges, kings, priests and prophets, the leaders of this nation have no place in its history except by the rôle they played in the effects and the fulfilment of the Promise.

If it is the proper nature of man, as distinct from the animal, to anticipate his destiny both in desire and thought at every hour, in his anxiety to turn his eyes to a scrutiny of the future, then ancient times contain nothing more human than Israel; not even amidst the Greeks, the Romans, or the Chinese; for these as other people live with their eyes fixed upon their ancestors. The Jews, on the other hand, have their eyes fixed upon posterity. They are expecting and in spirit they contemplate the Son of Man, the Messiah who is to come, the

Saviour, and the Liberator of the human race—"from this attitude in the case of the Jews comes their passion to have children and their contempt of death". Amongst many others, Tacitus was astonished at this Jewish trait. It is of little concern that he found a difficulty in distinguishing them from the Christians and thinks that he has said everything when he mentions their belief in the immortality of the human soul. If he had read the story of Jephthah's daughter, he would have seen what he failed to see without it.

The blood of Israel, the blood of the Messiah! Happy is the man who has added to the number in whose veins runs that blood, if he has lived according to justice. Let him depart in peace to his fathers, "in Abraham's bosom". His sons, like the sons of old Tobias, can "bury him with joy". He has not failed in his task. For the rod of Jesse will not flourish in isolation in the desert. It is an ear of wheat in the midst of a plenteous harvest. For Him who is looked for there must be multitudes of His race for His apostolate and His sacrifice. He must suffer and die for them as an expiation for the sin, before He reigns over them a king, "to spread justice amongst the Gentiles and to carry salvation to the uttermost ends of the earth".

Then God shall pour out His Spirit on all flesh. "*For the law shall come forth from Sion: and the word of the Lord from Jerusalem. And he shall judge the Gentiles and rebuke many people: and they shall turn their swords into ploughshares and their spears into sickles.*"[1]

He, the new David, the faithful shepherd of the sheep of God, "*the government is upon his shoulder: and his name shall be called Wonderful, Counsellor, God the Mighty, the Father of the world to come, the Prince of Peace. His empire shall be multiplied and there shall be no end of peace.*"[2]

Such is the victory which makes the Jews "conquerors of the world" and leaders of the Human Caravan: "the Faith" of Israel.

[1] Isaias ii. 3–4.   [2] Isaias ix. 6–7.

II

JUDAISM IS PERMANENT

In all its essential points, this faith, which was that of Abraham and the Patriarchs, is also ours to-day. Its book is our book. We chant its psalms eight times during the day. Our liturgies put constantly on our lips and in our hearts its prophecies, its histories, its maxims, its poems and its canticles.₁ The least instructed of Christians, like the most learned, find in it food for their souls by reading and meditation. We reject as apocryphal or erroneous every writing and every doctrine which is not in agreement with it. The doctors, the scribes and the prophets of the Jews used to do the same. Could anything be more durable and permanent, more complete and more magnificent?

Judaism is presented as being the continuer of the initial religion of mankind. It is impossible to deny that it has as much right to this title as the other religions of antiquity. Nor indeed can one deny with any justice that these other religions, precisely because they were not exclusive, gradually altered and by accretion and development falsified the truths they had received. They enriched the trust handed to them but they corrupted it too—we have already observed the process in India, China and elsewhere—by a whole crowd of contradictions, arbitrary interpretations and meaningless subversive injunctions. Abraham on the contrary gave back to it its primitive purity. He set it free both from idolatry and from superstitions. He handed it down to Isaac, who in his turn handed it down with the divine blessing to Jacob and to all his posterity. This posterity preserved it, developed it and brought it to perfection during a period of twelve centuries, in the ¡very midst of pagan nations, without allowing any foreign element to be intermingled with it.

"The first religion of humanity?" You will ask: what was

s

the first religion? The worship of ancestors? The worship
of the forces of nature? The cult of the thousand and one
unknown forces of the world personified under the name of
spirits? "The first gods worshipped by mankind were fashioned
in its mind by fear." Or, if one speaks only of natural religion,
it is the reply of man endowed with intelligence who reasons
as to the great *why* and the great *how* which his consciousness
puts before him as soon as he begins to contemplate himself
and the whole universe which surrounds him. Theology may
discuss whether the first man knew all; history can give no
reply to that question. Even the Bible does not teach us very
much on the religion of Adam which Seth transmitted to the
Patriarchs, the Patriarchs to Noah, Noah to Shem and his
sons who into it introduced the errors and the idols which
Abraham in his turn eliminated from it. "What indeed was
man's first religion?"

The matter is simpler than it might appear. If the great
why leads our reason upwards from cause to cause until it
reaches the First Cause and if the great *How* takes it irresistibly
along the path towards Him who Is, it must also be that our
reason will discover beyond those ancestors whom we honour,
the First Ancestor, "Our Father who art in heaven"; above
the natural forces and spirits whose playground is nature, the
Supreme Force, the original motive force, the Sovereign
Spirit, "Jupiter the all-powerful Father of men and gods".
Such is natural religion. Add to it primitive revelation
which is its confirmation and which enlightens and completes
it. Add also the Sin and the Promise. They are indeed distant
memories but they are sure and without them man and history
would be merely an enigma and a derision: and there we have
the initial religion of humanity, that of Abraham, Isaac and
Jacob, that of Moses.

The pagans were but children whose careless and inattentive
minds allowed these memories to evaporate. When they went
upwards link by link along the chain of causes, of forces and
of lives, they paused by the roadside to gather gods like flowers
along the way. Amongst their rank and file only a few great

minds and a few stout hearts marched to the very end of the
road. The most limited in intelligence amongst the Jews left
them far behind.

To this tradition in fact, right through the long succession
of the ages, amidst all vicissitudes, and in spite of all the
obstacles it encountered, Israel kept itself true. It remained
faithful to it in spite of itself—for Israel had just as much inclination to superstitions and idols as the Gentiles. In very truth
it did not keep itself true and faithful, rather we should say
that it was kept true and faithful. Israel itself and the sacred
books of Israel furnish us with the evidence of this fact. A
whole series of miracles were necessary to pluck it free from
paganism and to constrain it to preserve intact the trust given
into its charge. The rigours of the Law were necessary and
its exclusive jealousy. The holiness, the authority, and the
incessant labour of the prophets were required to keep Israel
faithful to its religion.

The scholars who oppose Prophecy to the Priesthood and
celebrate its empire as a triumph of inspiration over ecclesias-
tical dogma are in direct conflict with the texts and the facts.
Certainly the prophet who had been seized by the spirit of
God sometimes experienced irresistible transports, an intoxi-
cation of enthusiasm, an annihilation almost of self. Neither
the Jews nor the prophet himself attached the least importance
to these things. There was nothing remarkable in the spectacle
of these fits of delirium, of these ecstasies in the eyes of the
Jews with their ministry of prophets, any more than there
was in the ascesis and the contemplation with which such
delirium and ecstasy were generally accompanied. The
Prophets were not Yogis, fakirs, dancing dervishes or
pythonesses. They were called "heralds, seers, watchers and
sentinels".

What were they on the watch for? Was it some idea
which must be seized upon as it flashed across the horizon of
the mind like the sudden illumination which revealed to
Descartes by his German stove the secret of his "Method"?
Not at all. On the contrary, they watched for events. They did

not sleep like the common man in the commonplace monotony of the regular course of human affairs. They were on the watch as sentinels. They looked at what was passing. They penetrated into its sense and they observed its range. They saw the results of what was passing into the distance of the future. They proclaimed what they saw, the causes underlying what was and what was going to happen, the harmful or advantageous results, the things which could not be escaped, or which were conditional, depending on the present and the past.

In their writings there are no theological speculations, systems of philosophy, inventions introduced by them into dogma, morality, mysticism, symbolism, liturgy, or social organization. Between them and such as Buddha, Plato, Mahomet, Luther there is an unbridgeable gulf. They never leave fact. They are historians. The utmost one can say in this respect is to attribute to them personal views in politics: and it is their calling which demands that deviation from their function as historians; but in the rest of their activities there is nothing which could be less individual than their inspiration.

The king's "Herald", the prophet is no more than the announcer and the interpreter of the law and the faith. He adds nothing of his own production. He repeats, develops, applies the law and the faith to life, gives them precision. Like Christ himself he could say: *"I am come not to destroy the law, but to fulfil it"*. The Law is the letter the spirit of which he maintains by throwing light upon its depths: the spirit and the letter go side by side in the prophetic revelation towards the complete and perfect fulfilment of the unchangeable Promise.

Moses once for all tells us by what signs we are to recognize the true prophet: it is he whose predictions are realized because he remains faithful and obedient within the four corners of the Law. The false prophet, on the contrary, is he who gets away from the Law, cuts it down, adds something to it or changes something, "a jot or tittle", according as it pleases his own sense, or whim, or is in accord with his self-esteem, or is agreeable to his own interests; and for these reasons his predictions remain unfulfilled.

The Law, the Priesthood, the Messianic Faith and Prophecy are all one: one single undivided spirit, one single letter and one single effort; and the result aimed at is achieved. Israel in spite of itself remains the witness of our origins and of our destiny.

Like all the rest the Promise is in fact not only unique, exclusive and universal; it bears the sign of permanence: "The power of the Messiah is a power which will not pass away and his reign will not know any decadence." And for this reason the people of the Promise, so long as they refuse to acknowledge its fulfilment, will remain in our midst, impossible of assimilation and at the same time indestructible, the sole survivors in the Western world of an antiquity which has disappeared. Israel has indeed been undone and scattered throughout the world but not dissolved; the Children of Israel have been mixed with all other nations but they have not been absorbed by them.

"God," says Bossuet, "has found this means of which there exists in the world but this one example, of preserving the Jews outside their own country and in the ruins of their fortunes, longer even than the peoples who conquered them . . . The ancient Assyrians are gone, and the Medes and Persians, and the Greeks and Romans of antiquity. The Jews who were of old times the prey of all these ancient races, so famous in the pages of history, have survived them."

III

JUDAISM IS PROGRESSIVE UNTIL THE COMING OF JESUS CHRIST

This prodigy which makes them invulnerable even in the midst of the destruction which has overwhelmed and still overwhelms them, appears the more astonishing because it does not arise from those factors which are creative of the

greatness of States and furnish clear evidence of the excellence
of civilizations.

Agriculture, industry, commerce, monuments, towns, ways
of communication, sciences, arts, philosophy, law, war,
diplomacy and politics, in none of all these things did the
Jews left to themselves surpass the common level or initiate
anything notable. They are learners merely, not originators.

Their excellence in poetry and in the social order does not
depend upon their natural genius. Is it even a consequence
of the superiority of their faith and of their law? This is a
question we ask ourselves when we see them lose that excellence,
not only through adulterating the traditions of their forefathers with foreign or personal inspirations as do the Sadducees, the Pharisees, the Alexandrists and the Talmudists,
but also, when the weeks of Daniel have been accomplished
through rejecting the message of Jesus Christ by a stubborn
attachment to the letter of their law and to their faith as they
understand them.

The beauty of Hebrew culture passes then to the Gospels,
to the Epistles of St. Paul and the Apocalypse of St. John the
Divine; and it surpasses itself therein. In them sings the
Divine King. He it was indeed who chanted of old times
through the books of Moses, David, Solomon, the sixteen
Prophets and the author of the poetic book of Job. A Book—
the Book—the diamond, in comparison with which the pearls
of India and the gold of Greece lose half their brilliance—
that is the literature of Israel. It is nothing but religion.
Beyond that there is no work in that literature which possesses
any remarkable excellence, not even the works of Philo, and
less still the Talmud or the Chronicles of Josephus.

The social organization of the Jews was simple, as was
natural to the requirements of a small nation of mountaineers
whose lives were spent in rearing sheep and cattle, in agriculture and in commerce; yet it also possessed a rare quality.
There was no slavery amongst them; there was no service
or debt the obligations of which extended beyond seven years,
unless the servitor or debtor consented to an extension of that

term. There was rest on the Sabbath day. There was mutual
assistance, public decency, good morals, even hygiene en-
forced by regulations which were precise and minute, under
efficient sanctions. The family was on a sound foundation
and was constituted on the basis of paternal authority. Work
was held in honour, the people were free within the rules
of law and order and worship was public and devoid of those
cruelties, immoral practices and superstitions which dis-
figured other cults. In all this again there was nothing but
religion—but a religion which Israel had neither invented
nor chosen, against which it had struggled for so long, but
which dominated Israel, penetrated it and drove it forward,
in spite of its resistance throughout the centuries, to the first
rank of the nations of the world in knowledge and observance
of the truth.

Where are these two qualities to be found as pure, as deep
and as full of life? We would search in vain in antiquity for
another people all of whom lowly and great, ignorant and
learned, heard the call, not only through their faith but also
through their Law, to become saints. I do not mean externally
by the accomplishment of certain rites, the uttering and
repeating of certain prayers, the profession of certain fixed
doctrines, but within their own beings, by loving God with an
upright heart—a love of service rather than a love of enjoyment—and by keeping their consciences clean of all actions,
words, lust or covetousness, thought or omission which God
condemns.

We should search in vain for another race like them amongst
whom human brotherhood—outside the bonds of family, of the
city, of hospitality, of personal interest or sympathy—is more
than a theme on which orators, philosophers, and poets embroidered all sorts of showy variations. And yet it was a race not
distinguished by any notable sensitiveness, tenderness of heart,
delicacy or goodness of soul. The race was rugged, sensual,
violent and avid for gain. Its hardness very soon became
proverbial in the world. But God risked this wager of imposing
upon Israel, "strong against God", having "a stony heart"

and rebelling against progress, the kingdom of divine love and of human brotherhood and that progress which alone counts, the absolute progress of humanity towards its goal, a moral and spiritual progress.

Along this way of progress what an ascent was made from Abraham to Moses, from Moses to David, from David to Jeremiah, from Jeremiah to John the Baptist and to Jesus! And whilst the progress is continued by the apostolate of the thirteen Jews to whom Jesus had confided the mission to preach "The Gospel of the Kingdom" to all the peoples of the world, Israel scattered amongst the nations sees the most enterprising of her sons, the strongest, those who emerge from the others, give themselves over body and soul to the false progress which to-day is intoxicating the whole of the West.

For others the "wall of wailing" and the "chimaera of Sionism". "For we," they say, "we have found the Messiah, the true 'Son of Man': it is Humanity itself upon which rests the Spirit which spoke by the prophets. That Spirit proceeds from Humanity; and behold by the roads of the Universal Revolution it carries Humanity along towards unity, towards collective dominion, towards complete independence."

In this wise they preach the divinity of Humanity. They arrest and falsify, both for themselves and for those whom they win over to this error, the whole development of the Law and the Promise. As their own people have been destroyed, they bend all their efforts upon the destruction of the Law and the Promise. This very action, however, of falsifying the testimony of their own people to drive them to worship the worst of idols, attests that the Law and the Promise, ever since the fall of man, have been for all mankind the only progress that is enduring in character. It also proves that Israel has been—and, though it no longer wishes to be, yet in spite of itself remains for ever—the witness of the Law and the Promise.

CHAPTER III

THE GREEKS AND THE ROMANS

I

THE GRAECO-ROMAN CIVILISATION IN ITSELF HAS NONE OF THE
MARKS WHICH ARE PECULIAR TO TRANSCENDENCE

THE faithful Jews, the great nephews of the companions of
Zorobabel and Nehemiah, seem to have accepted the sovereignty of Hellas without very much difficulty. Alexander took
by storm both Tyre and Gaza at either extremity of Palestine.
He then reduced to submission by force of arms the Samaritans
who were in revolt. To Jerusalem he came not merely as a
master but almost as a guest. We might almost say with
justice that he came as a friend.

What foreign conquerors and rulers—Syrians, Assyrians,
Babylonians and finally the Persians—had not succeeded in
doing, either by violence or by kindness, the Greeks of Alexander's age achieved in a very short time. Judaism then
underwent a process of Hellenization, first of all in the lands
of the Dispersion, then, from the second century before Christ,
in Palestine itself. The Holy Scriptures were translated into
Greek. The Jews became adepts in the philosophies of
Hellas and very soon began to borrow from the Greeks their
language and vocabulary, then their methods, and finally their
very ideas and processes of thought.

Into the mouths of the Greek Sybils they put the oracular
utterances of the Prophets; and that they might enter into
rivalry with the Academy and the Portico, they worked to
transfer the entire Bible, not into madrigals in the manner of
the frivolous and trivial Mascarille, but into allegories. There
were certain Jews who went as far as denying that there existed

any historic reality behind these allegories. There was even a gymnasium in Jerusalem not far from the Temple where priests abandoned the censer to take up the discus. Later on the Sadducees rejected the national tradition, extolling the practices of the Gentiles and, like the Athenian mob, jeering at any belief in the resurrection of the dead.

Such was the power and influence of the Greek genius. It conquered from within both victorious Rome and rebellious Judaea; but both of them, when they had received from it what they themselves lacked, gave to it in return what it did not formerly possess, neutralized those constituents in it which were soluble and thus transfigured it.

The Greek empire which differed in so many respects from other empires only achieved its development and attained perfection within the Roman universe; and the Graeco-Roman hegemony, unique in the world, unlike the theocracy of the Jews was not static or fixed, even for a time, in its realization. It was, on the contrary, always growing, spreading and developing. Its majestic façade, its solid bases, its walls and its framework, everything about it expressed strength, elegance and stability; yet everything was in a state of movement and in a perpetual becoming under exterior influences.

Both the Greeks and the Romans set up an active opposition to the Barbarians, as they called the peoples outside their own culture, just as the Jews did to the Gentiles. It was not merely being cultured or uncultured which counted in this antithesis: what the Barbarians lacked was Greek and Roman culture. Elamites, Chaldaeans, Egyptians, Hindus, Dravidians, Chinese, all these veterans of civilization were Barbarians to the minds of the new-comers. It seemed at first as if even the Jews showed themselves less jealous and exclusive. We shall see that Israel excluded the Gentiles by reason of their gods, and their gods because they were false, evil-doers and corrupt. On the other hand the Greeks and the Romans excluded the Barbarians and their gods because they were foreigners: and that was the sole reason for their exclusion. They said to the Barbarian: "Learn our language, frequent the palestra, follow our customs, adopt our gods, accept our laws, enter into our empire, acquire amongst us a right of citizenship: then your exclusion will cease, you may even preserve your own laws, your own manners and your own tongue. You shall become ours and one of us; and in order that no one may be ignorant of the fact we will find a place for your gods in our pantheon.''

Jewish exclusivism is separative. Without taking away from its king, its law and its faith their character of universality, it restricts and in some degree slows down their diffusion: but thereby it assures permanence in their progress with sovereign efficacy.

The exclusivism of the Greeks and Romans both absorbed and confused: there was an apparent progress, but an actual decadence; there was a continuous inflow of elements which mingled and which in the process lost their own nature, corrupted and were dissolved. It was at this cost that the Graeco-Roman civilization accelerated its diffusion throughout the world and realized its universality.

It must be admitted that there has never existed a civilization which was more human. It was perhaps too human, because it made of man the centre, the measure, the principle and the end of everything. Was the work it created, its peculiar and principal work, the total and perfect expression of its genius, a philosophy, a literature, a science, a monument, a religion, a book: Bible, Temple or Labyrinth? It was none of these things, though elsewhere and in other civilizations there existed no greater perfection in knowledge, no higher intelligence and no greater beauty. What then was the work it created? It created a House. Others pitch their tents and strike them, strengthen their roofs with straw or bark fastened upon a frame of pine sticks or bamboos, build walls with bricks dried in the sun, or with clay mingled with straw within a framework of wooden beams: what they build are mere lodgings for a day which the winds shake, or fire devours, even if insects and damp do not eat away the supports. Other people heap block upon block, in order to build the pyramids, terrestrial milestones along the pathways of the stars and the tombs of kings. The Greeks and Romans, however, built cities, edifices well cemented together, constructed with art in which there is mutual balance and support in the several parts; an abode capable of defying the efforts of all agents of demolition and of providing a shelter throughout the centuries for living man in joy and in grief; a hearth, a house, the House of Man.

The Roman genius calculated, formed plans and carried them out; the genius of the Greeks provided architectural ideas and, at one and the same time, fashioned materials and provided constructors: both were human in their essence and universal in character, the Greek because it was the very genius of reason and of nature, and the Roman because it was the very genius of action and of the city of man. Both of them drew to themselves and retained their hold over men by their sense of harmony and of measure, the one in the order of the intelligence, and the other in the order of politics and social life. They left the doors of their house wide open. Their pantheon from day to day became the pandemonium of idols; their philosophy became the great museum of wisdom, of fantasy and of error; their Western world became a mighty river in which flowed together, between strong high banks, all the passions, the vices, the vileness, the illusions and the splendours of humanity. There lay the secret of its permanence, even in dissolution. It captured everyone; Chaldaeans, Egyptians, Assyrians, Hittites, Persians, Arabians, Jews, Etruscans, Ligurians, Iberians, Celts, Numidians, Scythians, Sarmatians and Germans, but the mire which this flood of different peoples and races bore along its waves, into which the Greeks and Romans plunged, accumulated in an ever growing mass till in the end it burst the river-walls.

The empire broke down under its own weight, at the same time as it grew corrupt and by its corruption lost its strength. All the nations which lived within the vast embrace of the empire, one after the other, put a prince upon the throne of

Augustus; but though there were some great princes and a few clever administrators upon the throne, what a gallery of adventurers they were, what politicians, what brainless, characterless puppets, crowned brutes, madmen and monsters. Some of them even were amongst the cleverest in the discharge of their imperial duties, and yet, like Nero and Diocletian, were by no means the least cruel nor the least vicious of the band. The empire had the masters it deserved in its own image. Constantine and Theodosius came too late. Its ruin could no longer be stayed.

Yet that ruin meant no break in anything that mattered. It might even be said that it carried everything on, that it was simply a violent accident in the second of the five or six acts of that mighty Western drama of whose profound unity it brought into clear light. Byzantium was not altogether wrong in considering itself as the heir of Rome after Romulus Augustulus. In Byzantium subsisted the past, the old pagan confusion between the things of Caesar and the things of God which Caesar claimed to rule. Draped in her magnificence, her refinement and her exclusive pride Byzantium seemed to be like a tower left intact but close shut at the angle of a ruined fortress. Within Byzantium for more than a thousand years was concentrated the Greek genius. Thrown in upon itself, by a kind of in-breeding it grew distorted and rigid in the hypertrophy of its own defects. It became lost within its own subtlety, its taste for abstraction, its verbiage, its fine-spun speculations and disputes upon questions of ridiculously infinitesimal importance, needle points, and its disdain of the Barbarians. Within Byzantium you might have thought yourself to be in China. The understanding which once it had of humankind and of the universe shrank to nothing and shrivelled up for lack of sap. A narrow spirit of nationalism clouded it. Fascinated by luxury and enchanted by things that were precious, rare, artificial, fantastic, Byzantium took the place of Athens and Ionia, for whom beauty, common and simple in its essence, the daughter of reason and of life, was, even in the lightest play of fancy or allegory or myth, the resplendence of nature shining through the minds and hearts of man.

What to it remained of the Latin genius? Very little. It had suffered degradation even before the eclipse of the Greek genius, because it abounded excessively in its own special sense.

It carried its intellectual indifference and passivity to an extraordinary point. Its spirit of dry positivism, blinded by an anxiety to preserve the order of the world outside the empire and to satisfy the immediate demands of utility within, as also by its reliance upon force and political measures to secure these objectives, plunged it into the slough of formalism, of bureaucracy, of finance, of material well-being and carnal indulgence. Where could one find the fertility of the Roman strain, the chastity of the matrons of ancient Rome, the power of the father of the family which was like a block of living steel forged expressly for the support and defence of an empire? It had all gone to mud and dust. Domestic virtues, civic virtues, warlike virtues, all disappeared. The conquerors of Carthage in their decay took into their service mercenaries to defend the City of Rome. Soon these very paid defenders became the masters. They juggled with power. The name Lower Empire became synonymous with decadence.

The Germans in the fifth century of our era and the Turks in the fifteenth swept away all that was left of the rubbish of this decay. And what followed? Hellenism and Latinity found themselves in a position not much worse than before. Where are the Goths and the Burgundians, the Ripuarians and the Salians? Theodoric the Great was more a Roman than was Eliogabalus. Clovis bore the titles of *patricius* and *consul;* Charlemagne those of *Augustus* and *Imperator*. He was ambitious to restore the glories of the empire, to unite under the same sceptre the West and the East and to restore to the City of the Caesars its dignity as the Capital of the Universe. Germany was latinized and the Turkish broom, by sweeping away the dust of Byzantium, only succeeded in bringing back again to the knowledge of the world and in driving out in the direction of Italy those treasures which the Latins were always greedy to possess, the treasures of the Greek genius. The Renascence saw the rebirth of nothing, because nothing was dead; that which it saw was merely the reflowering of what had lain dormant.

Much might be said on the intentions and schemes of Charlemagne, the character of the Holy Roman Empire and the attitude of Clovis whom Gregory of Tours presents to us as "the most cunning of men"; but there is no need. It is the plain fact that mediaeval Christianity differed considerably from the Graeco-Roman empire and that the latter, which had met its end in the fifth century of the Christian era, did not return to life in the fifteenth century.

As for the epoch of the Renascence, during the 200 years of its duration it saw the disappearance of many things. It also saw just as many spring into life and develop; and also the rebirth of many: but what were they? A whole portion of antiquity survived, preserved by the Church, made use of by her, then by the legists against her and by the abettors of heresies. We cannot speak with justice of the resurrection of that part of antiquity which had always lived, had never suffered death, but on the other hand had been incorporated in the original Catholic civilization of the Middle Ages. There remains of course that other portion which had perished, paganism with its corruption, its egoism and its errors. That was in truth reborn with the Renascence. We have seen the consequences of that and how the Anglo-Saxons supplanted the Latins at the head of the Human Caravan.

These observations are enough. They enlighten us on the subject of the Graeco-Roman transcendence: that civilisation neither possessed the quality of permanence nor did it succeed in making any real progress.

This does not mean that the seeds of transcendence and of progress were lacking: there were fine ideas on the part of the Greeks and grandiose achievements on the part of the Romans. The hero and the sage, as they were conceived in the antiquity of the Mediterranean which its legends and sometimes its history depict to our eyes, embody certainly, in spite of many dark shadows and unpleasing deformities, a lofty ideal of moral value in the sphere that was purely human.

Sparta, the most virtuous of the cities, exhibits, it is true, a vain and excessive austerity which even at a great distance seems artificial. Athens is a finer thing in spite of the failings and vices chastized by Aristophanes in his satirical comedies. Greece and Rome practised very exalted domestic virtues, civic virtues and social virtues; yet they had also the most shameful, perhaps, of all the disorders of the antique classical world, the institution of slavery. The conception of life which Herodotus expresses with such good nature and with so charming a manner, in the famous dialogue between Solon and Croesus upon happiness, is evidence of the existence of an undeniable moral rightness. Nowhere in literature is there expressed with more ingenuous grace the exquisite sense of measure and the natural good taste which are characteristic of Greek genius and make it human amongst all men and in all ages.

In this school the Latin genius was cleansed of its original grossness. It was broadened and refined without losing anything of its energy or tenacity. And there we have it ready to build that political masterpiece the empire, and that juridical masterpiece the private law of the Antonines. Elegance and Ciceronian clarity are the interpreters of the healthiest conceptions of the Greek philosophers in polite society where they reduce them to harmony and make them popular. And such work is essentially humane and noble.

But we must not be deceived with regard to the real morality of the readers of the *De Officiis* and the *De Senectute* nor overrate the effect of these fine speeches, these generous and rational theories. The range of their influence seems to have been very limited. What are we to say of the Graeco-Roman world in its entirety (apart from the Christians) during the first three centuries of our era?

The unity and the holiness of God, the immortality of the soul, the identity of virtue and happiness, the brotherhood of humanity and the precepts of the natural law, the sanctions which divine justice and Providence, masters of the Universe, apply to transgressors—all these are merely subjects for school exercises and academic discussion, for the hypocritical pretence of worldlings and the amusement and diversion of the cultivated. Even in the centre of this élite these fine ideas have little place in the ordinary course of life. What fruit could the multitude of plebeians and slaves pluck from the boughs of such a tree?

The Stoics certainly could boast truly of having made some progress, more especially during the time when the influence of the Christian maxims and virtues came to their assistance; but what suggestions could they possibly make to the mob to rule their lives, that they might escape from slavery, from suffering and misery and suicide? To endure life and bear its burdens they could advance no support other than the pride of the human will, the vain denial of pain and of pleasure, and the gratuitous affirmation of an abstraction: virtue. Their law, which had no legislator, nor sanction, nor judge, lacked both force and foundation. Their faith went no further than the fatality of nature and the excellence of the ego.

Epicurus and Pyrrho drew from the same source easier teachings and, taking them by and large, more efficacious for common humanity. The upper classes leaned towards Stoicism, but neither Zeno, the founder of the system, nor Cicero, its advocate, nor Epictetus, the most exact amongst its faithful followers, nor Marcus Aurelius, the most distinguished amongst its disciples, surpass in moral value the "heroes" of the good Herodotus: Cleobis and Biton or Tellos the Athenian. With the exception of Epictetus they remain rather below them.

The remainder of the Graeco-Roman humanity, if they did not escape in the direction of Catholicism, stagnated in the Epicurean calm of soul or the Pyrrhonian scepticism—"What is truth?"—or the aberrations of magic and of Gnosis or the excesses of the lower passions.

"Their women have changed the natural use into that which is against nature. The men have burned in their lusts, one towards another, men with men working that which is filthy.

T

Delivered up to a reprobate sense, they were filled with all iniquity, malice, fornication, avarice, wickedness, fraud and lies; detractors, proud, haughty, inventors of evil things, disobedient to parents, without affection, without fidelity, without mercy." (Rom. 1. 26-31).

A thousand gods and goddesses led the dance. "Crime," says Bossuet, "was actually adored and recognized as necessary to the worship of the gods. The gravest amongst the philosophers forbids drinking to excess, except during the feasts of Bacchus and in his honour. Another philosopher, after having condemned all offensive and obscene pictures, makes an exception of those of the gods who desire to be honoured by these infamies. It is not without astonishment that one reads of the honours which it was necessary to render to Venus and the prostitutions established in her adoration."

In this manner, from the austerity of their primitive age the morals and the religion of antiquity gradually slipped down into the most bestial obscenities and cruelties. It is of great importance to observe that in spite of this failure and decadence in practical morals, the theory was by no means corrupted, and maintained the observances of natural morality amongst an élite, few in numbers, whom Catholicism absorbed into the Church and multiplied. We observe, however, that the virtues practised by this élite, though they were more effective than the eloquence of the theorists, nowhere possessed the force necessary to stem the tide of decadence or affect any regeneration whatever. Universality, diffusion, permanence and progress, the civilizations of Greece and Rome differ in no wise in their total result in any of these characteristics from the civilizations of India and China. Everywhere history is the same. Each and every race, according to its genius and environment, developed with more or less fidelity, clearness and amplitude the natural morality and religion included in a prehistoric and common tradition which experience of life, observation of nature, the speculations of the mind and the misuse of the passions both enrich and deform. Morality and religion, little by little, degenerate in this way. A multitude of beliefs and of foreign practices, of wretched superstitions, of contradictory opinions and of divergent systems spoil and distort them.

And what end for this decline? The fall into the animism and fetishism of the savage races; the stagnation of corruption. Sometimes by means of great effort there comes a return to past purity after which there is a second lapse into decay. It also sometimes happens that a great interior crisis, a war, an invasion by a foreign power, the appearance of an exceptional genius, abolishes the past to the advantage of a new morality and religion—which, however, had their origin elsewhere in the same sources and were subject to the same corruptions— or formed, by an amalgam of all kinds of doctrines, a chaos of truths and errors put in order to suit the taste of the day. Nowhere does that which has been distorted return in fullness to its original nature. That which has degenerated is nowhere regenerated.

The religions and the systems of morality which obtained in Egypt of the Pharaohs, in Chaldaea, in Assyria and in ancient Persia, amongst the Barbarians of the North and the civilizations of America have completely disappeared. Those of India and China—very broadly supplanted by others—Taoism, Shintoism, Buddhism and Islamism—have survived, thanks to the strong support afforded them by the deserts and the mountains, the climates, the castes and the routine amidst which they flourished; but many variations corrupted their purity. What transformations did they undergo in their very essences! What novelties at the very base of that which is to-day given to us as the development of a tradition as ancient as humanity! And what doctrinal abysses between the little and the great Vehicle; between the Tao-Tei-King and the mysticism of Ling Pao or the alchemy of the Pao-Pu-Tseu; between the Koran and its unchangeable text and the wavering and artificial ecstasies of the Sufis.

The evolution of ethics and religion in the Graeco-Roman world operates in a manner which is in no wise different. It is clearly to be seen that the sign of transcendence is not there.

CHAPTER IV

SIMON PETER

I

THE CLAIMS OF THE ROMAN CHURCH TO TRANSCENDENCE
ARE WORTHY OF EXAMINATION

AND what would the Western world, the Jews, the Greeks, the
Romans, be in history without the Fisherman of Galilee, Simon
called Peter by Christ, to whom Christ said: "Thou art Peter
and upon this rock will I build my church; and the gates of
hell shall not prevail against it. I will give unto thee the keys
of the kingdom of heaven and whatsoever thou shalt bind on
earth shall be bound also in heaven: and whatsoever thou shalt
loose on earth shall be loosed also in heaven."[1] And later: "I
have prayed for thee that thy faith fail not. And thou being converted, confirm thy brethren." And again: "Feed my lambs,
feed my sheep"?

Romans, Greeks, Jews are memories: the West is nothing.
In itself it does not differ from the East except by its aptitude
at the time of Christ to receive the seed of that great tree,
the Kingdom of Heaven. If it had not grown or if the frail
shoot had withered, the Orient and the Occident would be as
like as east wind and west. But the stalk grows green and the
tree shoots upwards. The Building—sheepfold, society, kingdom—is constructed. The Fisherman's bark is sailing across
the Mediterranean. Simon Peter steers his course for Rome,
lands there, reigns there. And there we see the Occident
placed, made distinct, unified, the leader of the Human
Caravan. Jews, Greeks and Romans survive, transfigured
in the Roman Catholic Church, which, strong in the promise

[1] Matthew xvi. 18–19.

which assure to the fold of Christ unique and universal permanence in progress, affirms its own transcendence.[1]

What is indeed the value of these claims? Critics have done
their utmost to reduce this great Church to the proportions of
a little chapel, a sect, a successful conspiracy, a party which
has had the luck on its side, a doctrinal school whose opportune
syncretism made its fortune. But all this is folly. You cannot
reduce the status of this Church in the history of the last 2,000
years, nor its place in the world of to-day; and in the face of
its miraculous success it is impossible to reject its claims without discussion.

There is another consideration: a remarkable coincidence,
embarrassing to those who deny the Church's claims. The titles
on which the Church of Rome prides herself, or as she says,
"the marks of the true Church" founded by the Lord Jesus
Christ on the "rock" Peter, turn out to be, under other names
and in a stricter sense, precisely the marks we have seen as
belonging to transcendence; although our method of approach
to the problem was quite different from hers.

Thus we analyzed the order of the march, the forces and the
movements, the goal and the itinerary of the Caravan. This
analysis showed us that if history has a direction, for lack of
which the words happiness and progress would mean nothing
whatsoever, one must somewhere find a society which is
altogether unique and universal, permanent and yet progressive. Having arrived at this conclusion we set out to look for
this society throughout the centuries.

The Church of Rome had quite different concerns. She
thinks of Christ. She is preoccupied with souls. It is not so
much a question for her to prove her transcendence as to
manifest her origin. She does not begin by saying, "If there
exists amongst the world of men a divine Church, she bears
upon her certain marks; now, these marks are mine; acknowledge therefore my divinity." She says: "Christ is God. There
is no salvation except in Him and it was I whom He founded

[1] For the whole of this chapter see the second part of the note placed at the end
of this volume.

to save your souls. He lives in me. If others claim to originate
in Him, they deceive themselves or they are liars. You shall
know it by this sign: Jesus made me one, holy, catholic and
apostolic. Every Church which does not possess those four
marks does not come from Him. Leave it, reject it, let it be
anathema.''

One and unique, therefore *exclusive*.

Catholic, that is to say *universal*.

Apostolic, bound by the Apostles to Judaism as the branch
is bound to the trunk, and by the means of this trunk to the
root, the original tradition ; *permanent* therefore as permanent
as the human race.

Holy, as Israel is holy and more than Israel, and therefore
progressive.

The Church of Rome in this manner claims a position of
transcendence because it claims its title from Christ. That is
logical, if Christ is God. Is He God? There is no other problem
to solve. The key we are looking for lies there. The Divinity
of Christ, the transcendency of the Church and the direction
of history are all one. If the claims of the Church are well
founded the remainder follows.

It is certainly worth our while, therefore, to examine them.

II

CATHOLICISM, THE LIVING SOCIETY, IS THE ONLY HISTORIC
RELIGION AND THE ONLY RELIGION OF AUTHORITY

Man is a religious animal. Religions flow forth from his
soul with the same abundance and the same infinite variety
as political systems, social organisms, the arts, literary forms
and technical inventions. Their different exteriors, however,
conceal a fundamental resemblance of structure—they all tend
to be modes of worship arising out of a doctrine.

Regard this as the effect of instinct or intelligence; give it
any origin you please—covetousness, fear, the imagination

which fabricates myths, poetical visions, the contemplation of mystics, the speculations of philosophers or all these things put together. The fact remains. They are doctrines expressed outwardly by rituals: doctrines and nothing else.

They tell us what we must believe and do; but not one of them alleges any other motive than tradition, personal inspiration, or the requirements of reason. This indeed is true even of Christianity, in so far as the innumerable swarms of Protestantism and (on more than one capital point) the national schisms and liberal chapels are concerned. Roman Catholicism alone, under analogous exteriors, offers to us a structure which is fully and radically different. It is in that direction first of all that the Roman Church is unique in the world. It puts itself forward in the order of facts and not in the order, or sphere, of ideas: it is a historic religion and there is none like it; a society which existed before its teaching; a Church anterior to its cult; a living body made of living men and organized for life. It is in possession of a theology, a philosophy, a morality. It develops them and it spreads them, but it remains distinct from them. They are the fruit of its being, the effects of its existence. They no more define its essence than the creation defines the essence of the Creator.

The edifice which was built upon Peter is not reducible to the meagre if venerable dimensions of temples and schools. It does not repose upon its doctors, the men whose task it is to instruct it, preserve it in health, adorn it and drive away the money-changers and merchants from its precincts. It rests upon the foundations of the martyrs and the apostles; and the apostles, like the martyrs, are nothing else but witnesses. The Prophets and Moses are also witnesses.

Their testimony is nothing else but the testimony of facts: the conversion of Abraham and his exodus at the command of God from the land of Canaan; that of the Twelve Tribes from Egypt; the events of Sinai; the unfaithfulness of Israel to the pact of Alliance with Jehovah and the disasters which resulted from that unfaithfulness; the life of Jesus, His miracles, His prophecies, His death on the Cross, His resurrection and ascension into Heaven, the exact concordance between this history and the predictions of the Scriptures.

Whether they are lying, deceiving themselves, or speaking the truth, for the moment it is of no importance to the question we are discussing. The important thing here is that their evidence bears upon the facts, not facts within the mind— intuitions, visions, dreams, and the words which are spoken within—but exterior facts. The testimony they bring is historical and the whole edifice depends upon that alone. That is not seen elsewhere.

What did Christ say at the very moment when He was leaving this world? *"And you shall be witnesses unto me . . . to the uttermost part of the earth."*[1] What did Peter say when he invited the Apostolic college to complete its numbers after the suicide of Judas? Whom did he wish to be chosen? One *"of these men who have companied with us, all the time that the Lord Jesus came in and went out among us, beginning from the baptism of John, until the day wherein he was taken up from us."*[2] Faith, virtue, intelligence, energy are indeed not sufficient. A witness is required. What said Paul the theologian, the apologist, of the close, deep, able reasoning, the master framer of dogma? *"If Christ is not risen, our preaching is in vain and vain also is our faith."*

All attempts at proof amount to nothing, if the fact is lacking. Here, now, is the central fact; Christ who was announced by the Prophets and was born in Bethlehem of Judaea, preached both in Galilee and in Judaea the Gospel of the Kingdom. He laid the foundations of His Church. He confirmed His message and the foundation of the Church by miracles. He declared Himself to be the Son of God. He predicted that to bear witness to this divine incarnation He would die in pain and in shame and would rise again on the third day. That prediction was accomplished. If the alleged fact were a forgery, everything would go to pieces. The witness would be reduced to silence and the Church to dissolution. Doctrinal or moral apologies

[1] Acts i. 8.　　　　　　　　[2] Acts i. 21–22.

would be of no avail whatsoever. They are useful, no more than that. One thing is necessary. For the one historic religion an historic apologetic is necessary.

"*I have not judged it necessary,*" said St. Paul, "*that I ought to know amongst you any other thing than Jesus Christ, and Jesus Christ crucified.*" After the lapse of fourteen centuries the youthful unlettered woman of Domrémy re-echoed his words before the men who knew all that the *Studium* teaches and who regarded themselves and it as the framework of the Church. "*It is my opinion,*" she replied to their questions, "*that Our Lord and the Church are all one. Why do you entertain in your minds any doubts that they are one?*"

In this idea and fact lies the essence of the Catholicism of Rome. It is in truth the Christ, "the Man who became God" and for this reason was tortured, the "Crucified who rose again", the Man who rose from the dead, to whom "all power was given in heaven and on earth" and who dwells with us "for always until the end of the world."

The exterior form which covers up this mysterious reality as with a garment is no less extraordinary.

Everywhere in the world of men since the dawn of things, religions have been formed and organized into societies. It was human nature itself which demanded this organization and the societies which resulted from it were secret or public, open or closed, ritual or spiritual. There were some which combined all these qualities: they were both public and open, and secret. Some through their esoteric quality were also spiritual and, as a consequence, universal. Buddhism and Islam possess both spirituality and universality.

The Catholicism of the Church of Rome also accumulates qualities in the same way, but it alone is a kingdom. Alone amongst other religions, to faith and to law it joins a king: a king who reigns and governs, a monarch, a visible authority, both sovereign and infallible in his sphere—the sphere of the spirit. Everywhere else spiritual authority is lacking or remains uncertain because it is invisible. If it indeed exists and appears, it is either indistinguishable from temporal authority, or else

it is lacking in sovereignty. Nowhere are there any sure
guarantees of its infallibility.

"*Render to Caesar the things that are Caesar's and to God the things
that are God's*": there lie the two distinct authorities and their
domains. The Jews still make too great a confusion of the two.
They have scarcely any conception of the triumph and universality of the spiritual kingdom except upon the analogy of the
triumph and universality of the temporal kingdom. Henceforth the confusion becomes impossible. Caesar has no longer
any hold except over temporal things. The authority of the
spirit remains an authority in the sphere of the spirit. And
the visible monarch who possessed it at the moment of entering
into the invisible, regulated His succession. "Bind and loose,"
said He to Peter, "I give you the keys of the Kingdom of
Heaven." "Confirm your brethren"—those brethren to whom
Christ had said: "He that heareth you heareth me, and he
that despiseth you despiseth me."

Vain words indeed if Christ were not God. If He is God
those words are an incomparable guarantee of spiritual infallibility. Roman Catholicism is then saved from all superstitious
or idolatrous degeneracies; from all the crowd of illusions and
fantasies of individual inspiration; and from all the variations,
uncertainties and contradictions of the philosophies. Roman
Catholicism alone is so preserved: for this authority which only
exists in Roman Catholicism is the sole effective preserver from
these dangers.

You will tell me that you need a religion within the soul.
It is worthy neither of God nor yourself that He should thrust
Himself upon you from outside. Your conscience is enough
for you. Your own inspiration guides you and you judge it
according to its fruits. Very well; but if you reach a judgment
of the fruits according to your conscience, you simply close
the vicious circle; and if you make your judgment of them on
the faith of another person, on what grounds will you judge
this authority whom your conscience chooses? It is absolutely
necessary for you to escape from the circle, to come out from
yourself, to find an authority who commands your obedience

and respect by itself and from outside. There is only the
Catholic Church which can make you this offer.

There lies the reason that the real mystics are athirst for
dogma and obedience. They never put any credence on what
takes place within themselves. To have a director and guide,
to submit themselves to him, such indeed is the first need of
their souls.

St. Theresa wanted her guide to be both a saint and a savant;
but it was for knowledge that she had the greater desire. Her
spirituality seemed to her subject to suspicion, if it were not
founded upon rigid affirmations and precise definitions, the
intellectual forms of the Roman faith.

Intuitions, inspirations, revelations, impulsions which motiv-
ate the will, sentimental effusions, conditions of ecstasy, visions
and words uttered within the mind, everything in fact which
the false mystics aspire to experience and to take as the rule
of their acts and their thoughts, all such things the true mystics
mistrust and shrink away from. To them simple contemplation
alone appears to possess the virtue of certainty and their
opinion is justly conceived, they say, because the individual
sense and the will-power in the proper sense of the word cannot of themselves raise themselves up. The simplicity of the
mind in contemplation, they add, since it can never attain
to divine realities under definite forms, renders more precious
the definitions pronounced by divine authority.

The loftier the flight of the soul into the sphere of love, the
more complete is its vision of the perfection with which the
intellectual dogma of the Church expresses its spiritual realities,
and at the same time adapts itself to the limited intelligence
and shallow minds of this world. The life of the soul becomes
absorbed to a degree which is constantly increasing into the
eternal life which Christ shares with His Church. It enters
into an ever closer and more perfect intimacy with the community of saints.

Dogma, like morality and that charity which is at the basis
of morality, is not a form of tyrannical domination, but rather
of unity and deliverance. The Kingdom of Christ and the

authority which rules over that kingdom still possess that unique quality.

The madman whom the old fox, Herod, tricked out in a white robe to amuse Pontius Pilate launched the Fisherman's bark on the deepest, the most irresistible and the most comprehensive of the currents of history. What 2,000 years of His work have succeeded in bringing before our eyes, He Himself saw before there was any indication of it whatsoever. He dared. What a depth of intelligence and what a vast treasure house of knowledge! What force of will-power! In the time when domination held the whole world within a unity which the world then believed would be eternal, He indeed understood that the human river had since its origin been flowing towards a unity which is both spiritual and free. He opens to all those who knock the door of His wonderful edifice. His kingdom of the spirit, where no one is a subject who does not wish to be. *"Holy Father let them be one as we are one."*

He can promise them duration and continuance. How could this kingdom come to an end before the world's end, if its essence is in this way the very goal towards which, with all the weight of accumulated centuries, the world is rushing? Dominations and tyrannies crumble away and separations are wiped out, or unity succeeds : the vast wave of unity mounts, flows back and then flows forward again, ceaselessly making its way and rising until it submerges everything beneath its waters.

III

CATHOLICISM IS EXCLUSIVE AND PERMANENT

By the principle of exclusivism, power and duration are retained in that unity, just as the weakness and decay of syncretistic religions and faiths come upon them because they do not possess the saving quality of exclusivism. What jealous care, what great vigilance are exorcized by the Catholic

Church at all times and seasons to keep intact the fruit of the tree of life. Bitter reproaches are levelled at her, but then she has always been the target of such reproaches. The pagans used to accuse the very martyrs of being intolerant. If we listen to them, it would seem that the martyrs subjected their torturers and executioners to torture.

Even now in our days, if the Church condemns a book, subjects a priest to an interdict, denounces heresy, condemns maxims, philosophies or laws which are incompatible with her doctrine, shrieks and cries are raised against her. Yet the question is of the merest common sense; a member of a union must obey its rules and regulations if he wishes to avoid exclusion or expulsion. And in that you have the whole atrocity (as it is called) of excommunications and anathemas. Excesses in this matter were undoubtedly committed in Spain and in the crusade against the Albigenses, but such excesses do not affect the soundness of the principle of exclusion.

The Church does not employ force. Much rather does she forbid her followers indiscreetly to disturb the consciences of schismatics, heretics and idolaters, as long as they are at peace and are sincere in their error. But she refuses to give herself to the monstrous contradiction of posing as the guardian of truth which is of necessity unique, and at the same time putting adverse, multiple, variable and discordant opinions upon a level with truth.

"Outside the Church there is no salvation." All those who have been saved belong to her, whether suffering in Purgatory or triumphant in Heaven, and all those human beings who live to be saved. The grand edifice has three doors: men may enter by water or blood or desire. That all men of good will may enter into peace, must there be other doors than these three—Baptism in Christ, death for Christ, life for Christ under whatever name or form the mind and the will adore Him when invincible obstacles prevent them from adoring Him under the name and form of Jesus, the Son of Mary? The answer is that if other doors were opened into the Church it would mean her demolition.

Such an exclusivism is neither more nor less than the instinct of self-preservation. Its aim is not to safeguard the Church alone, but before all else the spiritual trust received by her from God—religious truth in the souls of men.

The Church of Rome reckons the stages of her history by the decisive victories which her defenders have won against the forces of decadence and death: apostles and martyrs against the paganism of antiquity, the doctors of the Church against heresies, bishops and monks against the ignorance and superstitions of the barbarians; popes of mediaeval Christianity against secular usurpations and national schismatics; mystics, theologians, the religious orders, sovereign pontiffs with their defined infallibility, against the forces of free thought, of non-dogmatic morality and that denial of the supernatural which constitutes the modern form of paganism.

If this vital instinct were less strong in the Church we should see her, by reason of her universality, dissolving in the course of centuries and being lost in the universe instead of conquering the universe. She would not be permanent. And permanent she is; and to remain so she is as energetic, as careful as she has ever been to exclude corruption and drive away error.

In the innumerable voices by which her teachings are repeated there has been a measureless diversity of accents, of methods and of problems for the last 2,000 years. But from one end to another all the voices repeat the same theme.

It is the theme of doctrinal permanence; nothing new which has not its origin either in the Scriptures or in Tradition, just as the plant grows out of the seed, the conclusion from the premises, the effect from the cause. In that purpose lies the unceasing care of the popes, the perpetual duties of the councils of the Church, of the doctors of the Church, the fathers and the apostles, when it becomes their duty to define what Christians must believe and practise.

One after the other, the different denominations and confessions, the numerous sects and non-conformist Churches separated from the Roman Catholic Church, just as from a tall tree fall the dead branches broken or cut away from it.

Whether this happens in the twentieth century or the fifteenth or the sixteenth, in the eleventh or the fifth, it is of small importance: there comes a day in history when the dissidents, after having lived in the communion of the Roman Church, leave it or are driven out of it. They may compare themselves to Lot fleeing from Sodom, to Zorobabel returning from Babylon, to the Twelve Tribes of Israel leaving Egypt. Yet the day must come when they will recognize that they have in fact quitted the Church. They may claim that they have left the Church as the Church herself left the Synagogue; but the Church continues and completes the Synagogue, whereas the dissidents, far from continuing the Church of Rome and bringing it to greater perfection, have broken away from that "Egypt", that "Sodom", that "Babylon of Antichrist", as they call Rome.

They lay claim to a direct contact with Jesus Christ by vaulting over the intervening centuries. Their contention is that the Church of Rome has deviated from the track; that it has falsified, distorted and corrupted the practice and the doctrine taught by the Holy Apostles; but they cannot deny that this Church, adulterate and diabolical as they believe her to be, is the only one which is connected, without having to leap over one single day of history, with the Church of the Apostles founded by Christ and "confirmed" by St. Peter.

The promise of infallibility was made by Jesus to Peter and to His Church alone; all its claims are justified; beyond the Apostles, the Christ; beyond the Christ, Israel; beyond Israel, Noah, Abel, Adam, the eternal religion which unites in their common divinity the Father the Son and the Holy Spirit. "*I am descended from heaven*", said Jesus to the Jews. "*Abraham, your father, rejoiced that he might see my day. He saw it and was glad. . . . What dost thou say? Thou art not even fifty years of age and thou hast seen Abraham? . . . In truth, in truth I say unto you: before Abraham was, I am.*"

"*I am*"—It is the name of Jehovah Himself. He calls Himself "*I am.*" What madness, or what blasphemy, or what truth! If He is speaking the truth the duration of His Church is eternal. It is permanent. If He is lying or deceiving Himself, how can it be that He is the fulfilment of the Promise of Joy made to Abraham, to Isaac and to David and that in this manner He transfers to His Church the whole permanence of Israel?

Messiah, Son of God. He claims to be both. He offers to the world all the features of the Messiah and the Son of God. Could He have fabricated the evidences of His claim? Some few of the traits conceivably—but the greater part of them assuredly not: it was only after His death that the most decisive evidences became applicable to Him—His own resurrection, the destruction of the Temple by the Roman legions, the ruin of Jerusalem, the end of the Jews as a political entity and their dispersion, and the thronging of the Gentiles into the service of Jehovah. There is no question of illusion or imposture. The facts speak. The Catholic Church is the Kingdom of the Messiah, the league of God with men, the blossoming out of the earliest form of religion. Its permanence and the permanence of humanity are identical.

IV

CATHOLICISM IS PROGRESSIVE. ITS TRANSCENDENCE

And the sign of God is imprinted on the Church.

Reproaches have been levelled at her that she has not adapted herself, quickly enough or well enough to "the progress of civilization", that is to say to the changes of the world around her. But can it be shown that the Church would have been wise to adapt herself to these changes, enticing as they appear to be? What would have become of her and human souls and the world, if she had adapted herself in the sense of the criticism to every one of the intellectual, moral and social modes which the Church has seen come into existence and perish? There would be an end to all unity, to exclusivism and to permanence. The Cross would have been transformed into a wind-vane and the Kingdom of God into an inn.

The progress that the Church aims at and achieves is not measured according to this standard. It is absolute progress, as we have already defined it; it is holiness. That is its end or goal, that is the reason for the Church's existence and that is its mission, its dominating note and the objective of all its works. The Church is called "holy" just as it is called Catholic, Apostolic and Roman: these epithets do not so much express the claims of the Church as her very essence. She exists only to accomplish that which was in existence before her: the law and the prophets, the original religion of man, the people of God and the nature of mankind. *"Be perfect as your Heavenly Father is perfect."*

It is therefore in her doctrine that the Church is Holy. That cannot be contested, unless we go to the extent of modern paganisms and deny the holiness of the Church by perverting the very notion of holiness. For the Church, like its Master, never ceases to preach to all men and to all human societies the sublimest and most complete and perfect progress that can be conceived in the mind: the imitation of God. For twenty centuries, whether on Mount Thabor or in the Garden of Gethsemane, whether full of ardour or lukewarm, sinful or saintly, Peter urges men to become members of his Church and as soon as they have entered therein he says to them: "As obedient children, not fashioning yourselves according to the former lusts in your ignorance: but as he which hath called you is holy, so be ye holy in all manner of conversation; because it is written, Be ye holy for I am holy. . . . Ye are a chosen race, a royal priesthood, a people chosen to announce the perfections of him who hath called ye from the darkness to his admirable light."

Peter certainly did not himself invent that. He merely repeated it. He is reciting a speech of Jehovah made to the Hebrews by Moses. He gives to the Christians for reasons of holiness the divine choice and the ransom by Christ's blood which have made them heirs of Israel responsible for developing their heritage. But from Israel to the Church what progress there has been in the knowledge and understanding of love,

U

how many new achievements of perfection in the means of holiness!

The prayer mounts upwards, overflows and invades all the depths of the soul and every instant of our lives. The worship that is brought to the Father is no longer a ritual and national adoration, in a unique temple, on the Mountain of Sinai: it is a universal cult, in the temples and outside the temples; an adoration of the spirit as much and more than of gesture and voice; an adoration in very truth as much and more than in figures and symbols; the adoration of those pure hearts where Jesus lives with His Father and the Holy Spirit.

We no longer sacrifice bulls or rams or doves; but at each instant of time the Lamb of God somewhere renews His sacrifice. Even if they were merely symbols, what genius for love is in this Son of Man crucified, thus to make His Calvary eternal! What a superhuman tenderness in the invention of the Eucharist! What a psychological miracle in the gift of the sacraments! An unbelieving philosopher has justly observed: "In their own kind they remain unique, these sacraments. They are moulded to the intelligence and the sensibility of modern times", as well as upon those of the other ages of humanity, "and they bring within their own sway this intelligence and this sensibility. They go as far beyond pagan sacrifices and figurative rites as that which is both reasonable and real rises above the mere image and the imagination."

And beyond this it is impossible to think that any progress can be achieved. These things and the Mass open a door upon the infinite. It is their beauty, their fertility and their strength. Where, however, would such things as beauty, fertility and strength be, if they rested upon mere symbols? They are simply realities. "My flesh is meat indeed and my blood is drink indeed." It is unnecessary to look elsewhere for the secret of the marvellous blossoming which never for one moment since the exhortations of St. Peter and the Sermon on the Mount has ceased to develop in every season and on every separate branch of the mighty tree.

Here are indeed the fruits of the sacraments, of the Mass and of prayer: they are the apostles, the martyrs, the doctors, the pontiffs, the confessors, the virgins, the holy women, the innumerable crowd of saints whom all nations, epochs, temperaments, ages, callings and occupations and social classes contribute to augment and renew from day to day. They are known by the name of "the blessed," for happiness and holiness are but one thing which is the goal of the Human Caravan.

With what shining exactitude they all express and translate the holy doctrine into a holy life! Kindness, delicacy, uprightness and faith, pure hearts, generous souls, sages, ascetics, mystics can indeed be found in other religions; but heroes of virtue in such numbers, so diverse, so humble, so completely and wholly forgetful of themselves, so devoted for the love of God to other men, especially to those who are most wretched, can only belong to the Church of Rome. The unique importance of the part they have played in its history justifies beyond all measure its title of the "City of the Saints".

Even its faults furnish it with the opportunity of manifesting that it is at once holy and the artisan of progress. Divine in its leader, human in its members, it suffers, as we ourselves do in our common infirmities. Nothing that is a factor in the corruption of societies, religions and the civilizations of mankind is spared it: politics which are both ill-advised or too earthly, too materialistic, philosophies founded on sophistry, illusory or perverse mysticisms, passions and superstitions; but the Church finds a remedy and a cure for these diseases just as a living and healthy organism eliminates the poisons and destroys the evil germs. "*They shall not prevail*": that is the Promise of Christ which so far has been fulfilled.

The annals of the Church, the epic story of the saints, are scarcely anything more than a journal of their interior struggles and their victories over themselves, of personal reforms, purifications and spiritual ascensions. Their biographies also are of this nature and quality.

Those who practised Jewish rites, those who practised pagan rites and those who wished to become converts to gnosticism were reduced to obedience or driven out by the Church in the time of the apostolate and the persecutions. Peace did not lull the Church to slumber after these hard tasks had ceased to absorb her energies. Her popes, doctors and councils pursued even bishops when they were the aiders and abettors of heresies. They reduced them to obedience, or they drove them out of the Church.

In the same way the clerics, the monks and the laity whose ignorance, cruelty, deplorable lack of discipline, incontinence and superstitions obscured the doctrines of the Church and degraded the morals of the world at the time of the Barbarians, were either reduced to submission or expelled from her precincts. Those who spread disorders and created schisms in the Church—even if they occupied the see of St. Chrysostom, or the throne of Charlemagne or seemed to hold the very throne of St. Peter—were likewise brought to obedience or driven out: as were all those men, from the Lutherans to the Modernists, who opened wide the door to secular usurpation or to the renascent paganisms of the world.

Nothing like this had taken place in other religions or in other philosophies. Not one is to be found whose development is not subordinate to the flux and reflux of heterogeneous elements and contradictory teachings, as well as to radical transformations effected by foreign ideas and forces. They have to change in order to continue to exist. As soon as change ceases, death comes.

In the Roman Catholic Church the contrary obtains. As soon as any development begins to deviate from the straight path and to turn aside towards a change, it stops, it is corrupted and it falls into decay. A return to the Scriptures and to Tradition saves it. Its progress is merely an aspect of its permanence, of its catholicity, of its exclusiveness and its unity.

As a consequence it is not surprising that the Church from its origin should have claimed the future as her own and declared herself its mistress. The masses of the Gentiles will, declares the Church, be won. The Man of Sin who must arise will perish at the mere breath of Christ. The Jews will be converted to Christianity. Just as He once departed from us, the Lord Jesus will come again. He will descend from heaven to judge human beings according to their works.

It is for this that the Church is waiting and wishing, this is her work and prayer. Now, those claims which she announced whilst she was still as nothing, from century to century she maintains and realizes, in this fashion revealing herself as the transcendent society, without which history would remain devoid of sense and direction. She goes far beyond everything which our destinies and our natures demand for their accomplishment. In her excellence and her fullness there is a quality which opens up for us, beyond the depth of our decay and her mercy in our healing, perspectives which are superhuman in their nature.

Without Providence, it has been said, history would be unintelligible. I agree, but the statement must be made more precise. The Human Caravan does not propose to us for solution a riddle to which the answer is the word Providence. It bears testimony. This procession which from the dim and distant ages of the world has been ever moving onwards, spreading and constantly increasing the pace of its movement, is in truth a procession of witnesses to Christ. They may also be according to the epoch in which they live and the country which they inhabit, witnesses of Mahomet, of Confucius or of Buddha, as of Napoleon, or Genghis Khan, or Asoka or Alexander; but all of them, willingly or unwillingly knowingly or unknowingly, give evidence, not only of the existence and the genius of these great men but at the same time and with the same force of the divinity of Jesus Christ.

We must listen to them or stop up our ears and flee away towards bewildering negations—beyond pantheism, agnosticism, scepticism even to a nihilist and radical materialism. There is no other alternative: to deny, to deny without reason or proof, by denying the intelligence and reason themselves; or else to obey and be submissive to the divine fact, Jesus Christ, "the Word made flesh, whose glory we have seen, as the only son of the Father, full of grace and of truth."

THE PRINCE OF THIS WORLD

CHAPTER I

THE ANGEL AND THE BEAST

I

THE PROBLEM OF SATAN IN HISTORY

THE kingdom of Christ is not of this world: and for this reason it has not submitted to the law of this world, which is a law of regression, of dissolution, of transformation, of that type of evolution which revolves in a circle and is a law of death. Its best and most numerous citizens—the angels, the saints whom the Church has named, a host of unnamed saints and a multitude of souls saved from perdition and on the way of purification—live elsewhere a life very different from this.

The citizens who are of this world—exiles and pilgrims of the Caravan—are few in number; but it is through them that the kingdom of Christ exists in this world. In them it grows, advances, undergoes the law of sin, the original loss of equilibrium between the angel in man and the beast in man, the cruel war which is waged between spirit and flesh, death and life. It enters into and remains at war, by the permanence of its progress, against our excesses, our aberrations, our weaknesses and our inertia; against whosoever serves them and makes use of them for his own purposes; against their activities in itself and in the rest of the world.

These phenomena introduce some unity into the facts, otherwise incoherent, radically different and confused, by which the initial decay and fall of humanity become manifest to us. The chaos of waters which presses against the Church is moulded into her shape and bears the impress of her form. There is an order in the forces of evil which is primarily the counterpart of the essential order which exists in the forces of good. Zoroaster and Manes were wrong when they declared that there was a transcendent principal of Evil. No transcendence here is possible. We cannot define a God of Evil otherwise than by naming him "he who is not."

Are we then to deny that perverse intelligences, foreign to humanity, add to this evil order of the world the order of their designs and their action? Yes, if all the evil which exists in this world has an adequate reason in the state of man alone—a defeat in his being, the ignorance and the weakness of the angel which lives in him, the blindness and violence of the beast which also lives in him, and malice born of that triple cause through the attachment of his own affections to this depravity.

But if there is to be found in the history of the world something which can in no wise be explained by the triple cause defined above, a deeper and continuous and more connected malice, aberrations so contrary to the nature of man that they cannot be attributed merely to his original fall, then it looks as if Someone were pulling on the reins and pushing at the wheel, when the chariot of humanity plunges from the divine road into ways muddy, full of holes, torn by ruts and leading downwards into the abysses of destruction.

II

SATAN TAKES ADVANTAGE OF THE FALL OF HUMANITY

Someone.

As soon as reference is made to the devil, there are incredulous or pitying smiles. Our forefathers believed in him perhaps; but then our forefathers lived in the darkness of the Middle Ages. Some such folly as the belief in the devil was bound to be the companion of ignorance in the Dark Ages. But to us has come light. Darwin, Allan Kardec, Rudolf Steiner, Charcot, Hertz and Crookes, Freud and the rest have exorcized the devil from our imaginations. The devil is the unknown of yesterday, to-morrow he is known for what he really is—unknown forces, the eddies of vital currents, the boiling up of the sexual instinct, subconscious reactions, impulses of the nervous system, waves imperceptible to our senses; morbid animalities which we have inherited from our ancestors; the scattered elements of the dead, the obscure traces which those of whom we are formed, whose characters we have inherited, still preserve in us of their pre-existence outside ourselves.

Most assuredly we are subjected to these multiple influences —and also to many others besides, for the savants who are so keen on them insist upon ignoring the grace of God and the suggestions of good angels as of evil spirits. But our forefathers were no more foolish than we are. They were very intelligent and they drew a perfect distinction between an epileptic, a madman and one possessed by a devil. When they said: it is the devil, they had their reasons for the statement. On the other hand we have no reason for denying *a priori* the value of their experiences.

There are facts. At the point which we have now reached in the pursuit of our studies upon the direction of history, there is above all one fact: the Christ who declares Himself and proves Himself to be God, no less clearly affirms the existence of the devil, his actions and his empire over the world. He imposes His will upon evil spirits and compels them to perform it. He permits them to enter into the bodies of a herd of swine which at once rush down a steep place into the Sea of Galilee. He says to the Scribes and Pharisees: " *You are of your father the devil*"[1]; to His disciples He says; " *Drive out demons. I saw Satan like lightning falling from heaven.*"[2] " *For the Prince of this world cometh : and in me he hath not anything.*"[3]

The hostility evinced by the world to real progress and to those who are the pioneers of that progress, though they compel its admiration and its respect, is a problem that needs solving. I see what is best, I do the worst: it is the weakness of our human nature; but when we consider the whole of humanity and its history, this weakness seems to be exploited

[1] John viii. 44.   [2] Luke x. 18.   [3] John xiv. 30.

by some foreign malice which could not annul the transcendent order ordaining the foundation and building of the City of God, but which in revenge is determined upon creating in it internecine strife, spoiling the work, and stirring up the human race against the builders of the City.

We can observe this abnormal perversion early enough. To be under an illusion as to our goal in life, or as to the means of reaching it, is natural to us; but not to run contrary to our own nature, against the essential impulse which carries it towards life and to happiness through life. The beast and the angel are indeed in agreement on this point. The beast in us, as in animals, cries out aloud in its desire for joy and for life. It is to live that the angel within us aspires when he inflames our souls and even torments the flesh itself with a desire for God.

If we merely regarded this desire as vain, if we should call God and joy and life things unworthy of those names, then our action would still be human in character; but it is inhuman to carry error to the point of hatred of joy and of life and a despairing love of death and of evil.

If we should be atheists, and deny the existence of the Perfect Being infinitely wise, omniscient, just and good, it is possible for this blindness to come solely from ourselves; but, having denied God, how should we hate Him, unless the devil prompts us? Suppose we say and believe that life is a sinister farce, kindness a piece of trickery, virtue an empty word, happiness a chimera and religion a poetic falsehood: these follies belong to us; but if the devil does not mix himself up in it, how comes it that we should go as far as denying our own nature, hating it and striving against it by doing everything possible to pervert it in us and around us, and finding in this destruction a bitter joy?

Such rancour against human nature cannot possibly be imputed to humanity alone. We must recognize in it him whom the Bible and the Church agree in calling "the Devil and Satan", the enemy of the human race, the calumniator, the very spirit that from the beginning of mankind has had the

quality and intentions of a murderer. He plays his part in the
work of sin and death, in the work of disruption and dissolution, of the perpetual acts and events of destruction which fill
the pages of history. Against this work of evil the building of
the Holy City goes on, permanent in its progress.

III

MAN CONSTRUCTS THE CITY OF THIS WORLD

Let us endeavour to define the rôle played by the evil one,
and for that purpose, let us begin by seeing more precisely the
rôle played by man. One word will be sufficient to establish
the precise definition: selfishness. All that we can adequately
explain as the result of unrestrained love of self is human and
nothing but human. It is no doubt true that the Prince of this
world derives an advantage from it. If he did not intervene
in such actions, the evil would be less and the decay which
followed neither so swift nor so profound. The social instinct
would in that case offer a better resistance to the instinct for
anarchy and disorder which saps and mines it, though in the
end it would give way to anarchy and disorder, would allow
itself to be led astray, corrupted and destroyed. The angel
and the beast conspire within us to render the defeat of the
social instinct inevitable.

The angel in us—the spiritual part of us—is simply devoured
with pride and is passionately in love with illusion. It poses
as the centre of everything. Whether or not the angel recognizes that failing in itself, it aspires with all the forces of its
being to exercise domination, even when it is under the
delusion that it is acting solely from a desire for equality
or a love of independence, even the sentiment of brotherhood. And so you see it in contradiction with reality. Overcome by the harsh logic of fact, it takes refuge in a land of
dreams, changes its desires into ideas, its prophecies into utopias,
and fabricates for itself in the abstract "felicities which make it

shed tears of tenderness" at the very moment when it sets all things on fire and sheds oceans of blood for the achievement of the marvellous future it has dreamed. In China, in Greece, in Rome, in India, in Germany, in England, France and Russia, everywhere there have been upheavals of States, their transformation and their ruin. The tribulations suffered by the Kingdom of God in those countries come in the first instance from that cause.

In such a situation the beast finds his opportunity. Let us write down to his liability the madness of pillage and of lust, cruelties, rancours, vengeance, revolts stirred up by the spirit of envy, the lust after carnal enjoyment, the worship of matter and of brute force, the blindness of souls which no longer have any vision of the divine, and the downfall of all that animality into very rottenness.

Such then is what develops from self-love and selfishness. "*You shall be as the gods* knowing good and evil," is a tempting saying: what meaning would it have for man if, without it, he did not aim at growing to that status? In reality God created him and put him in this world to achieve a divine life. Man makes a mistake if he looks for his destiny too low, as Antiquity deceived itself in looking for and adoring the source of human life under the figure of an ancestor or of some obscene symbol. He desires to find within himself the divinity towards which his being gravitates. He makes himself a god of his head, of his heart or of his belly; of his money which obtains for him enjoyment and power; of his power, finally, as a State or Prince whose condition appears to him as the manifestation of the divine essence, immanent in humanity.

His deviation from the true path is sufficient to explain all this. St. Augustine has expressed it definitely for all time: "*Two loves have created these two cities, namely, self-love to the extent of despising God: the earthly; love of God to the extent of despising one's self: the heavenly city.*"[1] This is a profound view of things because in its ultimate secrets it penetrates to the reality of history. The love of oneself tends to become con-

[1] Przywara, *An Augustine Synthesis*, p. 265. Sheed & Ward, London, 1936.

tempt for God. Call it as you will, free-thought, free-criticism, individualism, humanism or humanitarianism, the mere name is of no importance to the question. It aims at self-deification, under its form of power. Idolatry—adoration of the creature—conceals and engenders everywhere that adoration of the self in man which is also the basis of pantheism, of atheism, of anthropomorphism and of magic. It is the most ancient and the most constant of phenomena which thrusts itself upon our attention, that sooner or later the father of the family, the chief of the tribe or clan, the king and the State usurp the divinity of the Creator. At this end or limit Occidental polytheism and Chinese monotheism join company, the political-religious system of Confucius and the religious politics of the Caesars.

And even that remained human.

IV

SATAN IS THE HIDDEN PRINCE OF THE CITY OF THIS
WORLD

But it has disappeared and no longer exists: nowhere does man adore himself in this way, unless he is also a worshipper of demons. Bossuet's saying with regard to the ancients is well known. "When they apply themselves to religion," he declares, "they appear as if possessed by some exterior spirit and they seem to abandon the light of their natural intelligence." In direct proportion to the lack of that vigour of exclusion which saved Judaism and of that infallible authority which was conjoined with exclusivism to preserve the Catholic Church, all religions open wide their doors to errors which begin as human and puerile and end as diabolic. They tolerate them in the masses of their adherents, perhaps because they are unable to eliminate them, or perhaps they attach but little importance to such aberrations, or put no value upon the masses of the common people. It often happens that they themselves are entirely absorbed by them. They slip downwards from illusory mysticism, proud or sensual mysticism to the depths of diabolical mysticism; from magic to sorcery and fetishism, from the cult of nature, of the dead and of idols to the worship of demons. The natural light is put out. The foreign spirit from outside is installed and begins his work in the darkness.

Sometimes the stranger spirit reveals himself wholly or partially. Mr. H. G. Wells and the followers of what he calls the modern religion; certain savages who think it reasonable to render worship to evil spirits because they are dangerous—the Yezidis, for example, worshippers of Satan; those Satanists who exalt Lucifer as the perpetual champion of pride and revolt, know that their god, their "invisible king", their "captain of humanity", is not "the Infinite, Absolute, Unconditioned", the Creator, "the veiled Being enigmatic, incomprehensible, who hides himself right at the back of existence and scarcely ever bends over the mirror where the busy shapes of life are dying".[1]

Generally speaking, however, it is Jehovah who manifests Himself openly in the universe. The Other seeks concealment behind the city of this world, behind the screen of man's egoism. But ever and again a shaft of hatred directed at Jehovah or the Church of Christ reveals his presence: hatred so atrocious, so tenacious, so universal, so contrary to all reason, to all the true interests of men and to the instincts of humanity amongst those who are intoxicated by it, that we cannot help recognizing in it the stranger spirit.

This stranger spirit has no abiding city. He builds nothing. His only occupation is to overthrow and turn upside down every piece of the divine work he can find to attack. He is the spirit of evil, that is to say of darkness, chaos and nothingness; he is capable only of destruction; but he has seized upon and he monopolizes the City of the world. He is its lord and master. For his own purposes of death and destruction he exploits the mistakes, the weaknesses and the malice of men;

[1] Wells, *God, the Invisible King.*

their virtues even and their thirst after divinity; the ambitions of their masters, whether they be States or princes, whose
aim is identical with his own desire, namely to supplant God. He
acts under and behind a multitude of masks; he is treacherous,
cunning and secret in all his doings, which are often difficult to
detect in their genuine character, as we find in the texts of St.
John in which Jesus expounds what may be described as the
theory of the world.

It is a human world.   At the beginning of things there exists
in it only the family of Adam which is separated from God by
the barrier of man's original sin.   God so loves the world of
men that he gives His only begotten Son to save it from
the consequences of that original sin.   In itself then the
world would be no more the enemy of God than it is the
kingdom of God.   It appears upon the scene simply as
the "enclosed field", the lists or tournament-ground where the
"Kingdom of Heaven" and the "mystery of evil" confront
one another.

Jesus makes the choice of the witnesses and the apostles of
His kingdom in the very heart of the world, and He leaves them
there: "*And now I am not in the world, and these are in the world,
and I come to thee.*" They remain in the world in order that
the world may have faith and that the kingdom, preached by
them, shall grow until it covers the whole earth.   "*And not for
them only do I pray, but for them also who through their word shall
believe in me, that they all may be one as thou, Father, in me and I
in thee ; that they also may be one in us ; that the world may believe
that thou hast sent me.*" (John xvii, 11, 20, 21).

Whence then came the antagonism which exists between God
and this world?   It began in the scorn of the world for God:
an expressed contempt for the salvation which God offered to
the world, a contempt for the apostolic evidence, for prophecy
and for the miracle of the "Spirit of truth which the world
could not receive because it was unwilling, either to see it, or
to understand it." This deliberate blindness, this refusal to
submit to facts which are divine and to believe in the eternal
realities brought about the change from the redemption which

x

had just been effected through the Christ to the condemnation of the world.

"He that believeth in him is not judged. But he that doth not believe is already judged: because he believeth not in the name of the only begotten Son of God. And this is the judgment: because the light is come into the world and men loved darkness rather than the light. For their works were evil. For every one that doth evil hateth the light and cometh not to the light, that his works may not be reproved."[1]

"If I had not come and spoken to them, they would not have sin: but now they have no excuse for their sin. . . . If I had not done among them the works that no other man hath to do, they would not have sin; but now they have both seen and hated both me and my Father."[2]

It is not then in the course of a mere speculative discussion that the world is judged and condemned, nor upon its errors, nor the things of which it is ignorant. It is judged on the facts. It is condemned for lack of sincerity and double-dealing in face of the realities of life and of those testimonies which prove the divinity of the Christ in his own person and in the person of His Church.

"If the world hate you," declared Jesus to His Apostles, *"know ye that it hath hated me before you. If you had been of the world, the world would love its own; but because you are not of the world, but I have chosen you out of the world, therefore the world hateth you."*[3]

This hatred which is the condemnation of the world puts it to death by delivering it to the domination of Satan. From that moment the work of redemption, the sacrifice offered to God to save the world and to deliver it from the power of Satan overcomes at one and the same time both Satan and the world. *"Now,"* said Jesus at the moment of leaving the Last Supper to go to the Garden of Gethsemane and to Calvary, *"is the judgment of the world: now shall the prince of this world be cast out."*[4]

[1] John iii. 18-20.
[2] ,, xv. 22, 24.
[3] John xv. 18, 19.
[4] ,, xii. 31.

The Prince of this world: he who exploits the miseries of humanity, the king of hatred and falsehood, he who dominated Antiquity in the bosom of which a little people reduced by its misfortunes to nothing, on the confines of the desert, preserved intact the spiritual trust, the truth, charity and the understanding of life and of history which had been entrusted to it.

The Prince of this world still; the Lord and Master of the City of this world, the Caesar, the State and the usurper of divine rights; just as the other was cast out, so this one will be cast out, wherever his domain is found. He is indeed already cast out. Christ Jesus has put into his proper place him who was being deified everywhere in the world. Render to Caesar the thing which is Caesar's, that which is exterior and ephemeral. To God render that which is God's, the interior domain of immortal souls. Then when this was done, there began, in this world below, between the Kingdom of God and the City of the world where Satan is in hiding, the struggle for divinity.

Nations dispute for empire with one another; empires dispute for dominion over the whole world. In this way is history made; it is the result of struggles for power, wealth, glory and deification. This time it is no longer deification which is at stake, but actually divinity itself. The question at issue is whether the Church of Christ is divine, or merely deified, as the State and the princes of the world are deified. If she is divine the Church is invincible: nothing shall prevail against her, she shall never be dissolved. If she were merely deified, she would be human only and sooner or later she would undergo the lot which is common to all things human.

What then could possibly remain in this universe which we might name Very Good and Very Great, Very High, Supreme Master, Sovereign Lord Universal, Invisible King and God? Nothing whatsoever unless it were the humanity which remains whilst the generations of mankind pass away: humanity and its "Captain", the God of the religion of our modern times, of free-thought, of free morals, of sin without a hell awaiting it, of history without a Providence to guide it, of the omnipotent and universal State; the world and the Prince of this world would then at length "have vanquished the Jehovah of the priests" and cast His Christ outside.

CHAPTER II

THE STRUGGLE FOR DIVINITY

I

THE FIRST WORLD-WIDE ASSAULT (33–313)

WE now have the first combat with all its splendour—the triumph of Him who suffers and dies over him who slays.

From the year 30 to the year 313 for two centuries and a half the Kingdom of God continued to extend, and actually invaded the realm of Caesar; it placed itself above that realm and increased the number of its people in the very heart of the empire in spite of the persecutions which decimated it. It was not the agent of destruction; rather what is capable of being saved from decay is preserved by the Kingdom of God. It lifts up, brings light into the world as well as health and order. It serves mankind, and yet it is the Kingdom of God that the world is determined upon destroying.

And what a strange spectacle this is! The same doctrine, the same Church, the same Christ arouse in the hearts of some that marvellous love which enraptures them with joy under the very kisses of pain and death; amongst others they arouse a hatred which is as ardent and as inflexible as that love. Why does it happen that those who love are so fiercely execrated if they draw everyone to them and compel none?

A reason is doubtless to be found in jealousy, in self-interest, unreasoning fears, secret shame, prejudices and popular superstitions. But this is not a complete explanation of the hatred directed against the Kingdom of God, from the time of Nero to Diocletian and Julian the Apostate.

Was the hatred of the Church and of Christ caused by calumnies on the part of pagans and Jews? Without doubt;

but the persecuting power knew full well that Christians did
not indulge in unnatural orgies, did not eat little children,
did not worship a crucified man with an ass's head, did not
enter into conspiracies against Caesar. It was not Christians
but pagans who practised the bacchanalian rites, the Saturnalia
and prostitutions in honour of some god or goddesses, who
immolated their children on the altars to Moloch, deified
animals and dethroned emperors. There was no great difficulty
in discovering that.

Why was there so deep a hatred exhibited against the
Church? It is easily comprehensible that the Jews should be
subjected to persecution: they monopolized wealth. They had
the reputation of hating other nations and fomenting revolts.[1]
They dreamed of a temporal Messiah who should trample the
kings of the world underfoot and should rule over the Gentiles
with a rod of iron. But the Church? It preaches obedience,
respect for established order, fidelity to the established prince,
probity and zeal in the service of the State. St. Paul who was
thrice beaten with rods teaches us to see in its worst enemies
on the throne only the "ministers of God for good". He
declares that if we resist their power when the divine law is
not at issue, "we indeed resist the order of God."

Yet those men who tolerated everything else did not tolerate
the Church. It seems that there was to be found for the
Church no place amongst those civilized societies whose
development made them hospitable to so many religions. The
world passes on easily from one doctrine to another, embracing
and then detesting easily. But in its detestation of Catholicism
the world is obstinate and this hatred is the greater inasmuch
as the Crucified One and His martyrs, bleeding from their
tortures, fascinate, captivate and draw away from the world
the élite of mankind.

In this never varying division of the universe upon the
subject of Christ and His Church between a violent passion
of hatred and a corresponding passion of love, in spite of the

[1] These are the reproaches levelled at them by Tacitus (*Hist.*, v. 5). With regard
to their constant revolts, see the Chronicles of Josephus.

differences of times, countries, races and civilizations, there is something manifested which goes beyond our human nature.

It is the same as in the example of the martyrs, all of whom are heroically similar in every epoch and under all latitudes, whatever may be their age, sex or colour. We see them in our own days. Chinese or Bagandas, they are quite ignorant of the deeds and sufferings of their brothers who lived and died so many centuries before them in the empire of the Caesars; and yet feature by feature, very often word by word, they reproduce them. There is the same firmness in their faith, the same lucidity when they face their judges, the same peace of mind and calmness in the tortures they suffer, the same pardon for those who torture them and the same impulse of joy and love towards God who is quite near to them.

In very truth Jesus' promise is realized: "*When they shall deliver you up, take not thought how or what to speak: for it shall be given you in that hour what to speak. For it is not you that speak, but the Spirit of your Father that speaketh in you.*"[1] One sole Spirit for all, one sole energy. "It is not my flesh which is suffering, it is the flesh of Jesus Christ", said the old unlettered ignorant woman, Liou-Wang-Chou, under the Boxer's swords when they were cutting her to pieces from head to foot according to the rules of the art and were astonished at her motionless silence. At an interval of 1,700 years, and as if in another world, the Spirit repeats through her the famous words with which it inspired Felicity, the young slave, three days before the feast of Caesar Geta in whose honour she was thrown to the beasts in the amphitheatre of Carthage.

The Spirit of the Father, the flesh of Jesus Christ: there lies the secret of this unsophisticated, simple and quiet heroism, of those joyful sufferings and those joyous deaths. Even in the absence of those humble women and of the Gospel itself the numerous children of from two to twelve years of age who perished in a similar manner in the course of the ages rather than deny the Roman faith would also reveal the secret with sufficient clearness. Neither the stubbornness of pride or

[1] Matthew x. 19-20.

fanaticism, nor the callousness which is the result of ascesis, nor that physical insensibility which is natural to certain temperaments and to certain races could be alleged as a cause of such martyrdom. There is undoubtedly something super-human in it.

In a similar manner, even if it is natural that the first rapid progress of the Christian faith should provoke a reaction, it is unnatural that this reaction should be produced in so short a space of time and with such violence, perfidy, method and unity throughout the whole world. It is very evident that a foreign spirit is playing a part therein.

And he interferes and plays a part in the sphere of doctrine as well as in the sphere of action. At first, force does not occupy the front of the stage, except to be found mistress of the world and ready for the struggle at the first advance of the apostolate into action. When the martyrs for Christ vanquished force, heresy took its place; already, however, that new enemy was on the move behind scenes preparing to make its future assaults.

Heresy sprang from syncretism which had made an amal-gam of all the religions of the Orient ever since the Orient became Greek and especially since Rome surrendered to its power. It emerged from Gnosticism, which was the issue of this syncretism and which was doing its utmost to extend it to Western paganism, to the religion of Moses and to the faith of Jesus Christ.

What then is this Gnosticism which claimed to absorb all doctrines, to interpret them in their depth, to initiate the élite into the joys of ecstasy and the light of traditional secrets, to bring salvation to all men and to reveal the mystery of God? It was a vast religious advance, the secular movement of an army which for numbers was as the sands of the sea-shore, infinitely supple, wave-like in its movements, diverse, deployed upon a universal front, as ready for the manœuvre of infil-tration as for mass frontal attacks.

Simon Magus of Samaria, Basilides the Gnostic of Alexandria, Valentine of Rome were leaders of movements and manœuvres against the Church of St. Peter. There were others who conducted operations on other fronts. For whose benefit and in what direction? To have an answer to these questions there is no need whatever to explore their labyrinthine subtleties from end to end. We already see how they belittled God and relegated Him to the background. Under the pretence of magnifying Him and escaping from anthropomorphism in the conception of His nature they made capital out of His wisdom and His power. They personified His attributes. They interposed between Him and the universe lesser gods, divine beings that were emanations of His being. These do everything; He does nothing. He exists.

Thus they drove Him into the exile of His own being. They drew a veil in front of Him, just as the modern religion of H. G. Wells drops a veil in front of God; but they raised that veil to reveal to us the gods whom they had painted as angels of Light and the "Archontes", the demons, evil spirits and princes of the world, whose leader and chief, according to Basilides, is none other than Jehovah. And so we have the God of the Jews and of the Christians set amongst the ranks of the devils, though He may be at their head. As for the Scriptures they were interpreted according to a fictitious, arbitrary and unbridled system of symbolism.

Nicolaites, followers of Cerinthus, Docetists, Marcionites, Montanists, Manicheans, all the heretics of the time gravitated around this Gnosis. All of them more or less issued from it, and their numbers never ceased to grow in proportion as the chance of destroying the Church by violence diminished. The very defenders of the Church—Clement of Alexandria and Origen, that powerful genius—did not escape from the contagion of this heresy.

What was the basis of all this? At the point of departure and all along the route—the self-confidence of the philosopher and of the exegete, the startling feats of the ascetic and the magician, the uncontrolled delirium of the false mystic, individual fantasy, hungry for secrets, for initiations, for prestige and mysterious intoxications—there was simply love

of self. In the end dualism, emanationism, magic—three
pantheistic ideas from Iran and from India; in a word
contempt for God, and behind it all, he who is adored
under the name of God. Truly St. Paul was justified when
he said "already the mystery of iniquity is at work".

The mystery of iniquity—foundation, way and goal—makes
the unity of heresies, of paganisms and of all spiritual usurpations. It is easy enough to jest about the worship of animals
or about "God the cobbler who mends God the old shoe". But
if everything is God, then in its claim to divinity on earth
humanity has hold of the right end of the stick, and the Prince
of this world likewise: "Thou art that, I am thou. We are
God." Their situation is much better in that respect than if
the assertions of the atheists are true.

A fruit attractive and appetizing to the eyes, pleasant to eat
and desirable as a means to the acquisition of intelligence is
there once more, under the hands of the daughters of Eve
and of the sons of Life. "Eat thereof," says the Tempter.
"Far from dying therefrom, you shall be like gods—And I
shall be on equality in rank with the Highest."

II

TRENCH WARFARE (313–1517)

The attack which had been made en masse, was fiercely
delivered and tenaciously sustained yet it came to an end in a
disorderly retreat. From 311 to 323 Galerius, Diocletian,
Maximian and Licinius who headed the last columns of
assaults—the most dangerous in their co-ordination and
violence—saw with their own eyes Constantine on the throne
of Nero, the Labarum carried before the Eagles, the Church
at last set free and a Christian empire.

And was it peace that followed? There is no peace in this
world for that which is not of this world. The struggle had
scarcely begun. It had to be a long struggle, from the hour

when the most powerful force which up to that age had made its appearance in the world of humanity found itself incapable, even by putting the whole of its battalions in the field, of assuring the victory of the attackers.

Did this force pass over to the conqueror? It could be turned into weakness. It was a human force: decadence and death were on the watch for it. And then there exist other forces amongst men: they could be stirred up against it. It is possible to create dissension and division amongst the victors, to lead them astray, to weaken and corrupt them. The assailant does not belong to those who suffer discouragement: he has nothing to lose. Fixed for ever in his hatred, he brings into this struggle the fury and the stubbornness of his despair.

He also brings his subtlety, his depth of cunning, his knowledge and his dissimulation. For outside of this world he has no power against our souls: the mere will is sufficient to conquer him with the grace of God, and their own scorn soon gains the upper hand over this tempter, who is "strong in will and weak in force" in the phrase of St. Ignatius Loyola; but in this world, whether we wish it or not, he is the Prince and his perversion has not deprived him of his intelligence.

What a complex and consummate art he displays in his manœuvres. What foresight and what promptitude. If we consider them in isolation and one by one, or in little groups, the movements which are made use of by his foresight and promptitude can be explained by local and purely human reactions; but it is the Prince of this world who stimulates those movements, gives them their direction, co-ordinates their efforts or sets them at variance for their worse confusion; and, for these reasons, it is clear that the whole hostile movement, considered without prejudice, furnishes evidence of the action of a single commander-in-chief, remarkably powerful, stubborn and ingenious.

The great attack had failed. To reconquer by a surprise attack and at one single stroke the ground which had been lost, the vanquished foe immediately attempted a counter-attack against the weakest points in the victor's lines. The defence

of Christianity is now in the hands of men who but yesterday
were pagans, who have joined the Church because it is now a
social advantage or because everyone else is doing so; for the
venturesome theologians fascinated by philosophical speculations and very ready to think that their genius will succeed in
defining and illuminating dogma; the civil power recently bap-
tized and always ready and willing to covet the rôle played by
God: there were plenty of leaders and a crowd of followers to
bring reinforcements to the vanquished Prince of the world in
his plan to ruin the Roman faith from inside.

In the fourth century we have the priest Arius, the bishops
who followed him and the whole tribe of his posterity of
heresiarchs, supported by Constantine, Julian the Apostate
and Valens. In the fifth century we have the Arian kings of
the Goths, Vandals and Burgundians; the monk Pelagius and
his acolyte Celestius; Nestorius, patriarch of Byzantium and the
archimandrite Eutyches. At the beginning of the seventh
century the patriarch Sergius and his accomplices, the emperors Heraclius and Constantine II.

The times were favourable for the attack on the Church
when the advance of the Huns resulted in the mobilization of
the Barbarians; when the empire of the West, invaded, was
going to pieces, when the Pope and the bishops of the Latin
world, engulfed in this shipwreck, had to save civilization in
its dire peril; to prevent Italy, Gaul and Spain from foundering
in this ocean of anarchy; to convert to Christianity the newly-
arrived peoples in the Latin world and to transform their
wandering tribes into States.

It will no doubt be said that there was nothing supernatural
about this advance or its consequences; that heresies are
inevitable; that in the development of dogma they play a rôle
which is providential; that the spirit of routine, of innovation
or of contradiction which heresies engender have nothing about
them specially demoniacal. One cries out to go one way,
another cries out to go another way. People grow angry
and stubborn; and on both sides excesses are multiplied. That
is only human nature. That certainly is true, but what about

the unity, the continuity and the method which throughout the centuries bend so many hostile sects and parties to the same plan and reduce to the same denominator so many irreducible fractions?

They fight one with another and they hate one another, but they all of them in short time involve themselves in the same mystery of evil as the Gnostics: they strive to humanize God, to turn man into a god by deifying humanity, the State or matter; they strive to subordinate the spiritual to the temporal, the universal to that which is merely national, the Church to the civil power; to sum it all up, they strive to abolish "Him who Is" or to relegate Him into the abyss of silence so that they may leave the field free to the stranger spirit.

Arius denied the divinity of Christ thereby reducing the church to the purely human level,—reducing also to the same level you also see the condemnation that Jesus uttered against this world and the Prince of this world. Change becomes their law. Faith and opinion are mingled in a "confusion worse confounded". History no longer has any direction.

Nestorius denied that man and God in the person of Jesus Christ are one person: He thus emerges by another door upon the same road.

Eutyches denied that Christ had two natures; later on Sergius defined this more clearly, by denying that He had two wills: the second confusion opened the way to the first and the first opened the way to all the confusions which are engendered by pagan pantheism.

Pelagius and Celestius denied the necessity of grace and of original sin: this also is a confusion, a pagan confusion between what is supernatural and what is natural; it is the initial confusion of Lucifer who, in the madness of his pride, declared that unaided he would acquire the perfection of the Highest.

Such were the tactics of the Prince of this world during the course of these 300 years. They very nearly succeeded in their objective and they broke down only in part. The Nestorians and the Jacobites of Syria, masters of Mesopotamia and Persia,

barred to Catholicism the ways which lead to China and the
Indies. Their Christ, thus belittled in power and influence,
carried into those lands only diminished and corrupted versions
of the truth. To rival Buddha and Brahma in the full enjoyment of their empire, or merely to avoid being absorbed by
them, a very different force was necessary and a knowledge
possessing higher qualities of illumination. In this way it
occurred that the whole vast extent of Asia was forbidden
ground to Simon Peter for many centuries.

He would have seen himself reduced to terrible extremities
if the Arians and Pelagians had triumphed in Europe and in
Africa. Luckily in these lands the Prince of this world suffered
defeat upon defeat. Just as Irenaeus, the martyred bishop
of Lyons, won a victory over the Gnostics, so Athanasius,
Jerome, Ambrose, and Augustine gained decisive victories
against the new heresies. The Franks in Gaul were converted
to the Roman faith and laid the foundation of France, the
eldest daughter of the Church. The Lombards in Italy beat
the Ostrogoths and were converted. The Pope and the
bishops who acted as the defenders of the cities made up for
the negligence of the empire. Mediaeval Christendom springs
up from the soil straight, strong and thick as a field of new wheat.
Once more the Kingdom of God had proved itself the victor in
the struggle.

There was a fresh retreat for the spirit of evil and then new
tactics were adopted. Paganism was found to be too heavy
with errors for souls which were athirst for the truth. The
world fell back upon heresy, but a heresy at last unmasked and
revealing its true features. Souls now turned away from the
pleasant road which they saw would lead them back to the
ancient falsehoods. The Prince of the world in his newly
adopted tactics must hide himself more skilfully, be still more
cunning, look more like truth. For lack of any thing better
he must content himself with sowing tares amongst the wheat
as it grows. Schism had already tried itself out at the back
of the stage. Let it now come to the front. It must now be
multiplied, diversified, renewed. Sooner or later it will weaken

unity, render authority feeble and uncertain if not actually blind and guilty. Shocked and scandalized souls will in their complete desperation turn to the austere sort of heresy or to the new paganism.

The Barbarians of the North allowed themselves to be converted; but there were others who would not be converted. For them specially a religion was made in their own image and to their measure; it was simple and rigid in its worship, but supple and bending in its morality. It was Islam, or rather, beneath that pious name, Mahometanism, which since the death of Kadija was wholly given up to its temporal and warlike ambitions.

In the first rank of the idolators whom the followers of Islam were ordered to hold in contempt and hatred, and to kill like dogs were placed the Christians, infidels as far as the Scriptures were concerned (according to the Moslems) and worshippers of three Gods: Allah, the Christ and His Mother. The holy war was preached to the followers of Mahomet. They were hurled from Arabia into Syria, against Egypt and thence against the West. Jerusalem, Alexandria and Carthage fell before their victorious arms: Byzantium was besieged, Persia invaded as well as northern Africa and Spain; finally Aquitaine.

The circle of steel would have closed round Rome if the Hammer of the Franks had not broken through it at Poitiers. That victory marked the arrest of the advance of the false Prophet in the West and was a prelude to the Crusade which was to thrust back the Moslem hosts towards Africa, until the Crusaders advanced to seek them on the Orontes and the Jordan's banks, in Egypt and in Tunis. But from this time for more than a thousand years the Churches of Cyprian and of Athanasius remained the prey of Islam and for seven centuries schisms worked their revenge upon the Church by disrupting without respite the unity of the Eastern Church.

There were the national schisms of the Iconoclasts (726-842), of Photius (867-886), of Cerularius (1054): Byzantium, though she had many times recognized it, denied the primacy of Rome; and in this way we see Christianity broken into little pieces—amongst the Greeks and Slavs into as many pieces as there are nations. Being an annex of the State, the Church was shut up within the walls of the State. There were schisms, discords, political revolutions and a renascence of pagan law: Marozia, Crescentius and Tusculum, Roger of Sicily, the Roman republic; the quarrel with regard to investitures, the jurists of Frederick II, of Philip the Fair and of Charles V.

In addition to these there were pontifical schisms, finally there were schisms amongst the cardinals and the councils of the Church: there were two, three and four popes at once, with men unable to discern the true pope; there were schisms at Bâle, at Constance and at Pisa. The University of Paris appropriated to itself the saying of Christ: "I am the light of the world," and laid claim to confirming him whom the Christ had charged with the duty of confirming his brothers. Everywhere there was turbulence; there were abuses, sterility, corruption and a welter of disorder. Reform became necessary. It was urgent but impossible.

Only 700 years, centuries of faith, centuries of love of which men of genius were the creators and architects—Charlemagne, Bernard, Francis, Dominic and Thomas Aquinas, Gregory VII and Innocent III—only 700 years, and behold Christendom in chaos, at an impasse. In such a catastrophe there is too much cunning and vigilance, too constant, too purposeful a concentration, too persevering a method to be the resultant of mere chance, of the force of circumstances and the logic of events and of passions. A master hand must have been at work.

From 1418 it became clear that the Prince of this world had this time gained a victory. Doubtless he would not prevail against the Church. He would not demolish her. He would be unable to prevent her from effecting a reform and from growing in extent and influence. But he did not go so far in his demands. He desired to open the doors to heresy and paganism; and that was precisely what was to happen.

Pass on to the year 1450. Mahomet had invaded Thrace and was threatening Constantinople. The paganism in Italy submerged everything. Wyclif, the Lollards, John Huss, Jerome of Prague and John Wessel had blazed a trail for Luther. The Medicis, the Farnese and the Borgias had already raised themselves to power in the Church. Under the apparent chaos of the battlefield a new attack of great extent was in preparation. The time was at hand when the work of St. Leo IX and of St. Gregory the Great was to be undone and the mastery of the struggle pass into the hands of that world for which Jesus Christ did not pray.

III

THE SECOND WORLD-WIDE ASSAULT (SINCE 1517)

What more need be said? The facts that have been enumerated are eloquent of themselves. What we have learned by following the world-march of the Human Caravan and by examining its leader of to-day, the Occident, with regard to the direction taken by history in this march and to the destinies of the human race, goes to prove that everything holds together, is linked together and co-operates in the winning of the same ends in the confused mêlée of the City of the World warring against the City of God.

The disorder caused by schism carried the nations of Christendom along the broad road which leads to apostasy. Apostasy made the disruption of Christendom inevitable. The Reformation was the beginning both of the apostasy and the disruption in Germany, in France and amongst the Anglo-Saxons, opening up the path for "philosophy," for naturalism, and for pantheism; whilst the ephemeral Renascence weakened the faith of the Roman Church, supplied pretexts to the Reformation for its policy against Rome and urged on the Latins and the French towards that modern paganism which was the child of Rousseau and the "philosophic church" and

Y

the grandchild of the Renascence, of Calvin and of Luther. Letters, arts, sciences, law, philosophy, theology and politics, naturalism and pantheism, disguised and camouflaged as laïcism, socialism, and humanitarianism, invaded everything in human life, deifying under the name of the State or of Humanity, the City of this World.

And now the issues in the struggle, the spirit of the contest, its plan and method appear in full light. There is nothing new under the sun, neither Renascence, nor Reformation, nor Revolution, nor modernity, nor modernism. There is, however, "the mystery of evil" which was already at work at the time of St. Paul and since that time has continued and developed its campaign under our very eyes, in its haste towards the fulfilment of its designs. The struggle is waged round divinity. That fact becomes evident in the centuries when the State is elevated into a deity rather than in the centuries when individualism was in control, or the centuries of the schisms, of invasions, of heresies, or even of persecutions and of the Gnostics. The Adversary certainly has not yet thrown aside his mask. "I believe in the devil" is a *credo* which will not figure so soon on the list of the innumerable acts of faith which the credulity of unbelievers imposes upon themselves. It is part of the devil's policy thus to deceive the multitude into whose hands great power has come, through the universal upward flight of democracy in the world of to-day; but he acts behind the veil, delivering the mass of men over to the errors, lies, dreams and idle speculations of the half-baked scientists and savants of the modern world, to politicians, journalists, showmen. As far as possible he conceals himself as in the past; but the disguise is wearing thinner.

For the lists are now the whole universe. They have grown too vast, the combat too desperate. Those who have knowledge see only too well the inter-relation of facts in time and space and the common end or goal towards which these facts are all in movement, in spite of their contradictions; the unity of their origin, or at least the unity of method of the men who are exploiting them, in spite of their diversity or of their incoherence; the insidious, specious part played in the universal mêlée by the old Oriental paganism and by Islam, the skilled occult help they lend to the new paganism of the West, for all the scorn they pour on it. Does not the Western world ever since the time of Luther bear upon its forehead the double sign—hatred of God and subversion of His divine work—by which we can recognize the "stranger spirit"?

Everything Christ preached during His mission on earth: truth, liberty, justice, peace, brotherly love, constant progress, the renunciation of self for others, has been taken from Him, overturned, and perverted. Of these abstractions, they manufacture "immanent forces", superior forces which are sufficient in themselves and which must be conciliated by means of a cult entirely verbal: they are idols. They have been placed on pedestals in the modern pantheon where other deities have been enthroned according to times and places: civilization, culture, race, fatherland, class, strength, law, science, revolution, free-thought, humanity and democracy. What magnificent names the immortals bear in this new Olympus. But above them all hovers that all-powerful Jupiter, the absolute master and lord of men and things, the god of gods, the prince of this world, the State.

The "lay State"—it is evident that everything has been secularized with the most intense thoroughness, even Christ Himself. Since that day when Simon Magus thought that Christ was for sale, the world has found satisfaction in presenting the Christ in one form or another and in varied terms as "the first of the sans-culottes". And so you have men in the place of God. The only thing that now remains to be accomplished is to put the beast in the place of man. That is easy, for the beast is already installed within man. It is enough to give the beast precedence over the angel, and for that end to set free the beast in man.

And so the world is breaking in pieces the two chains which restrain the beast: morality and the family. Divorce, worse indeed than concubinage or polygamy, is there, waiting for the advent of free unions to multiply the discords of the married state, to encourage free love, to legalize lust and abandon children to their fate. The supporters of the State will rob parents of their rights, if indeed the parents do not abandon them of their own accord. The State itself will mould and furnish in its secular style the minds of the people of the future world.

In this fashion will grow and develop that generation which in the full meaning of the world will be modern, for whom legality, hygiene and solidarity in lust and covetousness will be the alpha and the omega of morality. Every way which leads towards the ultimate goal of its journey, towards the only progress which does not bear within itself the seeds of decadence, and necessarily ends in happiness, will be shut against the Human Caravan. Whether it then follows the roads of prosperity or of poverty, whether it falls away into savagery or achieves a unity under some form or other of "culture" and of "civilization", the Caravan will no longer be a Human Caravan, it will be a Herd of Cattle.

In the meantime revolutions are on the increase throughout the world; they extend and grow more serious. Just as outside Catholicism the whole of philosophy since the *Discours de la Méthode* of Descartes tends to make a god of man and the whole of sociology since Rousseau has tended to make a god of the State, in the same way since Karl Marx and his *Capital* the whole of political and social democracy has tended to render incarnate these divinities in the mass of the manual toilers and then to hand over to them "all the kingdoms of the world", especially the Kingdom of God.

The first of the attempts proved to be abortive because favourable circumstances, adequate preparation, mutual understanding and energy and fidelity amongst their accomplices, were lacking in the revolutionaries, but a day came when all that had hitherto been lacking was found as united and combined as could be desired. On the 7th November, 1917, Lenin put his hand on Russia and from that very moment his aim was a revolutionary world. He knew precisely what he was doing and what he wanted to do. He thought what he was later to say openly: "The Russian revolution is a mere prologue to the world revolution. If the revolution does not break out in other countries very shortly we shall be destroyed." His successors were to hold on to this watchword. From 1918 Moscow neglected nothing to carry it out everywhere possible. In Finland, Germany, Austria, Hungary, Bavaria, Turkey, Italy, France, Bulgaria, Esthonia, Morocco, Great Britain, China, Mexico, the Indies, in the United States of America and in Spain, everywhere throughout the world the Soviets carried on their intrigues; they bribed, they pursued their campaigns of propaganda, they stirred up risings as soon as the propitious time arrived and the hour struck. The fact that they suffered defeat after defeat made no difference to their actions. "If the West holds out against us", said Lenin, "we will turn our efforts towards Asia. We shall come to the end of the West by the instrumentality of the East." And at the Baku conference held in 1920, Zinovieff repeated: "The 800 millions of Asiatics are necessary to Russia to crush European imperialism and capitalism."

In Russia, however, the subversion has been achieved. In every direction the Christian notion of man, of marriage, of the family, of society and of the State has been eliminated. The contrary view has been taken to that which obtains in Christian States. Schools, the law, those who govern, all work at the task of creating a new humanity, unique on earth and unique in history: a godless humanity. All are to be atheists. At once the child of matter and its master, the human race must free itself completely from belief in the Spirit. In it animality alone must dominate and excel itself in order to exercise its final empire over the world. That is the principle underlying Marxism and the goal it aims at reaching. It is difficult to know to-day what exactly is happening in the Land of the Soviets. Whatever it may be, whatever the course of events there, he who strives to establish in this manner the soulless and Godless empire of man belongs to the beast in man.

The finger of God is perhaps there; but most certainly we see the claw of the Prince of this world. "There is not the slightest doubt that the spirit of the Tcheka is the most diabolical spirit which has ever reigned on the earth", wrote the German Keyserling quite recently; and elsewhere in his books he gives incidentally this definition which illustrates his thought— "the tendency of the Bolshevists, by denying and combating the deepest elements in the nature of men, is to bring about the reign of a Satanic spirit." To deny, to combat, to overturn the work of God, to confuse and corrupt those aspirations which are essential to human souls and the very order and nature of things, is undoubtedly to furnish undeniable evidence for the recognition of Satan in such activities.

IV

THE UNLEASHING OF HATRED

What lies beneath these proceedings is no longer weakness, nor ignorance, nor folly; it is hatred, a reasoned hatred, intended and complete; a hatred which lives in the head and in the heart, a hatred of the intellect and of the emotions, lucid and implacable.

To crush the Church was the aim of the eighteenth-century Encyclopaedists in France; of the fifteenth-century Humanists in Italy—Poggio, Filelfo, Marsuppius, Valla, Beccadelli, Platina, Pomponius Laetus and others. It was the aim of Wyclif and John Huss, the aim of Luther when he was at grips with his Catholic and sacerdotal conscience which he called the devil. It was the aim of John of Leyden, of Calvin and of all the other sectaries. To find a motive for that cry they did not hesitate to accuse the Church of all kinds of error, false-hoods and idolatries of which she had never been guilty even in the tenth century, or during the Great Schism, or during the time of Alexander VI and Leo X.

In France, once the wars of religion had been settled, there was no outburst of this hatred amongst the Libertines and the Huguenots, except from time to time in the intimacy of some conventicle, or in forbidden leaflets passed furtively from hand to hand. It grew bolder under the Regency; then it broke out in the fireworks of the Encyclopaedists. Let us not forget the part taken in this pyrotechnic exhibition by the soi-disant deist, Frederick of Prussia and the wits of his court, those who fluttered like butterflies around Catherine of Russia, the "Semiramis of the North", and those of England who attracted men to them to listen to the lessons they had to teach.

"In twenty years God will see fine sport," cried the patriarch of Ferney, carried away by an impulse of joyous sincerity. Twenty years afterwards God saw the French Revolution and the atrocities there committed in the name of humanity. He saw the sack of convents and monasteries, the churches of the land profaned and polluted, the faithful priests driven out and several thousands of martyrs guillotined, massacred or made to perish by slow death. The revolution sang its blasphemous songs in "full throated ease" and elevated upon the high altar of Notre Dame de Paris a dancing woman as the symbol of the goddess of reason.

What followed these events is well known. The lay religion of which Quinet and Michelet remain the prophets in France and the modern religion of which Mr. H. G. Wells has made himself the evangelist in England are unmistakably religions of hatred directed against the Church, Christ and God.

This hatred pierces in all directions through and through the works of these writers and their imitators who are equally unrestrained as detractors or apologists of Western Civilization. It also pierces through the laws of Masonic Jacobinism. It is hatred that flames forth in many a passage of that Bible of Science which Wells claims to have bestowed upon humanity in his *Outline of the History of the World*. His *God the Invisible King* draws all its eloquence from it. Hatred crawls about amidst the obscurities of theosophy and occultism, when Satan does not enter upon the scene to disperse them by displaying himself there in its company. There are no other depths but depths of hatred in the initiative secrets of Masonry wherever it is found. Upon hatred reposes all the hope of a world-wide revolution: "What is needed," said Lunatcharsky, "is hatred. We must learn to hate. Then only when we have learned that lesson shall we be able to conquer the world."

And what a commentary this is on the word of Christ with regard to the bonds and the resemblance existing between human charity and divine charity. Everything is bound together and abides. Everything is revealed. We now begin to understand the anguish suffered by Pius X when he ascended the throne of Simon Peter.

"The thing which terrified us more than everything else," he wrote, "is the present condition of mankind which is extremely deplorable. Is it possible to ignore that human society is engaged in a struggle, more terrible now than in past centuries, with a very grave and very deep-seated malady which grows worse from day to day, is corroding humanity to its very heart and is dragging it down to ruin? You know quite well what this malady is: it is a falling away from God, an apostasy. . . . In very truth, against their Creator 'the nations are distracted in tumult and the peoples of the earth meditate vain projects' to such an extent that it has become almost commonplace to hear the cry of God's enemies: 'Withdraw from us.' With what audacity and fury everywhere in the world the people rush to attack religion and its practice. A breach has been made in the teachings of the revealed faith; it is demanded that man should be set free from his duties towards God; and there is a stubborn struggle being waged to achieve the total abolition of such duties. In return, man himself, by a temerity unparalleled, puts himself in the place of God, to such an extent and so completely that he dedicates this visible world to himself, as if it were a temple in which everybody must adore him."

The World War and its frightful consequences have made no difference whatsoever in this condition of affairs; yet it is possible to get a glimpse of great days coming for the Kingdom of God in the future. The struggle for divinity is moving forward rapidly towards its decisive battles.

Between the Invisible King of Hatred, the Prince of this World, and Jesus Christ, the Invisible King of Love, the issue of these battles is not in doubt. The Church knows that the crucifixion of Our Lord followed Palm Sunday and was a prelude to the resurrection. It is awaiting with equanimity its holy week and its Easter, repeating to itself the words of the Master: "*In the world you shall have distress. But have confidence: I have overcome the world.*"

SIXTH PART

THE REMAINDER OF THE ROAD

CHAPTER I

THE DIRECTION OF HISTORY

I

FUTURE OSCILLATIONS

WHAT is the remainder of the way to be?

"*What is it that hath been? The same thing that shall be. What is it that hath been done? The same that shall be done. Nothing under the sun is new.*"[1] Give to the words of Ecclesiastes all their depth and plenitude. We must scrutinize the future by the light of the past and we shall be able in the shadows to catch a glimpse of something that is going to happen.

Nothing permits us to think that the laws which govern the Human Caravan are ever abrogated, any more than the laws which govern the fall of material bodies or the ascensions of souls. Since the first origin of human things such laws have been in operation without exception. They still play their part, but with a force accumulated from all the weight of a long past. They will continue to play their part in the world until the end of things and their power will never cease from growing.

The elements of the transcendent and of the supernatural in history are added to the elements of the natural and perfect them without destroying them. They are the work of the same Craftsman; "He saw everything that he had made, and, behold, it was very good." Why should He unmake it all? If, when He comes down to this lower world for the purpose of accomplishing a work which is still better, He appears in the midst of the sons of Adam as "a sign of contradiction", this can be only because of the errors which flow from human

---

[1] Ecclesiastes i. 9–10.

331

liberty. He indeed denounces such errors and aspires to cure the evil consequences to mankind of the first of them. He takes all of them upon His own shoulders in order to expiate them all. His desire is to enfranchise men from evil and in this way to make them like God: and men refuse to receive the boon. The great efforts He makes to overcome this refusal and to deliver those who consent to receive His benefits, in spite of those who are unwilling, cannot make any change in His designs, as a creator, nor yet in the laws which ever since the beginning of the world have ruled over its fulfilment in the order of nature.

The first, which is the law of cyclic continuity, embraces and penetrates all the other laws. That which comes is born at all times from that which departs, and prolongs it. This process, cataclysms, miracles and revolutions cannot prevent. There are "turning points in history", but if they are "turning points", they are also "in history". What remains of the road is a part of the road—it is one journey and one road.

There is no going back. The Jacobins of France thought to raise Brutus from the dead; the Lutherans thought they had brought back to life Silas, Barsabas or Apollos; the Clers of the year 800 thought they had brought back Theodosius; but Charlemagne, his peoples and his work belong for ever to the ninth century and the kingdom of Eastern Gaul; Luther, his people and his work belong for ever to the sixteenth century and the country of Germany; just as Chaumette, Marat, Danton and Robespierre and their associates in crime, their Jean-Jacques Rousseau and their revolution belong to the eighteenth century and the country of France.

To-morrow will only have the seven colours of to-day with which to paint its own picture. At the most, only the shade and the composition will be changed in that picture. We can therefore think of nothing whose seed cannot be found in the present, we can dream of no building for which the materials are not already heaped one upon another before our very eyes, no renovation or destruction which is not already in preparation. Napoleon was, first of all, the sub-lieutenant

Bonaparte. A little later he took his rank amongst the political generals of the Directorate. His "18th Brumaire" was nothing but the inevitable consequence of the "18th Fructidor". His armies were the armies of the Convention and his policy towards Great Britain merely that of the Bourbons and the Ancien Régime.

The struggle for divinity will be fought over the whole globe. It is of small importance whether man himself, or the State, or some Caesar should claim the status and dignity of a god, or declare that everything is God, or allege that there is no God. It is of little importance that Satan remains behind this veil, as he hid behind the old paganism, or shows himself in the open. It is the fact alone and not the word that counts.

As soon as man refuses to God what is His due and usurps His place, he deifies himself even if he denies the existence of the soul and in this way puts himself upon the level of the animal. As soon as he abrogates the law of God, legalizes sin, canonizes egoism and selfishness, speaks evil of the Christ and the Church of Christ, persecutes their faithful followers, works to corrupt, divide and overturn the divine work, he becomes the worshipper of Satan and serves him, whether he realizes it or not.

When we speak of the deification of the State, or of the prince, it is mere puerility to imagine the Kingdom of God as victor upon earth, like a universal Salentium, where the sons of Adam are all saints. There will always be idolatry under numberless forms, and until the end of things good and wicked will live together, just as the rich and poor, the diseased and the healthy, fools and wise men.

Events are clearly not moving to the immediate and complete ruin of the City of God, nor to the immediate and complete destruction (or conversion) of the City of the World. Everything is conspiring, it is true, against the first; and, like Pierre Loti at the end of his journey in Palestine, we could well believe in the approaching advent of "tyrannous and frightful democracies in which the disinherited shall no longer even know what prayer is". We must, however, pay attention to the fact that God does not, generally speaking, make use of honest men to execute His justice upon those who are guilty and whom He has resolved to punish by driving them from the pages of history.

To build, to repair, to put in order, to pacify, to ameliorate, to civilize are tasks for honest men. It is the others, the wicked, whom God uses for the purpose of punishing the wicked. Those who destroyed Rome were not Christians: they were Barbarians; nor did Christians destroy Jerusalem: that was the work of the Roman legions; nor were the persecuting Girondins crushed by good and honest men: the Jacobins put an end to them; nor did good men bring about the fall of the Jacobin terrorists: they were suppressed by a *jeunesse dorée* who were themselves of no great value. Attila, Genghis Khan, Timour and Lenin were the scourges of God. When God desires to destroy the wicked He overwhelms them so that they shall devour one another.

It was necessary that the modern world should at length come to the apostasy of the nations, to the unchaining of egoism, of pride, of brutality and hatred; to the triumph of individualism, according to Luther, Rousseau, Kant and Marx, an ancestry greatly reinforced by the work of Hegel, Darwin and Nietzsche. Only after such apostasies could implacable wars break out in the midst of their posterity in the Human Caravan.

The Godless-State, radical democracy, absolute nationalism, socialism, humanitarianism, and their many different shades of thought, are to-day engaged within the chaos of the world in mortal combat without any other issue at stake than despotism or anarchy. In this fashion, in the present crisis, that which was produced in the great crisis of the sixteenth and eighteenth centuries is engaged in self-destruction by the achievement of its logical perfection. We are now liquidating four centuries of history: no other explanation of our time could possibly give its meaning in totality.

This places us at the end of one of the widest and unsteadiest oscillations which the law of cyclic continuity has yet traced out in the life of humanity; and because we are approaching the dead point, the play of this law becomes perceptible to us. Once more apostasy itself has prepared a triumph for the Galilean. Humanity aspires to enjoy peace, justice, mercy, and to arrive at the discovery of truth with an ardour which is all the keener since apostasy has completely thwarted humanity of the enjoyment of such boons and reduced mankind to the severest extremity. The City of God is the only possessor of the means to satisfy such aspirations. She alone can enlighten and preserve the consciences upon which reposes all that men can, without deluding themselves, call order, well-being and happiness.

Whether they know it and wish it or not, when once the dead point has been crossed, it is towards the Church that soon all the power of their desire and all the momentum of their past will hasten their march. Either that, or we shall see approaching the end of all things, eternal failure: for nature and the supernatural are mingled in such a manner in human destinies that humanity could not betray the supernatural without at the same stroke betraying its own nature and falling into mere animality. How can we believe in this dénouement twenty years after Might—better armed, better disciplined, better prepared than ever since the beginning of the world and surer of itself and its power to crush everything—gave way, apparently on the high road to victory on the banks of the Marne and the Ourcq, under the shock of an heroism determined to stay its advance and to snatch the future from it?

Since that day, doubtless, the struggle has changed its appearance and as it grows to its full magnitude, its direction is more clearly seen. Joffre's soldiers were not slow to perceive that they were fighting for a William Pitt against a Prussian Napoleon who possessed no genius. Foch's battalions saw very clearly that they were pulling the chestnuts out of the fire for the Entente—Anglo-American! I would not like to give my word with confidence that either Joffre's men or Foch's felt much satisfaction or were bursting with delight when they perused President Woodrow Wilson's Fourteen Points as the

z

foundation of peace. The upshot, anyhow, was that the democratic and mercantile individualism from over the sea broke
and defeated the despotic and military individualism from over
the Rhine.

But who shall destroy this individualism? After all is said,
the dictatorships are individualistic in principle. They are in
opposition to several of the laws which give irresistible force to
the profoundest movements of the Human Caravan. Including the dictatorship of the proletariat, they seem to be very
fragile. How could they succeed in doing what France of the
great Napoleon and Germany of Bismarck, of Hindenburg and
Tirpitz could not do? It is extremely doubtful if they will
have time to carry out their policies. The strongest amongst
them and the most advantageously placed, the dictatorship of
the Soviets, has already put its hand to the task; but there is
an awakening in Asia. Her hour is drawing near; yet before
that hour strikes the worm will have caused the fruit to drop
from the tree.

"He who takes the sword shall perish by the sword"; he who
causes division shall perish by division; he who preaches
demagogy and revolution and makes them last amongst other
people for the purpose of extending or consolidating his own
empire shall perish in his turn by them; he who intoxicates the
universe with the poison of speculation in order to exploit
it, shall perish by that same poison. The Soviets and Asia
will be only too ready to lend a strong hand to bring about
the rule of "immanent justice" as the simpletons of the day
call it.

There is no point in prophesying either collapses or restora-
tions which will last for ever; it is better to speak of transformations and of crises, struggles, assaults, successes and reverses,
of recoveries and the agonies of dissolution; these are the
ordinary run of human things. ever since there were men
upon this earth; only they have gained in speed and have
become worldwide. The dismemberment of Chistendom, the
apostasy of the nations, the world-wide conspiracy against
the Church, Christ and God, reveal in their totality too

powerful an offensive to be wiped out by a single blow. It is possible for such an offensive to be counterbalanced, as it was during the seventeenth century in France; but a triumph, even a brilliant and striking triumph, of God, of Christ and the Church would do no more than restore the equilibrium of things. This effect would become quite evident as soon as the victors relaxed their efforts. The peoples of the world have eaten the unripe fruit of pride, of envy and of hatred and their children's teeth shall be set on edge. Sooner or later they will be drunk on the wine which at the present moment is intoxicating their fathers. No. The immediate and total ruin of the City of the World is no more to be foreseen at the present moment than the ruin of the City of God.

The whole surface of the globe, the whole abyss which exists in human societies and hearts is filled by this battle. It leaves nothing aside, it enters into everything. Do not believe that one or two changes in the position of the champions will put an end to the conflict. The oscillation will continue with ever growing force, weight and rapidity in the universal struggle between anarchy, Catholicism and the despotism of the State. The human race is promised to them as the prize of victory: this results from their nature and the whole meaning of history.

Days are coming when the Gospel of the Kingdom shall be preached throughout the whole earth with sufficient force and authority for the nations to receive its testimony in all the power of truth and in their turn to be able to repeat it to others. Days are coming when the God-State, the new Caesar, shall in one guise or another possess the whole world as his domain (not excluding the United States) and shall have humanity at his mercy. But the days shall also come when this world-wide edifice of the City of the World, giving way in collapse, as formerly the Roman colossus on its feet of clay, shall crash down into anarchy.

II

TOWARDS A UNIVERSAL UNITY

There are other laws in operation, some against the first law, others merely diverging from it, but the majority acting in the same direction. The inter-play of their combinations does not present to us so many possibilities of equal likelihood as to preclude all prevision of their results.

At the very beginning it is fully clear that, if human affairs move towards universality; if they have always been approaching it afresh since the beginning of things; if their uniformity and concentration continue to grow at the same pace; if this pace is regulated by the multiplication of the numbers of men and their dispersion and the extension of their empire around the globe, thanks to the riches and the forces of nature which are ceaselessly used and on an ever-growing scale—then the conjectures which I have just formulated become, in their basic essentials, almost certitudes. Now in these there exist laws that are beyond conjecture in their certainty, permanent laws: we have already made this observation as we followed the march of the Caravan. Of its truth there remains not a shadow of a doubt.

Let us move forward on this firm ground. Not less permanent and sure in its operation is the law of political organization. The future of the world will obey its demands and requirements. It is an illusion to think that the great unities of future times, leaving intact the sovereignty of States, will limit their activities to gathering the States, so to speak, into sheaves in the economic, social, moral or political order.

We must not of course deny the power of national sentiment. Ireland, Poland, Finland, Germany, Italy, Spain and France have supplied us with too many proofs of it, to say nothing of Japan and Switzerland, and of the numerous independent States along the Danube. The star of nationalism is scarcely beginning to pale and decline over Europe. It is rising in its full brilliancy towards its zenith over America and Asia.

And what of the imperialisms of the world? It is the star of nationalism which sets them in movement over the four quarters of the globe and guides them by ways which converge towards that universal hegemony which one day they will fight over. The excesses of "separatism" must be favourable to their progress and guarantee victory to that one which shall know how to stir up exactly the agitation necessary against its rivals and to discipline such agitations in its own ranks or lull them asleep. There exactly lies the reason why the crowding together of the nations who are rushing towards the goal of independence or do not desire to lose any little fraction of it, will continue to result in grouping them into political platoons, the denser and livelier as the rush becomes more violent and the imperialisms more voracious and powerful.

It goes without saying that these ententes, alliances, and coalitions can be at the same time of an economic, social, moral, even spiritual nature. Sometimes the fabric of their relationship at the very beginning is woven on only one of these threads. The others follow and then comes the political thread in the fabric which is being woven. In this way too the imperialisms of the world take advantage of confusion; but the thread of politics is always brought in. Why should it not be on this occasion; since inevitably it is already in the fabric? It is indeed only waiting to be used. In the relationship of peoples and nations we shall most certainly see enlacements and weavings hitherto unknown in which the thread of politics will be the principal strength of the fabric.

I do not know what the League of Nations can become or bring about, nor the International Bureau of Labour, the International Institute of Intellectual Co-operation and the other Internationals of all orders, colours and calibres which flourish in our days. Their destinies are of less importance than their origins. They come into the life of the world by virtue of necessities which are unavoidable. We can prophesy as we choose with regard to them: miscarriage, growth, metamorphoses, disruption, universal supremacy. There remain the factors of peace and war, to-morrow as yesterday and to-day and on until the final crash—and these factors of necessity tend towards bringing the nations into groups and making these groups total and world-wide.

To trace upon this colossal plan the result of the forces which move the Human Caravan is a problem of history; but the solution of the problem is thrust upon us almost as clearly and certainly as the solutions of the science of mechanics. The Caravan is marching towards that major unity which Joseph de Maistre saluted from afar, without having yet perceived it. But we perceive it now. Whether it be an entente, a coalition, an alliance, a concert of Europe, a society, an imperial group, or a group of States of a new kind, it is above everything else thoroughly political. It is an ethnarchy, a State whose members are States gathered together under the aegis of one of them just like chickens under the wings of the mother hen—or driven there for shelter by the terror of the hawk. If there should rise amongst them a chief or leader, he will be the master of the earth; but the chief or chiefs are but men and that is where the fall and collapse will come: for nothing in human affairs escapes from the law of internal contradiction, the law of death, unless it be the Church of God made Man. The grand unity oscillates in its turn between Catholicism, anarchy and the despotism of the State.

Two other laws, moreover—that which lays upon the shoulders of humanity an increasing weight of matter and that which imposes upon its collective institutions an unceasing growth of complexity—make this destiny particularly irresistible.

We live under the weight of numbers, under the control of the machine and of money. That ability and value, either in good or evil, will some day dethrone mere numbers, can be regarded as certain. That day seems indeed to be very near. That capital and mechanical force will sooner or later change hands and employment is no more susceptible of doubt. But that His Majesty King Money and Her Majesty Queen

Machine, whose power is constantly strengthened and re-inforced by the operation of these two laws, should be so soon broken and destroyed can only be thought of in dreams. To put them back in their place amongst the simple tools used by humanity would require such a cataclysm, so complete an upheaval of everything, a depopulation of the globe so unlikely, a world revolution so profound and violent or of so long a duration, that it seems scarcely possible.

The analogy of the dead civilizations is not at this point of much use to us: the circumstances of to-day are too different from theirs. At the most we could call before our minds only the fall of Rome which appeared to those who witnessed it and its prophets as a general rehearsal for the end of the world. There are no longer any Barbarians, however, to overwhelm from outside the civilizations of to-day; and the barbarisms they conceal, like the civilizations themselves, have but one objective and one ambition: to possess themselves of both money and machinery in order to subdue them to their own uses.

Whether we consider the idea of replacing England by the United States of America, or of substituting the East for the West as leaders of the Caravan, or of putting the proletariat in the place of the bourgeoisie; of restoring as world powers Europe, Islam or China; of giving back Asia to the Asiatics or of handing the whole world over to the Universal Republic, it is upon the machine and money that we must count. It is vain for us to rely either at the same time or in the first place upon anything else whatsoever; we must submit to these two powers. We cannot neglect them. Even the Pope is compelled to have a budget. Just like the rest of the world Gandhi makes use of the press, without speaking of the other things which imply money and machinery; and the campaigns of propaganda which he undertakes must concern themselves with the possession of the sinews of war, equally indispensable whether war is carried on by the explosive power of shells or of ideas.

A great unity without money and machinery, reduced to domestic trades, to local cultures, to nearby markets, to slow

methods of communication, and to speculations upon the
money and coins hoarded away in stockings by a thrifty
peasantry cannot be thought of. Nor can a great anarchy. We
shall not see the Human Caravan moving off in that direction.
The miracle which should cause it suddenly to turn back again
along the path it has traversed would be unique in its history
and it would reverse the direction of that history. Such a
miracle has no place in the round of previsions, probabilities
and conjectures. God alone knows and could inform us if such
a miracle will or will not happen.

We must therefore regard it as an indubitable fact that
commerce, industry, finance, economic and social organization
of the production and consumption of real wealth, the natural
sciences and their practical applications in industry will continue to play a capital rôle in the march of the Caravan. The
preponderance of financial interests and material means,
already very great, will not cease to grow: it is the great trump
card of the Soviet and American republics, born of such a
preponderance and bound to continue it—in themselves almost
complete political and social realizations of our modern civilization, as it is offered to our eyes and minds when we follow
the recent advances of the Human Caravan around the globe.

Even in that same direction the complexity of things and the
rapidity of their movements are destined to increase. Time,
like space, will be reduced in its bounds: that is the law of
acceleration. Here is our new measure of time: in our own
days within a period of four years and three months of warfare
we settled a mightier dispute than that which a century back
disturbed the peace of Europe and the world for twenty-seven
years; and between the years 1792 and 1815 the face of Europe
was less changed than the face of the world between the years
1914 and 1920.

The future will be lived at a still greater pace than the
present. Just as our modern budgets juggle with thousands of
millions, our forecasts seem to juggle with centuries. It is
possible that the centuries of the future will pass away as
swiftly as those thousands of millions.

CHAPTER II

THE MARCH OF THE CARAVAN

I

SEPARATION OF THE TWO CITIES

THERE exists to-day a civilization which is of no country, of no race and of no colour; a human civilization. That civilization is the daughter of the West and has invaded the whole universe of man. The Orient, divided both for and against Western civilization, to-day toys with the ambitious dream of at one and the same time regenerating it and ridding the world of its presence. The Orient has rushed into Western paths and yet on the whole despises the civilization which comes out of Europe, execrates it and chafes against submission to it.

In this attitude the East is both wrong and right. The civilization of the West is double in its nature. Being the creation of the Church as well as the work of the Apostasy, it deserves the enthusiasms lavished upon it. They are, however, often addressed to its less deserving qualities and characteristics and even to those that are vulgar and vicious. Western civilization has also merited the anathemas hurled at it as its due, though they at times have been directed against its nobler and better attributes. The spirit of man, faulty, credulous and limited in capacity and vision, continually makes mistakes. The Prince of the world is fully aware of the fact and profits by it. He is also fully aware that between a society of just men and a conspiracy of those who are wicked and perverse, the game is no more equal than between an honest player and a rogue. He relies upon this fact and upon the success of the conspiracy of hatred entered into by the wicked.

His scheme is a simple one; it is to urge the ignorant multi-

343

tude on towards these errors by flattering its passions; to make
it regard the just as the unjust and the unjust as the just; and
by this method to assure himself of the alliance and the formidable power of a justice that has gone astray and been
deceived; to ruin in the work of the Church everything which
cannot be marked down in value to the advantage of the
apostasy; finally, by means of this depreciation and denigra-
tion of the work of the Church, to take forcible possession of
the part which the Church could still retain in a civilization
which has banished the Catholic religion from its midst. If
you study one after another the numerous assaults upon the
Church made by apostasy for some 500 years or so, you will
be unable to find one which is developed upon another plan
than this. Each attack in detail is a summary of the main
attack of the forces of apostasy and plays its rôle in it.

Next consider the direction of history, the revolutions which
have taken place *en route*, the awakening of Asia and of Islam,
the Catholic and apostolic renovation of the Holy City, the
gravitation of humanity towards her, the great unities which
are now in process of formation, the great unity of the day
after to-morrow and its normal crumbling away into universal
anarchy. In this entanglement and confusion you will perceive the gradual sketching out of the march of the Caravan.

In the first place there is an exodus, the exodus of its advance-
guard the Church. The liberals looked upon themselves as
eternal in a universe always in ecstasy when it contemplates
the progress and the liberties of the science and genius of the
West! To them Pius IX seemed to be a man of the Middle
Ages, possessing neither prudence nor moderation of judgment
in his condemnation of the axiom dear to their hearts: "that
the Roman pontiff can and must reconcile himself and put
himself into agreement with progress, liberalism and modern
civilization"; how out of date it seemed to them that Leo
XIII and his successors should wish, in the world of Bergson,
of Tolstoi and of Darwin, of Hegel, of Kant, of Spinosa and of
Descartes, to send the Church back again to the school of
Brother Thomas and that Pius X should proscribe Modernism

and leave to Protestants alone its fruitful principles and judicious methods! To-day we realize how profound were the views of these great popes and how wise their decisions.

The works to which they put their hands Pius XI seems to have hurried to perfect. One thought there is, one keen anxiety which dominates his mind: to set free the Church throughout the world from all temporal contingencies and from the dangers of the shores of Genesareth and to steer for the open sea. It is quite clear to us that He who enlightens him and gives him courage knows there are perils, more or less at hand, and necessities more or less vital for salvation and the apostolate, which make necessary this direction of the helm. The Church must free herself from such temporal contingencies. She even renounces the Seven Hills. She does not desire to be mixed up with secular powers, with merely human wars and political dissensions, with party struggles between governments whatever they may be, hostile or favourable, beneficent or the agents of persecution; she does not desire to be mixed up in economic rivalries and social discords, with alliances, ambitions and the jostling of nations, of empires and of races. Neither East nor West for her: only the human race.

She intends to remain at all costs what she has always been and must always remain: the kingdom which is not of this world, the Church Universal, the messenger of holiness sent to all people to bear to them the testimony, the sacraments, the precepts, the dogmas, the peace and the love of the Lord Jesus Christ.

Once more Gregory XI is leaving Avignon and Simon Peter is leaving Judaea. The very essence and the mission of Catholicism make this exodus unavoidable under the operation of four causes: first, the apostasy of the West, secondly, the growth of revolutions, thirdly the awakening of Asia and of Islam, and lastly the entry of the Human Caravan upon that world-wide stage of its journey which is leading it towards unity.

In this way, universal history brings its confirmation to

clear thinking minds and upright hearts who on both sides of
the Rhine and the Alps have been able to understand that
"the only force capable of offering resistance to the tradition
of dissolution of the Reformation, of modern individualism,
of religious nationalism, is Catholicism, but a Catholicism
deeper, more integral, which does not allow itself to be intimi-
dated by anything, which shows its acute scorn for petty
interests, tears all the masks from Satan's face and, cost what
it may, defends the rights of God."

What can possibly be the result of all this, if not a separation ever more complete, visible, decisive and intransigent
between the City of God and the City of this World in the
sphere of the spirit? "I represent to my mind the new epoch
which is coming, as opening up to man Two roads," writes
Nicolas Berdyaev, who arrived at the same conclusion as myself
by other ways than mine. "On this summit of history a definitive divergence is about to take place and operate. Man is
at liberty to take the first road, to subordinate his being to the
higher and divine principles of life and upon this earth to
strengthen his own human personality. He is equally at liberty
to subordinate his soul to other principles, neither divine nor
human but preter-human and wicked, and to make himself
their body-servant."[1]

There is no lack of historians and philosophers whose minds
are preoccupied with the future of humanity and who see it
under this aspect. It is of small importance that certain
amongst them invert the rôles played by the actors on this
scene and, giving a false interpretation to the words, glorify
the City of the World for having been the first to blaze a
trail. The fact is that we must make a choice. On the one
hand the Church and Jesus Christ; on the other hand the
ancient paganism of the East, Islam, the paganism of the
modern world and the Prince of this world. The separation
between the two sides will become so clear and the conspiracy
so manifest that it will be no longer possible to any of us not
to make a choice. The sheep will follow the Shepherd.

[1] *Der Sinn der Geschichte* (Darmstadt, 1925), p. 250.

II

THE ETHNARCHIES

In this wise the Human Caravan will continue to march along towards its supernatural end and, by the same action, will accomplish its own destiny in the natural sphere. In the realm of things temporal, however, the course of affairs seems also to be moving in the direction of other divisions.

On the one side let us consider the hegemony of the Anglo-Saxons; the power, the riches and the ambitions of the republic of the United States of America and the fact that the Americans live under the necessity of dumping their manufactured products upon the whole of the world, of forcing the world to consume their products; the increasing fragility of the British Empire and the indignation and hatred felt by Islam, India and China against the English; the awakening of Asia and its modernization on Western principles; the return of all the Russias to the vast bosom of the ancient continent and the consciousness at length aroused in Europe that it is running a fatal risk by remaining too long in a state of division against itself.

On the other side we must add to these considerations the world-wide condition of human affairs, the preponderance in them of the power of money and the machine; the artificial needs of humanity, its radical selfishness, its practical materialism, its automatic mercantilism both impersonal and international in its nature which are the fruits of money and the machine; the lust for gain, for speculation on the stock exchange and for domination which these fruits arouse; the unscrupulous collective competitions, the merciless struggles that obtain in commerce and industry, the mortal hatreds and finally the false and deceptive peace under the mask of which are stirred up those passions which lead to international brigandage.

We see upon the blackboard a whole system of complex equations, the solutions of which are not easily perceptible through the complicated network of expressions and symbols— among them those events which are entirely supernatural: Pilate could not, for example, foresee the resurrection of Jesus, nor Bedford the coming of Joan of Arc. It is within the logic and probabilities of facts that the Human Caravan will first assemble in the times which are coming in a small number of groups, combatants and competitors for the hegemony of the world : colossal powers at one and the same time political, economic and military in their natures and constitution, resembling those which existed at the beginning of the twentieth century, the British Empire, the Triple Alliance and the Triple Entente.

From now onward we are able to distinguish four of such colossal powers: the United States of America, Islam, Europe, and the East, though it is still impossible, at least for the last three named, to enumerate with precision their elements, their territories and domains and the way in which they will assume corporal entity. We catch a glimpse of their warfare upon one another and their mutual struggles which will inevitably be the prelude to the grand unity to follow. This unity next in the process of time will arouse the united attack of all the elements which make up the City of the World against the City of God, henceforth entirely separated from the rest of the universe. Like those that preceded it from the time of Christ to our own days, this assault does not set armies at grips with one another, but puts torturers and their victims face to face. It will be an assault in the nature of a persecution, leaving the victory, as always, to those who suffer persecution and to their children.

These are far distant perspectives: some will doubtfully shake their heads; others will openly declare that they are altogether chimerical. Distant perhaps they are; but the law of acceleration may very well bring them closer to us than we now think. Chimerical, perhaps they are; and yet the method I have adopted in this book and which I have studied, worked at and perfected for more than forty years has not proved fruitless in results.

What will the dénouement be? Whether it comes soon or late, history from the hour that it has taken its direction will affirm that dénouement in its entirety; but what will it be? "The days of Noah . . . little faith . . . the net cast over all those who live upon the face of the earth . . . the light which comes out of the East and shines even unto the West . . .?"

With regard to all that, history knows but one thing: the Gospel affirms that the Son of Man will come back, for the purpose of closing everything. The remainder is not within the domain of history. It has nothing to say of it. Along with history I am silent and in the silence I listen to the words of the Prophets, the Apostles and our Lord Jesus Christ.

A NOTE FOR THE READER WHO IS IN A HURRY

AA

A NOTE FOR THE READER WHO IS IN A HURRY

THE reader who is in a hurry has indeed no time for a discussion with the author. He admits that a statement in the book is true, or denies it with equal promptitude. He runs the risk of following his own ideas, rather than those which find expression in the words he reads and, in this manner, of putting into what he reads concepts and meanings which are not to be found therein. It is for the purpose of helping him to escape from this error on essential points, and to save his mind and his time, that the author's position is here summarized first as to historical determinism (First Part, Chapter I, para. 1); and then as to the position of the Roman Catholic Church in history (Fourth Part).

I

HISTORICAL DETERMINISM

(1) Divine liberty is perfect and absolute. It is subject to no limitations. The power of the divine will over the facts and movements of human history is absolute. (Cf. p. 7.)

(2) The liberty of the individual human being remains complete within the four walls of history. The only matter in question is the power of the individual human will to control the facts and movements of history. (Cf. pp. 4 and 5.)

(3) The power of the will of the individual human being over the facts and movements of history is limited by "the obscure and profound force of accumulated causes" and their effects. (Cf. p. 5.)

(4) The extent of this limitation:

(a) The power of the will of the individual human being over the facts and movements of history is limited, in direct proportion to the isolation of its actions, that is to say: the greater its isolation the greater the limitation of its power. (Cf. pp. 5, 6, 32, 33.)

(*b*) Its limitation is also in direct proportion to the amplitude of the facts or movements, having regard to the whole extent of history, that is to say: the greater the amplitude the greater the limitation of the power of the individual human will in this respect (Cf. pp. 4 and 6.)

(*c*) As far as the great historical movements are concerned the will of the individual human being is never absolutely without power (Cf. pp. 4 and 6; but :

Pitted *against* these great historical movements, the power of the individual will is always weak (Cf. pp. 5 and 6.)

Outside their scope the individual human will is capable of doing more; *with* them, that is to say by acting in the same direction as the great historical movements, or in some related direction in which the force of such movements can be made use of, the individual will is capable of acting very effectively. It sometimes even occurs that its action may be decisive and may indeed change the face and course of things: that depends upon its own qualities, upon its own means and upon the value of the other will-powers which act in its support. (Cf. pp. 5 and 6.)

(*d*) As far as the divisions of time are in question, the power of the individual will amounts to *nothing* at all over the past and its consequences; it is *direct* upon the present and *more or less great* according to people and circumstances; it is *indirect and more or less great* upon the future through the consequences of its present acts, but it has *no* power over those consequences themselves. (Cf. p. 7.)

(5) Demonstration of the preceding remarks. (Cf. Third, Fourth and Fifth Parts.)

(*a*) In the past there is not a single one of the great

movements of history in which the rôle of the individual human will has ever gone beyond the limits thus defined.

(*b*) Sudden catastrophic changes, even the most sudden, have all of them been in preparation for a long time and the effects they produce are entirely due to this lengthy preparation.

(*c*) The divine masterstroke of the Incarnation itself, the only one which since the original fall of man has really and definitively altered the course of things and brought the struggle to a definite conclusion, was prepared slowly and wisely during the thousands of years which intervened between Adam and Christ.

(*d*) On the contrary the masterstrokes that should have achieved success, having regard to their strength, but yet broke down in spite of their careful preparation (e.g. Xerxes, Hannibal, the persecutions and the invasions of the fifth century, the Hohenstauffens, the Mongols, the Lancastrians, the captivity of the Popes at Avignon, Charles V, the Hohenzollerns) failed because they were in opposition to still more powerful preparations and living historical currents, growing in force and in harmony with the central current of history, such as our observations with regard to the movements of the Human Caravan and its different stages have brought to our knowledge.

(*e*) To this objective and positive demonstration there can only be opposed an argument which is entirely subjective and negative: "Cleopatra's nose . . ." For example: If (conjecture) Henry VIII or Mahomet had not given way (negation of a fact) to pride, ambition, lust; England, Africa, the East would be Catholic (subjective opinion unproved and incapable of proof).

II

THE PART PLAYED BY THE ROMAN CATHOLIC CHURCH IN HISTORY

(1) If there exists in history one or more transcendental religious societies devoted to the absolute progress of the human race, then history has a direction and meaning; if not, then history has no such direction. (Cf. Second Part, especially Fourth Part, Chap. I, No. IX.)

(2) The Roman Catholic Church declares: "I am transcendent, that is to say, divine, because I am the Church of Christ; and the proof that I am the Church of Christ is that I am at the same time one, holy, catholic and apostolic."

(3) Now:

(*a*) If Christ is God, the Church of Christ must be divine and transcendent.

(*b*) The four marks which the Roman Catholic Church claims for itself are precisely and definitely those of the transcendent religious society which the direction and meaning of history postulate (unity, and so exclusivism; universality; permanence; absolute progress). (Cf. Fourth Part, Chap. IV, No. 1.)

(4) And so:

(*a*) To know if history has a direction and meaning or not, it is indispensable to examine the claim of the Roman Catholic Church to be the only Church which possesses all of these four marks. (Cf. ibid.)

(*b*) If this claim is well founded it proves both the transcendence of the Roman Catholic Church and the divinity of Christ.

(*c*) The three problems—the divinity of Christ, the

transcendence of the Church and the direction and meaning of history—are in fact but one problem (cf. ibid.)—and it can be approached by one of its two first terms: either the divinity of Christ (whence comes the transcendence of the Church and the direction and meaning to history); or the transcendence of the Church (which proves the divinity of Christ and gives direction and meaning to history—and this is the manner of the author's reasoning); but not by the third term (the direction of history) which can only be laid down if the second term (the transcendence of the Roman Catholic Church) is first demonstrated and proved. (Cf. Second Part, Chap. IV.)

(5) Now the Roman Catholic Church realizes both excellently and superabundantly all the necessary conditions of the transcendent religious society which is postulated by the direction and meaning of history. Therefore the Church is transcendent, Christ is God and history has a direction. (Cf. Third Part, Chap. IV; Fourth Part, Chap. IV; Fifth Part, Chap. II.)

(6) It is true that the Roman Catholic Church satisfies these conditions in a sense stricter than is required. And so other religious societies would be able to satisfy them in another manner and alongside her to lay claim to transcendence; but such religious societies cannot be found, for:

(a) Outside Christianity and Judaism no society possesses in combination the four marks or signs of transcendence. (Cf. Third Part, Chap. I, and Fourth Part, Chap. III.)

(b) Judaism possesses them only in an imperfect fashion, progressively before the coming of Christ and acting as the Christ, as preparation for the Christ. (Cf. Third Part, Chap. IV, and Fourth Part, Chap. II.)

(c) In Christianity the Churches which are not in union with the Church of Rome form no part of the Apostolic Unity, because they have separated themselves from the

Apostolic Church (Cf. Third Part, Chap. IV and V; Fourth Part, Chaps. I and IV; Fifth Part, Chap. II) and because the Apostolic Church has excluded them. (Cf. Fourth Part, Chap. IV.) It is then manifest that two of the four marks or signs, the unity and the permanence or apostolicity, is lacking to them: this fact gets rid of any necessity of examining whether they possess the two other marks or symbols; holiness and catholicity.

(7) So it follows that the Roman Catholic Church is the only one which is both transcendent and divine.

(8) Two texts in support of this method which the author has here adopted: The words of Our Lord Jesus Christ in the Gospel according to St. John (v. 36; x. 37, 38).

"For the works which the Father hath given me to perfect, the works themselves which I do, give testimony of me, that the Father hath sent me. . . . If I do not the works of my Father, believe me not; but if I do, though you believe not me, believe the works, that you may know and believe that the Father is in me and I in him."

The Oecumenical Council of the Vatican, XXth, Session III, 24th April, 1870, Chap. III, *de Fide*. (Denziger, Nos. 1793, 1794):

". . . It is our duty to embrace the true faith and to persevere in it with constancy. That we may be able to fulfil that duty, God by His only Son has instituted the Church and has bestowed upon it marks which make manifest this institution, that all men may be able to recognize it, as the guardian and the teacher of the revealed word."

"To the Catholic Church alone are related in effect all the marvels so great and numerous which God has prepared to make evident the credibility of the Christian faith. Much more, the Church by herself by reason of her admirable propagation, of her unparalleled holiness and her inexhaustible fruitfulness in all kinds of good things, by reason of her Catholic unity and her unshakable stability is a great

and *perpetual motive for belief and an irrefutable proof of its divine mission.*

"As a standard for the nations" (Is. xi. 12), the Church calls to her those who do not yet believe and she gives to her children one more certitude that the faith which they profess rests upon the firmest foundations.

INDEX

A

Abd-el-Melik, 174
Abdur-Rahman II, 174
Abraham, 86, 99, 116, 253, 255, 256, 277
Accad:
  Sargon the Ancient, 114
  Naram-Sin, 114, 115
  Tiglath-Pileser III, 126
Adam, 81–5, 88, 89, 303
Ader, 40
Aha, 112
Alaric the Goth, 151
Albigenses, 191, 283
Alcibiades, 138
Alexander the Great, 43, 44, 128, 129, 135, 138–42, 146, 248, 263
Alexander VI, Pope, 182
Al-Hallaj, 172
Alp-Arslan, 177
Amasis, 128
Ambrose, St., 316
Amenemhat I, 116
Amenemhat III, 117
Amenophis IV, 122
America, United States of, 43, 44, 45, 46, 90, 341, 347, 348
Amon-Ra, 121, 122
Anabaptists, 192, 202
Anaxagoras, 22, 131
An-Cheu-Kao, 142
Antiochus the Great, 142
Antipater, 141
Antony, 147
Aquinas, St. Thomas, 162, 180, 203, 318, 344
  Quoted, 40, 83
Arabia and the Arabs, 96, 164, 168, 177, 212, 266
Archimedes, 22
Aristotle, 22, 24, 34, 131, 139, 140
Arius and the Arians, 163, 314, 315, 316
Arnaud, Angélique, 185
Aryans, 106, 107, 112, 118, 119, 124, 125, 131, 143, 166, 177

Asoka, 143–4, 153
Assurbanipal, 127
Assyria and the Assyrians:
  St. Augustine on, 41
  Early kings, 116
  Conquered by Egypt, 121
  The founding of the Empire, 125–6
  Fall of Nineveh, 127
  Bossuet on, 259
  Absorbed in Roman Empire, 266
Astyages, 129
Athanasius, 316, 317
Atoti, 112
Attila, 151, 334
Augustine, St., 54, 17, 316
  Quoted, 41, 58, 64, 300
Aurelius, Marcus, 150, 271

B

Babylon:
  Area, 109
  Early kings, 111, 116
  Hammurabi, 115
  Dominated by Assyria, 126, 127
  Destroys Nineveh, 127
  Nebuchadnezzar, 128
  Fall of Babylon, 128, 129, 135
  Alexander dies at, 141
Barbarossa (Frederick I), 191
Basilides, 310, 311
Beccadelli, 324
Benedict XV, Pope, 203
Berdjaev, Nicholas, 54, 346
Bernard, St., 180, 318
Berosus, 94
Bindusara, 143
Bossuet, 10, 54
  Quoted, 75, 259, 272, 301
Brahmins, 22, 26, 124, 132, 133, 140, 153, 216, 226, 229, 316
Brutus, 147
Buddhism, (see also Gautama Sakya Muni), 22, 23, 44, 48, 133, 134, 143, 149, 153, 226, 229, 230, 273, 279, 316
Byzantium, 24, 151, 163–4, 175, 267, 268, 317–18

361